RUDOLF STEIN]
TO THE BR

RUDOLF STEINER SPEAKS TO THE BRITISH

Lectures and Addresses in England and Wales

RUDOLF STEINER

Translated by J. Collis

RUDOLF STEINER PRESS
LONDON

Rudolf Steiner Press
51 Queen Caroline Street
London W6 9QL

Published by Rudolf Steiner Press 1998

Originally published in German, principally in various volumes of the GA (*Gesamtausgabe* or collected works of Rudolf Steiner) by Rudolf Steiner Verlag, Dornach, and *Rudolf Steiner und die Zivilisationsaufgabe der Anthroposophie* (RSZA), private printing, Dornach 1943. PART ONE: chapters 1 and 2 in GA 211; chapters 3 and 4 in GA 218; chapter 5 in GA 228. PART TWO: chapters 1–4 in GA 305. PART THREE: chapter 1 in GA 304a; chapter 2 in RSZA; chapter 3 in GA 259; chapters 4–8 in RSZA; chapter 9 in *Das Goetheanum*, vol. 3, nos. 5 and 6. PART FOUR: chapters 1 and 2, original English, previously unpublished; chapter 3 in RSZA; chapter 4 in GA 218 (1992 edition), note to p. 179; chapter 5 in *Nachrichtenblatt*, Vol. 11, no. 41; chapter 6 in GA 260a.

Translation © Rudolf Steiner Press 1998

A catalogue record for this book is available from the British Library

The Publishers wish to acknowledge the generous legacy left to our work by Amy Tibbits of Sheffield. Her gift has helped to support this publication.

ISBN 1 85584 047 2

Cover by Trisha Connolly
Typeset by DP Photosetting, Aylesbury, Bucks.
Printed and bound in Great Britain by Cromwell Press Limited, Trowbridge, Wiltshire

Published in commemoration of the seventy-fifth anniversary of the founding of the Anthroposophical Society in Great Britain

CONTENTS

PART FOUR: MEETINGS AND ADDRESSES

INTRODUCTION

Rudolf Steiner had visited Britain for Theosophical Society Congresses in 1902, 1903 and 1905, but it was after he parted from that Society that he came to London in May 1913 at the request of the newly formed anthroposophical group and gave two lectures, since published as *Occult Science and Occult Development*. The tragedy and social aftermath of the First World War prevented his return for several years and he did not come back until April 1922.

He was able to speak to the British in a very direct and lively way. He did not need to give a long introductory build-up to his main theme, as was expected of him in Germany for instance, but could plunge straight into his lecture with quite esoteric material. He found the British particularly receptive to what he had to bring.

The first four lectures given in London, and included here, can be seen as a preparation for the material later given at Penmaenmawr—the theme of Christ, stages of consciousness, the meaning of initiation and how to embark upon it.

Part Two contains three lectures on social and educational themes. In August 1922 Steiner was invited to an important conference on education at Oxford University, hosted by Millicent Mackenzie, Professor of Education at University College, Cardiff. The historian H. A. L. Fisher also took part. The main education lectures were published as *The Spiritual Ground of Education*. The two lectures on social themes are likely to be particularly relevant to women's issues because, as in his work *The Philosophy of Spiritual Activity (Intuitive Thinking as a Spiritual Path)*, Steiner makes clear that women themselves must determine their future direction and needs, simply to copy men being no solution. Also, whilst describing the need to integrate industrial life—for he is speaking to a people at the heart of industry and commerce—he gives a very Blakean image of the factory as a kind of solitary demon. On a later visit he was to be much moved by the plight of dwellers in their tiny back-to-back houses in the blackened industrial towns.

The year 1923 became a decisive one for the history of the Anthroposophical Society. The First Goetheanum building had burned down on New Year's Eve 1922, and Rudolf Steiner had to consider the next step forward. It was a year in which a number of national societies were founded—by August, Switzerland, Germany, Czechoslovakia and Norway—and now it was the turn of Great Britain. Representatives from all these countries would be present later at the re-founding of the General Society. In August, Steiner visited Ilkley to give the lectures *A Modern Art of Education* and from there he went on to Penmaenmawr for a members' conference at which he gave the lectures *The Evolution of Consciousness*.

The choice of subject and location had been made by Daniel Nicol Dunlop, the Scot with whom Steiner felt a strong personal link. Dunlop, who was General Secretary of the Society in Britain, went on to establish the World Power Conferences—now World Energy Conferences. The experience of the ancient and remote Druidic Mystery Centre at Penmaenmawr—the stone circle—was to give Steiner very special insights into the development of European civilization and the part played by these Mysteries of the North and West, which date back beyond the period normally thought of as Druidic—to the megalithic period of *c.* 3000 BC.

In that period the exoteric and esoteric were still combined. The Druid priests and priestesses were in close communion with spiritual beings from whom they received the enlightenment needed to arrange the affairs of daily life for the benefit of the people in their community. Following this epoch earthly life became more separated from the spiritual, so that it grew harder for people to communicate with spiritual beings in the right way. This lasted until the end of the nineteenth century. The period of darkening, referred to in esotericism as Kali Yuga, was over. Rudolf Steiner set out to make it possible for initiate consciousness and spiritual insights to be drawn into the practical arrangements of earthly life once more.

The Penmaenmawr conference proved to be of the utmost significance for the anthroposophical medical movement also. Whilst there, the physician Ita Wegman awakened to a further realization of her own karmic destiny in connection with Rudolf Steiner and asked him whether a new form of medicine could be developed out of Mystery wisdom, as had been the case in early Greek times for instance. This decisive question enabled Steiner to give further medical courses (including two medical lectures in London) and he and Ita Wegman collaborated on the book *Extending Practical Medicine (Fundamentals of Therapy)* to bring to birth new medical insights and treatment arising from new Mystery knowledge. Following his return to Dornach, Steiner gave members an account of his visit. Previously unpublished in English, this is included in Part Three.

The experiences of these ancient sites of spirituality (Ilkley Moor was another), where 'Imaginations do not so easily dissolve', was one of the encouragements Steiner received which prepared him for the re-founding of the Anthroposophical Society at Christmas 1923, when he united his own destiny with the Society and founded a modern Mystery School.

Before leaving Britain, however, Steiner travelled back to London for the founding of the Anthroposophical Society in Great Britain. He was asked to become its President for life. The transcript of the meeting and address has not appeared in English before. Already certain underlying tensions between members are hinted at, which surfaced by the end of the 1920s and were to play a tragic part in the splitting of the

General Society in the 1930s. Steiner's lecture to the members in London following the founding meeting, *Man as a Picture of the Living Spirit*, previously issued as a single lecture, is included here in Part One.

Steiner came to Britain for the last time in 1924. Torquay was chosen as the venue for the members' summer conference. Again it was a pertinent choice, probably by Daniel Dunlop and his close friend Eleanor Merry, artist, writer and conference secretary. It enabled Steiner to visit Tintagel, where his experiences of the spiritual imprint of the Mystery wisdom of King Arthur and his Round Table Knights inspired him to speak on this in connection with karmic streams in lectures which form part of the *Karmic Relationships* series. Steiner was excited to discover 'a Christianity before Christ', a 'pagan Christianity' (not for him a contradiction in terms), which was still lingering in the spiritual atmosphere of North Cornwall.

In Torquay Steiner also gave the lectures *True and False Paths in Spiritual Investigation*, apparently requested by English members because of the attraction at that time (as indeed now) of holding seances and practising automatic writing. Steiner spoke about the kinds of elemental spirits that take part in these gatherings.

The Torquay event reveals how extremely active Steiner was by 1924—three lectures a day when his health had already seriously deteriorated. The third group of lectures was another on education—*The Kingdom of Childhood*, which inspired the young Cecil Harwood to join forces with the newly opened Rudolf Steiner School at Streatham, London. He was later Chairman of the British Society for 37 years.

The intention of this book is to give a fuller picture of how and on what Rudolf Steiner spoke to the British people. The major lecture series have been published for a long time, but the Questions and Answers and concluding addresses were hitherto known only to a few. A complete list of all the lectures and addresses given in Britain is included.

It is hoped that this book will be a valuable background work which can lead to a fuller understanding of how anthroposophy has developed in the British Isles and of the role of the English-speaking peoples.

More than 70 years on there is a pressing need for healthier arrangements in socio-economic life and in the management of the environment. Connected to this is the longing people experience for a deeper understanding of nature and its subtle energies or 'etheric', which leads many into joining neo-pagan movements.

The rituals through which one can contact gods and goddesses of old offer a deep sense of satisfaction. However, times have changed, spiritual beings evolve also and are known by other names. Christ, the Sun God, who was known by earlier peoples under names such as Ahura Mazda, Hu or Balder, has now united himself with the earth and its future evolution.[1] A new awareness of the being of the Earth Mother has arisen—an extremely relevant reference to this appears in the last lecture given at Penmaenmawr.

> From among those who in these first centuries were still initiated in Christian Mysteries there came ... a wonderful poem. It told of the coming of Christ to earth ... After these pictures had revealed something of what the gods had decreed from the Sun ... and the descent of Christ into the man Jesus had been impressively described, the poem went on to picture how in human evolution there was to be, in a new, metamorphosed form, a revitalizing of the old Demeter-Isis being. It was shown how this being was to be revered in a special, powerfully depicted human form, coming in the future as a solemn promise to mankind ... Together with all that came definitely from the Gnosis, [the poem] was rooted out later by the Church.[2]

The spirits of the elements who work into nature also await recognition again to inspire a better understanding of how to care for the earth's resources. In northern Europe they were traditionally (and in some areas may still be) seen and understood as old clairvoyant faculties linger on. Steiner wanted people to develop new forms of clairvoyance and realized that the peoples of Britain (and also Scandinavia and their descendants who inhabit the American and Australasian continents) particularly offered a rich and fertile potential.

Margaret Jonas
January 1998

PART ONE

LONDON

After a long absence occasioned by the Great War and its after-math, Rudolf Steiner once again visited England in April 1922. He had been invited to lecture at Stratford upon Avon, the occasion being a celebration of Shakespeare's birthday organized by the Society for New Ideals in Education. The two lectures he gave were on 'Drama and Education' and 'Shakespeare and the New Ideals'. He spoke directly out of anthroposophy and referred to the immense educational influence Shakespeare had had on Goethe . . . Rudolf Steiner stayed in Stratford for a week, during which time he enjoyed visiting the places linked with the memory of the great poet, and each evening attending performances of the plays that are presented there much more simply than in Germany, with a refreshing and healthy sense of humour. Prior to this he had given two public lectures in London (on 14 and 15 April), and after Stratford he gave a third lecture in London on 24 April 1922 on 'The Threefold Sun and the Risen Christ', this time for members of the Society only.

Marie Steiner[3]

1. KNOWLEDGE AND INITIATION[4]

London, 14 April 1922

The anthroposophy it is my task to represent in our time rests on the same foundations as any initiation science of bygone ages. In the course of humanity's evolution, however, human souls have undergone many and varied metamorphoses of disposition, so that in each age of human evolution one specific such disposition has been predominant. It is by this specific disposition of soul that initiation science must be guided as it endeavours to discover what is eternal in the being of man and in the being of the universe. The initiation science we need today differs from the one needed in the Middle Ages, or in the times of ancient Greece, let alone in even more distant eras of human civilization. What anthroposophy wants to be is an initiation science that is appropriate for the needs and longings of human souls as they are constituted today. In keeping with our present age, it has to work with the fact that today's scientific outlook does not enable human beings to learn anything about what is eternal either in themselves or in the universe. It also has to take account of the fact that when people turn from outer science and look into themselves in mystical contemplation they will equally fail to reach any kind of satisfactory result. Outer science does not go far enough to reach the eternal, and while inner contemplation may lead to some mystical belief it does not achieve real knowledge of the kind needed by human beings today.

It would be possible to prove in detail what I have indicated in these few introductory remarks. However, I shall assume that you who are present here today have discovered from your own experience of soul how external science cannot give you any satisfactory information either about your own eternal nature or about the eternal in the universe when what you seek is genuine knowledge rather than a mystical illusion. Therefore I shall instead speak in detail about how the anthroposophy I am discussing relates on the one hand to science and on the other to mysticism—which is where people often expect to find it. Taking the spirit and soul disposition of civilized human beings today as its starting-point, anthroposophy is striving for something that I would like to call 'exact or precise clairvoyance', and it is because this is its aim that it is encountering so many opponents. People find it so hard to comprehend even though in fact all souls are longing for it today. Why is it so misunderstood? It is misunderstood because the judgements and feelings people entertain consciously today do not yet extend to the unconscious yearnings that now exist in every thoughtful human soul.

This indeterminate longing, these unconscious aims make it necessary to strive for a deeper science, a higher knowledge of the eternal—to strive for this by means of quite specific exercises and a definite training of the human soul and its capacity for knowledge. Moreover, it is necessary for these exercises and this training to be given a form that is as precise as that with which we approach all knowledge nowadays. As does science, so anthroposophy also aims to present itself to contemporary human beings with scientific precision. At the same time it also wants to take the form of knowledge that is available even to the most unsophisticated souls, so that none need be excluded from knowledge about what is eternal and imperishable in the inner human being. After this brief preparation I shall now go straight to a simple description of how anthroposophy, today's initiation science, arrives at its path of knowledge.

In the first place it rests on our gaining a clear idea of how the three fundamental powers of soul life, thinking, feeling and will, are related to one another. When we look into our inner life in the ordinary course of things we speak of thinking, feeling and will. When we speak of thinking, of making inner pictures, we are aware of reflecting on something that makes us awake as human beings. This life of ideas and inner pictures is stilled while we sleep; from the moment we fall asleep to the moment when we wake up again our whole consciousness is in a dulled state. If we can let a clear light shine into our ordinary consciousness, we see the world as though bathed in a clear light if this consciousness is filled with wide-awake ideas and thoughts.

Next we come to our feelings. They are less clear than thoughts and ideas, though humanly speaking they are perhaps the most important to us of all our inner life. Feelings well up from unknown depths in the soul's life. They are to a certain extent illumined by our thoughts, but they are not as clear as the thoughts themselves. And how dark, how far from clear, is everything that is bound up with the impulses of human will, of which we shall have more to say later. They rise up from unknown depths, fill us entirely and lead us to act as human beings. Only in the rarest cases can we state clearly what goes on within us when an impulse of will is present.

These three fundamental powers of human soul life are thus distinguishable by their varying degrees of clarity and by other features as well. At the same time they also form a unit within the soul life of the human being taken as a whole. On the one hand we can speak of our life of thoughts and ideas as one pole. Yet we know that we are using our will when we move from one inner picture to the next, or when we allow one picture to emerge from another. So our will plays a part in our life of thought and ideas. The opposite pole is that of the will, the impulses of will, while feeling has its place in the middle between the two. We should not be truly human beings if we did not knowingly shape the most important actions of our lives, if we did not receive impulses from the realm of thoughts and inner pictures. So on the other hand we can agree that our will is also filled with our life of thought.

We must undertake to train and develop our thought life on the one hand and our life of will on the other if we want to achieve what I termed 'exact or precise clairvoyance' and modern initiation science in the sense of anthroposophy. We must carry out exercises in thought and exercises in will if the portals of the supersensible world are to open for us. It is this world that we must enter if we want to know the eternal aspect of ourselves and of the universe.

To carry out the thought exercises, we have to make ourselves attentive to the way an element of will always plays into our thinking life. To carry out the will exercises, on the other hand, we must pay attention to the thought element that plays into the will. In ordinary life the will element in thought goes unnoticed; yet in order to reach modern initiation it is precisely this slight unnoticed element of will present in our life of thought to which we must pay heed. This we gradually achieve by the exercises I have described in my book *Knowledge of the Higher Worlds*.[5] I mean by this that we have to push aside what generally concerns us most in our thought life, namely, the content of our thoughts, and learn instead to make conscious use of the element of will in our thinking. To do this we proceed as follows although, as I said, I can only indicate it in principle here. Further details are to be found in my books *Occult Science*[6] and *Knowledge of the Higher Worlds*, and in others as well.

Think of an inner picture, an idea that is easily and fully comprehended, one that is altogether clear, such as, let us say, a triangle in mathematics. Place this at the centre of a whole complex of ideas. It is not the content of the idea that matters, but the entire concentration of the soul on the one idea or complex of ideas in a thought meditation. We must attain the power to withdraw our attention from everything else in the world until nothing exists for our consciousness except the one idea or complex of ideas. A strong and vigorous effort of soul is needed to carry this through. Just as a single muscle grows stronger with repeated use, so does the power of the soul grow strong if we apply it again and again in this manner. Some take months, others years to achieve it. If we repeat the exercise again and again, concentrating the whole strength of our soul upon the one idea or complex of ideas, then our power of soul is gradually strengthened. Eventually a moment will come when we gain a new experience, an inner experience at first, one that deeply moves us. We find that we have strengthened and energized our inner life to the point of awakening a kind of thinking that is altogether new—a thinking that we never had before.

What we have thus achieved may most easily be described as follows. In our encounters with the ordinary, everyday world we have sense impressions that are strong and vivid. We live vigorously in our sense impressions in the world of colour and sound, or of heat and cold and all the other stimulations of the senses. The thoughts we have in ordinary consciousness are feeble in comparison with all this. It is easy to notice how much weaker your thought life is than the life you live in your sense perceptions. What we achieve at length is a thought life that is as lively and vivid as the life we experience through the senses. This is a transition of great importance on the path of human knowledge, for our thinking life no longer appears in pale and outlined thoughts like those we have in ordinary consciousness. The thoughts are now as vivid, pictorial, inwardly intense and full to the brim as are our external sense perceptions. By comparison with ordinary abstract or objective thought, what we have now achieved may be termed Imaginative Thinking. It is not that we give ourselves up to idle fancies. We can now see into worlds that we know live as lightly in the soul as do the pictures of our dreams. But they are not dream pictures, for they are filled with an inner reality.

When we have learnt through a period of finely honed training to live in Imaginative Thinking, when we can engage the whole of our being in this Imaginative Thinking, we find that it immerses us in a reality hitherto unknown to us. With this Imaginative Thinking we can now reach the first stage of the supersensible world. Through this Imaginative Thinking we gradually begin to experience a second human being within us, a human being who is as real as the one familiar to us in external, physical space. The external, physical human being is an organism in which the various members interrelate with one another; the head is dependent on the hands and the hands on the head, the right hand is dependent on the left. All the parts of the spatial human being are interdependent. But now we discover a second human being, one that I shall have to call a temporal organism. It is a temporal and not a spatial organism. It is spread out before the eyes of our soul like an immense vista. Once we have gone far enough in developing Imaginative Thinking we no longer look back to individual reminiscences in our memory because we see before us the whole of our life on earth, initially right back to the early years of childhood. We look back, seeing everything at once as in a single picture, yet we are aware that this is not a picture in space. If we were to paint it we should have to paint something like lightning, something that can only momentarily be held steady. This is what I have termed the body of creative forces, the ether body. It is impossible to paint a picture of it, or if we did we should have to be aware that we were painting only a momentary cross-section of a time organism.

We now discover how we were equipped in childhood with forces that were inborn in us. These forces sculpted our brain and found the transition from the brain to the organisms of breathing and circulation, working their way into the whole spatial organism until they were able to take control of it. Through the organism we get to know in Imaginative Knowledge as the time organism, the child increasingly takes possession of the whole of his spatial organism. As its powers gradually unfold the ether body fills us entirely. In ordinary consciousness we are aware of its effects though not of the ether body itself. But through Imaginative Knowledge we do become aware of this time organism. We learn to recognize why we have a particular kind of character or, to mention only a few possibilities, why one person is more disposed to become a painter, another a mathematician; we discover that something supersensible is working on us and on our earthly existence.

In this way we come to investigate the first supersensible element in our being. Through systematic exercising of our thinking faculties we can train ourselves for exact clairvoyance. Imaginative Knowledge is the first step in supersensible perception, and through it we reach the first element of the supersensible it is possible for us to reach, namely, the supersensible body that we bear within our earthly body in physical space.

I have been trying to explain to you how we can come to a first stage of the supersensible through Imaginative Perception. It is something supersensible that still has its being within the sense-perceptible. We have not yet gone beyond the earthly body, yet within this earthly body we find there is a supersensible part that I have here described at least in principle. Having got to know it through Imaginative Perception we have been able to describe the first stage of supersensible perception. So now we can continue, and we find that we can in a sense reach further towards the human being's higher nature that lives beyond birth and beyond death: the eternal in human nature.

In ordinary life, working with the will into our capacity to think, into our powers of thinking, can lead to Imaginative Perception. We can go still further along the path to the supersensible world if we now pursue these exercises in, you might say, the opposite direction. We know even from ordinary life that we have to achieve a sufficient degree of attentiveness if we want to concentrate on an inner picture or an object of some kind; we must also have it in our power, though, to turn our soul away from something we have been concentrating on. This leads us to the next exercise.

Having systematically applied our inner powers of soul to concentrating on something in a way that has led to Imaginative Perception, we then have to apply an even stronger force so as to avoid getting caught up in the inner picture or complex of pictures. We have to apply this stronger force to proceed further along the path of knowledge. Having succeeded in creating living thoughts, we need an even stronger power to remove them from our consciousness, to sweep them away by choice and in full awareness. By working on this we eventually come to the point of being able to take all the vivid inner pictures we have gained in our consciousness through concentration or meditation and push them out again, so that we end up in a state of complete wakefulness yet with a consciousness emptied of all content.

Try to imagine what it means to live in a consciousness that is emptied of all content. We know that in ordinary life we fall asleep or become unconscious if we receive no sense impressions or if no memories rise up in our soul. We can avoid such a loss of consciousness by strengthening our thinking life and then extinguishing it again. We remain awake and yet have an empty consciousness ready to receive whatever might come towards us. It is not sense impressions that can now come to us, for we have extinguished them through our strengthened thinking. Neither do memories prevail against our strengthened thinking. I have already explained how Imaginative Thinking brings us all that has hitherto happened not as memories but as a vista where in a single sweep of vision we can take it all in at a glance and see it as a unity.

What now enters our consciousness is something entirely new, something we never expected to find in our surroundings. Our emptied consciousness becomes aware of a supersensible environment which surrounds us as in ordinary life we are surrounded by colours and sounds. Actual beings of spirituality now, you might say, sprout from everything around us. We no longer watch the clouds moving across the sky as we do with our ordinary eyes. In every sense-perceptible thing we now see something supersensible. It is not a world of the 'beyond' but a world spread out before us just as our ordinary, sense-perceptible world is spread before us, a world to be reached through initiation, a truly supersensible world.

By immersing ourselves with our consciousness in a supersensible world, we now learn a new kind of thinking, a new life of mental pictures, one that is not dependent on the nervous system in the way ordinary thinking is. We know that previously we have had to make use of our nervous system, but now we no longer need our brain. Now we think thoughts that are brought to life in our consciousness solely by the powers of our own soul.

Once this has been attained we make other discoveries as well. These show us how from old thinking we have engendered a new kind of thinking with new experiences. It becomes obvious that this new thinking outside the brain cannot be compared with our old thinking that was attached to the brain, for this new thinking possesses no memories in the ordinary sense, whereas our ordinary thinking is only healthy if it brings memories, the power to remember, with it. Strange though it may seem, nevertheless it is true that initially no memory of the new experience is forthcoming. This sometimes surprises pupils of initiation science. Having reached a degree of clairvoyance, they presume that they will be able to retain a memory of what they have learnt from it and retrieve it at will, as they can with other thoughts. They are disappointed when they find they cannot do so. All they know is that they have been there, but once they are back in their physical organism they cannot remember it.

This is entirely characteristic of experiencing a reality rather than a thought. If I have had a sensory experience I can remember the thoughts I had in connection with this experience. I can store my thoughts about the rose, but if I want to see it before me again in all its vivid redness I shall have to go back and look at it again. If I have trained my ordinary consciousness through the effort of initiation and have attained a new way of seeing, then, if I want to have this spiritual experience over again, I shall have to repeat the steps that led me to it in the first place. Then, precisely as the rose is there again for my physical eyes to see, so will the spiritual experience appear before me again. Anyone who speaks out of the spiritual world itself, telling not merely what he has learnt about it but what he knows from his own spiritual vision, is aware that every time he speaks he must create something new in his soul by exact clairvoyance.

While someone who is working out of ordinary science can speak from memory, the scientist of the spirit has to repeat the steps that once led him to the experience or discovery of which he is speaking. The whole process must be generated over again, as a fresh, original experience. This is the sense in which the conditions of spiritual experience are different from those of ordinary consciousness in ordinary life.

In order to find our bearings in the spiritual worlds and see truly what is there for us to see, we need a further inner trait in our character, a quality I should like to term 'presence of mind'. In ordinary life this is the trait we need when faced with a situation that requires us to make an immediate decision without hesitation. Many exercises in presence of mind are necessary if we want to learn how to observe the supersensible world. Without such presence of mind we should not be quick enough to grasp the experience; we would only have caught up with it once it had flashed by. When we have reached the stage of being able to think without our brain we must be capable of immensely speedy reactions in intense alertness.

Having progressed in this way to the spiritual beings in our surroundings via the empty consciousness, in full wakefulness, we can then also learn to do something else, if we develop these powers a little further. As we go on practising, we can extinguish even the body of pictures, the ether body itself. We can now extinguish not only individual mental pictures but also the whole of the ether body. Then it is that we have achieved an emptied consciousness in a higher sense. Before this emptied consciousness, our life of spirit and soul appears as it was in a world of spirit and soul before we as a soul descended from supersensible worlds into this earthly body. We come to know pre-natal life through Inspired Knowledge, what I should like to call Inspirational Perception. Just as outer air enters our lungs by inhalation, by inspiration, so does the spiritual world enter our emptied consciousness. Now, spiritually speaking, we inhale the spiritual worlds as we knew them before descending from spiritual heights into physical existence on the earth.

We have now got to know one aspect of our being. I shall speak about the other aspect, that of spiritual immortality, in the third part of this lecture. Immortality is the negation of death. We do not usually speak about 'innatality'—about having not yet been born—yet this is something we would have to regard as the other aspect of the human soul. We are just as unborn as we are immortal. Being a modern initiation science, anthroposophy does not proceed along the lines of a philosophy that makes deductions and wants to extrapolate more knowledge on the basis of something it already knows. Anthroposophy seeks to prepare the soul so that through training it may raise itself to an altogether higher plane of perception. Having developed to a higher standpoint than that of ordinary life, the soul becomes able to perceive and recognize its eternal being.

This is one aspect of Inspired Perception and is related to our own humanity. There is another aspect, which I will endeavour to describe in the following way, though only in outline. Through Inspired Perception we also learn to know what is spiritual in the outer world. Look for example at the sun. To ordinary science it is a finite body in space. This finite body, however, is merely one part of the sun's whole being, just as the physical body is one part of the whole human being. In the case of the human being we say that the spirit and soul live within the body. With the sun it is different. Here we have to say that the supersensible, spiritual part of the sun is outside it, filling the whole of space with the sun quality. When we look at the sun with our physical senses we see a physical concentration of the sun quality that exists everywhere, in minerals, plants and animals as well as ourselves. But with Inspired Perception we get to know that sun quality itself in plants, animals and man; and we get to know it in every part of ourselves, our lungs, heart, liver, brain and so on. In this way we discover the spiritual quality not only of the sun but of all external creation. The moon, like the sun, is not limited by the sharply defined outlines of what is physically seen. The moon we see is only the physical concentration, whereas the moon quality fills the whole of space. Although such things are regarded as superstitions nowadays, they are in fact as scientifically precise as any other knowledge once we have learnt to understand them properly. We see the physical aspects of plants, animals and man as belonging to the physical universe, but Inspired Perception shows us their inner nature. The same goes for every hand, lung, liver and so on. In each of them the sun quality and the moon quality live on, the sun quality in all that sprouts, grows and flourishes, and the moon quality in the degeneration and decrease that is also necessary for us. Life would be impossible for us without both the sun quality and the moon quality. So we learn to recognize the sun and moon qualities in the outer world, the former in all increasing and growing life, the latter in decrease and degeneration.

Similarly we begin to recognize what it means to be ill in the outer world. An organ falls ill when there is too much sun quality or too much moon quality in it. It is the forces of the universe that make human beings fall ill. Having learnt to recognize how sun qualities and moon qualities live in plants, animals and minerals, we discover how we can find counterforces and also individual natural forces that point us towards medicines for specific internal illnesses. Anthroposophy begins to play a part in matters of practical, external life, such as a new science of medicine. This can be developed by looking into the spirit of the universe and thus recognizing the human being in sickness and in health. In these few words I am referring to the anthroposophical science of medicine, which is in fact already in existence. No medical science, no psychology or therapy can be more than an empirical result of experimentation unless we can proceed to a spiritual understanding of the universe.

I have shown how we can arrive at true self-knowledge through Inspired Perception and also how this can prove its value in a practical domain of life. The same goes for other domains as well. To sum up we can say that initiation science on the one hand provides the foundation for the deepest longings of the human soul, while on the other it gives us what we need to enter more practically into this world's life, sharing in it more fully than is possible through the science of the outer senses.

All this is true of the second stage of human understanding, Inspired Perception, which leads into the spirit of the universe. But there is something that leads us still further on, to the understanding of the human being passing through the gate of death.

The Inspired Perception just described teaches us about the true soul nature of the human being, the being of soul that exists even when we are outside our body, indeed even before we descend from the worlds of spirit and soul to take on a physical, earthly body. Nevertheless, our knowledge of the soul and spirit of the human being remains one-sided if we advance only as far as Inspired Perception, for in it we discover only the elements of soul and spirit that exist before birth. If we want to find out what follows after death, we must continue with the exercises that help us develop supersensible perception.

We can do this by now going in the other direction, taking our powers of thought into our will, just as in the concentration exercises prior to this we have been taking our will into thought. As I did with the concentration exercises, I shall now once again describe in simple terms how we can manage gradually to take our powers of thought into our will. Let us begin with a simple example. It is something each one of us can do every day. We sit down quietly and think about something we have experienced during the day. Instead of beginning with the morning and letting the events pass before us in the ordinary sequence of time, we look back over our day beginning with the final experience in the evening and working our way back to the morning in the smallest steps possible. At first we may find we are only able to pick out a single episode. Later on the whole vista of memory will appear of its own accord.

The important point is this. We are accustomed to let our thinking follow the outer sequence of events passively, allowing what happened later to follow on from what took place earlier. The power of will which we thus develop through our thinking is only feeble. We can develop a far stronger will by taking the opposite course, by extricating our thinking from the external, natural sequence and exercising our will by going backwards through the sequence of events. Something else you can do is think a melody in reverse, or a drama from the fifth act to the first. The important thing is to use our strong will to break loose from the external sequence of events. This strengthens our will and helps us develop the ability to propel our thinking into our will, just as in the concentration exercises we have propelled our will into our thinking. This is described in more detail in the books I mentioned earlier.

I will now indicate one or two more points to make things clearer. We can undertake a powerful self-training of the will if we do not simply give ourselves up to our external life and to all that education and environment have made of us, but instead take our own education in hand through mature understanding. We take ourselves in hand to the point where we can break ourselves of a habit and acquire a fresh habit in its place. Such exercises can continue for years. We can tell ourselves that purely through the power of our thinking and the power of our will that lives in our life of inner pictures we shall try to acquire a characteristic we do not possess at all and make it into a permanent feature. This might take seven years. But if we go on doing such things decade after decade, then we shall be strengthening our will. There are many other will exercises that enable us to enter the supersensible world in a similar degree from the other side.

But what does our consciousness have to do with these impulses of will? We can elucidate this as follows. If I lift my hand or arm, this is an impulse of will; it is an impulse that goes down into the depths of my being. It is hidden from ordinary consciousness just as consciousness itself is extinguished in sleep. Although we might dream in our feeling life, we are asleep with regard to our impulses of will.

In a sense, therefore, we are untransparent in our soul. Just as an object can be untransparent for physical light, so do we find our body untransparent when it comes to looking at our will. We cannot look into the will. Physically, in our physical sense of sight, we see with our eyes because the eyes themselves are transparent. If we suffer from cataract we can no longer see.

Without suggesting that we are ill in our physical organism when it comes to ordinary life, for anthroposophy is not a matter of false asceticism, it could nevertheless be said that if we could make our body transparent—not physically of course, but from the point of view of the soul—then we should indeed succeed in seeing our will-impulses flow into the physical organism from our thoughts. Our physical organism being transparent, we should at length be able to penetrate the working of our impulses of will with consciousness.

This is what we attain eventually through the will exercises. We come to see ourselves as human beings of will and at the same time, in that external element which we make transparent through our will exercises, we see into the spiritual world of will to which we belong. For someone who has reached the stage of knowledge where the physical body is transparent to the soul, where the will is seen and penetrated, there comes a point when the physical body becomes invisible.

Strengthened in the way described, endeavouring to see ever further and further, we come to the point when we have before us, in a picture, the moment of death, the moment when we give our physical body to the earth and pass with our soul and spirit through the gate of death. It is this picture of stepping across the threshold of death that we have before us when we succeed in making our physical body transparent in order to look beyond into the spirit. We then understand what this physical body no longer possesses and that we are not only looking into the spiritual world but actually living in it as we enter it. This stage of knowledge is what we call Intuitive Perception, true Intuitive Perception. This is where we see immortality, deathlessness. Having attained this stage by passing through those of Imagination and Inspiration, we now know that we belong to the universe as an eternal spiritual being and that we are looking at the spiritual in the universe with the eternal spiritual soul we carry within us.

Although entirely adapted to modern consciousness, this is where initiation science takes us. In the past it was a dreaming atavistic knowledge, but today it is a fully conscious knowledge that lifts us from transience to eternity. Initiation knowledge can be generated out of a modern attitude of soul. This anthroposophy will be recognized not only by those who have done all the exercises in order to attain their own vision of the eternal spiritual world and its beings. Imagination, Inspiration and Intuition are necessary for research. The scientist of the spirit has brought from spiritual worlds what he was able to investigate. He has clothed it in ordinary logic and language and thus brought it into modern times and placed it before his contemporaries. The results of his research will become intelligible to anyone who possesses a healthy sense of what is true. Just as you do not have to be a painter in order to appreciate a work of art, but merely need a healthy sense for it, so will all the results of this research be accepted by ordinary common sense if they are brought forward in the right manner and received without prejudice. We must not ourselves add misunderstanding to misunderstanding as happens so often, with the result that Imaginative, Inspired and Intuitive Perception as described here come to be confused with hallucinations that arise from pathological conditions. Then people might be inclined to claim that the Imaginations striven for here are nothing but figments of the mind, illusory visions or hallucinations and so on, or else something brought on by a mediumistic state. What is said here about meditation, concentration and so on is the very opposite of these states. Somebody with hallucinations becomes totally immersed in them, whereas if you ascend through Imagination, Inspiration and Intuition to higher faculties of knowledge as the result of doing the exercises, you are not immersed in hallucinations but remain present all the time due to your sound common sense. If you proceed on the basis of sound common sense you remain critical and in control and therefore are not in danger of getting lost in floating fantasies or meaningless hallucinations. The states of Imagination, Inspiration and Intuition are the opposite of pathological conditions. They lead on from modern consciousness to a conviction about the reality of spiritual life. Anthroposophical initiation science takes us to supersensible knowledge that is in keeping with modern life.

We must proceed via modern consciousness, for we need to have gone through all the triumphs of external science. We need a knowledge about the supersensible world that can serve the civilization of our present time and especially that of the future. Many people are already clamouring for supersensible knowledge, and they would be able to attain such knowledge through anthroposophy. Anthroposophy desires to serve this new call of humanity, also in regard to religion. Tomorrow I shall be speaking about this when I go into the path anthroposophical initiation science follows towards the Mystery of Golgotha and a right understanding of Christianity.

My purpose today was to indicate the general task of

anthroposophical initiation science. When we encounter another human being and see him with our physical eyes we gain an impression of his outer physiognomy. This is not an exhaustive impression of the whole individual, for we do not see the whole until we can look with the eyes of our heart and soul into the other's spirit and soul. Equally, we cannot see the world itself and humanity as a whole with the physical eyes of outer knowledge. We need a consciousness that outer knowledge cannot give us; we need a form of perception, initiation knowledge, if we are to perceive the soul and spirit of the universe.

We must become entirely convinced of this, for not until we have this conviction can we really satisfy the deepest needs of the human soul. We shall be working towards satisfying the needs of the human soul when we add something to the great and wonderful progress already made by outer science, all of which is readily recognized by anthroposophy. What we have to add to this is a knowledge of the inner nature of soul and spirit in the universe and in humanity. The inner spirit is what the anthroposophy intended here wants to place side by side with outer knowledge, it wants to add the supersensible to what can be discovered through the senses. Just as a complete view of the human being must place the inner soul side by side with external life, so does anthroposophy want to be the soul and spirit, the inner being of modern knowledge.

2. KNOWLEDGE OF CHRIST THROUGH ANTHROPOSOPHY

London, 15 April 1922

Yesterday I spoke about the path leading into the super-sensible world from the physical world of the senses, the path that today's anthroposophy describes as the one leading to exact clairvoyance. I spoke about such exact clairvoyance because it is in effect an imperative requirement of our age. Clairvoyance, which is the basis of the modern science of initiation, has always existed. In past ages it was something that rose up within the human being like an elemental force, and on the path of initiation those who had gone through fewer stages were essentially dependent for their progress upon the authority of those who had gone through more stages than they.

To meet the needs of the human soul of today we cannot build on authority; to do so would be to contradict the stage the soul has now reached. For the last three or four or five centuries we have been in possession of an exact science, which is obviously not yet an initiation science. But it exercises some degree of control over the whole method of our thought and our research. It is above all out of the full consciousness of the human personality that science exercises its control, and this is the kind of control that must be the perpetual practice of those who want to attain exact clairvoyance in the anthroposophical sense.

By exact clairvoyance many insights have been gained into the universe and into the nature of the human being. This knowledge has not merely the effect of a theoretical conception of the world, a sum of ideas about spiritual, supersensible worlds, held as a body of theoretical knowledge. Modern initiation science works also as a living spiritual power, able to permeate and inspire the whole human being in all his faculties. In a certain respect it has already been possible to prove that this is so. What would otherwise come forward only in the form of ideas about the spiritual world, we have been able to show in reality through creative art. The Goetheanum building in Dornach, which houses the School of Spiritual Science, is being built through the self-sacrifice of many friends of the anthroposophical movement. Though still under construction it has progressed far enough to have been in use for some time.[7] If another spiritual movement had wanted to erect a building it would have commissioned an architect to design one in Classical, Renaissance, Gothic or some other style, but with the Goetheanum at Dornach in Switzerland it was impossible to take this course. To have done so would have contradicted the very spirit of the anthroposophical conception which not only desires to manifest in the realm of ideas, but wants to be life itself in the sphere of human will and action.

It hardly needs saying that the Goetheanum is imperfect. In this respect I am my own severest critic. But imperfect as it is as a building or as a work of art taken as a whole, it was none the less necessary for the Goetheanum to be built in a new architectural style and in a new style of art. It was necessary for the simple reason that anthroposophy has to place this building before the humanity of our time as a new example and a new beginning. Thus it is that the architectural forms you will find in the Goetheanum in Dornach spring from the same fountain of life out of which the ideas about the super-sensible, expressed in words, are also taken. Everything in the Goetheanum, including the sculpture and the painting too, is carried by a new style, which has its source in the same modern life from which anthroposophy itself is born. Those who visit the School of Spiritual Science will find that the words spoken from the platform about the anthroposophical view of the world are expressions of the very thing shown by the shapes of the building and the painted works of art inside it. What comes from the platform is an expression of these same things in words. Anthroposophy cannot seek expression in words alone, for the root from which it springs lies very deep inside human life. Theoretical anthroposophy is only one of the branches springing from this root. Others are those of art and education. Anthroposophical life is a factor in the various spheres of human existence.

The Waldorf School has come into being in Stuttgart. This is not a school in which adults teach the children about anthroposophy, for it is not a school for propagating a philosophy of life. Religion lessons there are given by Catholic priests for the Catholic children and by Protestant pastors for the Protestant children. Those who require no particular religious education, and there are many of these in Germany now, receive their religious instruction in a suitable religious adaptation of anthroposophical thought. What the Waldorf School really sets out to achieve, however, arises when anthroposophy goes over into life, into the practicalities of teaching and method and the whole way the education is built up. What the teachers do, how they educate the children and give their lessons, comes out of their whole personality, which is fired by anthroposophy.

I have made special mention of education as an example of how anthroposophy aims to work in the most varied spheres of life in a living and vital way. One of these spheres in which it has already worked a good deal is that of people's religious needs. What I would like to speak about today is how it works for the religious needs of that part of the civilized world that adheres to what has arisen out of the Mystery of Golgotha. I shall be linking this with what I described yesterday as the anthroposophical path to the spiritual world.

I showed how it is possible first of all to achieve Imaginative Perception by means of specific exercises of the soul. This Imaginative Perception lives in the soul in a way that enables us to use our ordinary thinking power—which otherwise provides us with thoughts that are shadowy and abstract—to generate inner pictures that are as vivid and intense as the images we see with our eyes when we look at something. In Imaginative Perception we experience our thoughts as vividly as when we think of colours in allowing our eyes to bring impressions to us, or sounds when we listen to what our ears enable us to hear. We are in Imaginative Perception when we can actually experience our thoughts inwardly as pictures full of content instead of rather pale or abstract outlines.

Yesterday I pointed out that Imaginative Perception enables us to see our time organism, our picture body. We must be aware, though, that when we can progress to Imaginative Perception it is because we have something of Imagination within ourselves. What distinguishes the anthroposophical researcher from someone with hallucinations or from a medium is the fact that the former achieves exact clairvoyance and is capable of realizing that the pictures he sees are solely within himself. Even when we succeed in seeing the body of formative forces through which we recognize how a sculptural shaping power has been working on our earthly organism since our birth, we are still only seeing something subjective. I then told you that you can extinguish these pictures and make your consciousness empty. You then no longer have the subjective pictures that were there initially. But this emptied consciousness possesses the power to receive similar pictures from outside.

As anthroposophical researchers we must be fully aware that we have to extinguish the initial form of Imaginations. Then we gain an emptied consciousness that is wide awake and energetic enough to receive purely spiritual pictures from the real world outside of ourselves. The first picture that comes is that of our own life of soul and spirit before we descended from the spiritual worlds in order to take up residence in our physical body. Then we also notice objective pictures of the spirit and soul world around us. We come to such objective pictures when we have Inspired Consciousness. The anthroposophical researcher receives revelations of the spiritual world into his emptied consciousness; these are objective pictures, in the same way that prior to this he created subjective pictures through strengthening his thinking by means of precise exercises.

What is it we learn about ourselves if our emptied consciousness becomes filled in this way with objective Imaginations through Inspired Perception? We learn what we knew before we descended out of the spiritual world into a physical one. Another thing we learn is what we have brought with us into physical existence from the spiritual world. Initially the only part we can consciously know of this is our power of thinking, but it is an important discovery. Philosophers have wondered a great deal about how thinking can have come into being. Anthroposophists know that it could never appear out of the physical body, since it is a power that the human being has brought in from the spiritual world before descending to the earth. In that spiritual world it was something entirely different from what it is in ordinary earthly consciousness. Here our thoughts are abstract and thus well suited to thinking about what is lifeless. It means that a person who is serious about initiation science is obliged to speak to people about something they perhaps do not wish to hear. I would like to describe an example to clarify what I have been saying:

At the end of the span of time we spend on earth death awaits us, and death brings it about that we leave a corpse behind. The corpse is what remains of our physical body after death. Either via cremation or by burial it is returned to the element from which it was derived, the earth. Once death has taken place, the body ceases to obey the laws to which it has been subjected by the human being's soul life since birth. It now obeys the laws of the earth. Having nothing more within it that belongs to the soul and spiritual life of the human being, it obeys the same laws to which the minerals existing in nature are subject. This is the destiny of our physical body when death takes place.

What we now have to realize is that a death of a similar kind takes place when the soul descends from the realm of spirit and soul in order to become embodied in a physical body through birth. The soul enters into this physical body in the same way that the physical body enters into the elements of the earth after death. Of all that we had in the spiritual world it is our thoughts, our power of thought, of which we are immediately aware in our consciousness here on earth. Our power of thought is the corpse of what was there in the realm of spirit and soul. Before we came down to earth, our life of spirit and soul had its own existence in the spiritual world, but now we only take into ourselves that part of thinking that is its corpse. Just as the earth carries our physical corpse when we have died, so do we carry in our physical body our thoughts, which are the soul corpse of the life of soul.

This is the reason why the knowledge we possess today is so unsatisfying. Since we have in us the corpse of our soul we can only grasp lifeless nature, and it is an illusion to believe that we shall discover anything other than lifeless nature through our experiments. No doubt we shall progress beyond discovering only what is lifeless and shall also be able to describe organic things of a physical kind. But with our undeveloped thinking we shall be unable to comprehend them even if we have produced them in the laboratory ourselves. With this thinking, which is the corpse of the soul and thus spiritually dead, we shall only be capable of comprehending what is dead.

This is a truth that we shall simply have to accept, for we cannot escape the fact that there was a period in human evolution when human beings took into themselves this dead, abstract thinking. However, it is solely through this abstract thinking, which has no inner life of its own and exercises no compulsion over our inner being, that we can attain freedom. Hence human freedom has been evolving ever since death began.

What I still intend to say will show how we can only attain Imagination, Inspiration and Intuition through thinking, as I suggested yesterday. These are the real result of bringing dead thinking back to life. If the exercises we do progress to the point where Imagination appears before us, then thinking is alive in us once again. Then we can say to ourselves: 'Prior to this our thinking gave us no inner pictures showing what we were before we descended to the earth from the spiritual realm, but now that our thinking is alive again we can look back through Imaginative and Inspired Thinking to our existence in the spiritual world before birth; now we see that before we were somehow taken into the physical world through conception we lived in a spiritual existence.'

In that spiritual world existence is alive, but in the way we think about it in our individual consciousness in the physical body it is dead. Imagination brings it to life again. We bring to life our pre-natal soul. The spiritual world we reach through Imagination and Inspiration in which we then live, this higher, true capacity of thinking, this perception of spiritual figures, spiritual beings, spiritual events is nothing other than a re-enlivening of what is dead for our ordinary thinking.

In this enlivening of ordinary thinking that leads to Imagination and Inspiration, something happens today that could never have happened for those seeking initiation knowledge in the days of ancient Greece, or of the Egyptians or Persians or any others before the time of the Mystery of Golgotha. Before Christ descended to the earth from spiritual heights, initiation science brought life into thinking in a manner that differed entirely from what happens today. History is now seen to be a matter of external deeds and it takes no account of the changes occurring in the state of the human soul as time has progressed. This can only become known to us through initiation science, through exact clairvoyance.

Having attained Imagination and Inspiration, we begin to realize that something has happened that makes us feel ill at ease. This is something I have to mention as a remarkable fact and one that is alarming. Having attained Imagination and Inspiration, we begin to feel quite ill at ease. This is because once we become clairvoyant we have to admit that our development has made us too egoistic, our ego has become too intense, too strong.

No one who knows about these things, no one who is not describing illusions, will give you any different information on this point. Everyone who is familiar with the facts knows that this feeling of disquiet comes over us when we have to admit: My ego is working too strongly, too intensely. Before the Mystery of Golgotha, on the other hand, people had the opposite experience. They found that initiation science made them weaker in their ego. They felt less conscious, less within themselves, as though they had less hold of themselves as human beings. They felt they were strengthening their ego when they did not work at initiation science. There is a natural, healthy egoism that is a part of ordinary life, and prior to the Mystery of Golgotha this was extinguished by initiation. People felt as though they were being poured out into the world, and the intensity of their consciousness was dulled. Today, initiation makes people feel more conscious; their ego becomes more aware and stronger.

The first human being to sense that when receiving initiation the ego needs something to prevent it from becoming excessively strong was Paul. He sensed this from the moment described in the New Testament as the experience of Damascus. What Paul knew through his initiation, through the Mystery of Golgotha, was that he had become able to see into the spiritual world, and in order to bear this experience without danger he needed to make his ego less intense. He expressed this for the world in a universal formulation stating what a newly initiated individual must say: Not I, but Christ in me.[8]

To work in a way that is in keeping with the power of Christ we have to recognize that, by taking Christ into our ego when it has become too forceful, we fill ourselves with the power of Christ which has entered the earth through the Mystery of Golgotha. Then our ego is switched back into the right place within us. Paul's words are universal: Not I, but Christ in me. They give direction and orientation to someone who experiences the power of Christ through modern initiation. My description of today's abstract thinking as a corpse living in our physical body, when compared with what thinking was like before birth, only applies to human beings at the present time. By this I mean the state of soul that has been gradually evolving since the Mystery of Golgotha. Thinking only gradually began to take on the character it has today, beginning perhaps not until the third or fourth century after the Mystery of Golgotha. Prior to that it was still alive, it still brought with it a living quality in all the ancient peoples.

It is easy to discover that this was so if you study the evolution of humanity with regard to the inner qualities of soul. Look at all the ancient conceptions of the world that emanated from initiation science, and even those that had no initiation science. In all of them people saw what was spiritual in the mineral world, in rivers and streams, clouds, thunder and lightning, plants and animals. It is quite superficial to suppose, as people do today, that the spiritual in nature, what we call animism, is a poetic fantasy. Animism in this sense has never existed. What did exist in human souls was a way of thinking that enabled human beings to look at a plant and see the spirit working within it. Just as we today see the green of the leaves or the red of the flower, so did people in ancient times see the spirit and soul in everything. The clouds, rivers, mountains and valleys we see today devoid of spirit they saw filled with spirit.

Why did they see these things filled with inner spirit? Because they had within themselves a living power that had entered into them. Their thinking reached out spiritually to the things, just as we today reach out with our hands when we touch something. Reaching out with living organs of thinking like spiritual organs of touch, as you might say, was how they grasped the world. But the living element in thinking that was so vivid in ancient times gradually diminished. It became increasingly muffled, so that from the fourth century onwards we have come to possess a thinking capacity that is inwardly dead; when we look at things our lifeless thinking only sees what is lifeless in living plants and animals and indeed even in the outward aspects of the human being.

When people in ancient times looked at their inner life they saw there a living thinking that was simply a continuation of what their being had been in the spiritual world before birth. They were able to express this quite consciously by saying: I live in the same element I lived in before I had life on earth. They felt within them something that had been born with them and had merely entered with them into their physical body. But for human beings living since the third or fourth century things are quite different. When they look into themselves they sense the presence of lifeless thinking. This gradual dying of thinking is a most important and significant historical event.

Let us imagine that nothing else had taken place in the course of the earth's existence other than that in the constitution of the human soul thinking had continued to appear ever more and more involved in death. Imagine for a moment that earthly evolution had continued as it had begun, progressing beyond the third or fourth century after Christ, but as though there had been no Mystery of Golgotha. What would have happened to the human soul if no Cross had been set up on Golgotha? Human beings would have begun to feel dead within their earthly bodies. Seeing the death of the physical body they would have had to say: 'From the moment of my birth my soul begins to die, it participates in the death of my physical body.'

Had there been no Mystery of Golgotha, it would have been the fate of humanity on earth that when physical bodies died the souls would have died with them, gradually at first but then spreading over the whole earth. We can recognize increasingly how tragic it would be if we had to say to ourselves: 'We human beings are so bound up with the earth that we die when our body dies. The living element that was within us up to the third or fourth century no longer belongs to us. Now our soul can only share in the fate of our body and die.' At best we would have found that life continued for a while, since death had not yet taken hold of everyone. But in the end death would have caught up with us all. But this did not happen. The Mystery of Golgotha took place, so evolution no longer continues in the old way.

Those who have undergone initiation will be able to view the Mystery of Golgotha in a way that differs from that of ordinary hearts and minds who approach it through the Gospels. This is not to imply that there is anything to be said against approaching it through the Gospels, for it is the way you have to follow initially in order to take root in Christianity. Nevertheless what even the simplest soul learns from the Gospels can be further developed by those who go towards initiation science. For those who do not hold on to faith alone, but press forward from Inspiration to Intuition, a spiritual world arises that shows the Mystery of Golgotha to be for them the great comfort in world existence. Having passed through Imagination and Inspiration in the right way, the initiate knows that his ego has become too strong, not so much because it provides the basis on which human freedom can be developed, but because it can interfere with what must develop if human beings are to be rescued from the results of dead thinking. More than any other, the viewpoint given us by initiation science is capable of revealing the tragedy of dying thinking. But in the background the truth of the Mystery of Golgotha rises up. On the one hand there is in human feeling and experience the understanding that says: My ego has grown too strong, but here I stand as a firm and consolidated spiritual being. On the other hand, as a historical event coming at the right moment in history, we see supersensibly how the divine being of Christ goes first through incarnation in the body of Jesus of Nazareth and then through the death on Golgotha.

If you go through initiation in the right way, you experience on the one hand a strengthening of the ego and on the other the truth of the Mystery of Golgotha. Beyond the Gospels, beyond the content that is accessible through ordinary reading, an Intuitive Perception arises. It is from such perception that the Gospels themselves emanated. Then the initiate is no longer dependent on what the Gospels tell him. From the power he has gained, which gives him the awareness already described of his own existence after death, from Inspiration and Intuition, he derives objectively the Imagination and the truth of the world outside himself, so that he would be capable of writing the Gospels himself if they had not already been written.

He even becomes properly aware of the Gospel writers themselves and realizes that in the first three or four centuries after Christ there was still so much vitality left over from ancient times that some individuals, even if they had not gone through initiation, were able to view the Mystery of Golgotha and interpret it in the right way. If those old initiates of the first four centuries, in the Gnosis of the time—which was similar though not identical with today's anthroposophy— had not interpreted the Mystery of Golgotha there would have been no Gospels, for the Gospels were written out of the old kind of initiation science. Having before us in spirit the events written into the Gospels by those first evangelists, we learn to recognize the Mystery of Golgotha as well as the origin of the Gospels.

In this way we learn to understand the Mystery of Golgotha, we learn to understand how it was possible for Paul to say: If Christ had not risen, our faith would be in vain and therefore our soul dead. We discover what would have happened if the Mystery of Golgotha had not taken place, if a God had not descended in order to enter a human body and in this body suffer death and then unite with the forces of the earth. For since that event, Christ has been united with the forces of the earth. Since the Mystery of Golgotha forces have been united with the earth and especially with human evolution on earth, Christ-forces which were not there prior to that event. This is what Paul meant by the risen Christ. Christ had to experience death and he did suffer death, and he gained victory over death. In the Resurrection he emerged victorious as a living spirit being, and since then he has continued to live with and for humanity, who would have possessed only dead thinking if Christ had not done these things. Now human beings can remember that a God, Christ, descended to the earth and is living here. Whilst in ancient times thinking itself brought its own vitality with it to the earth, since the third or fourth century—before that it was easier—earthly souls have been able to reawaken their own thinking by a direct vision of the Mystery of Golgotha. The death and resurrection of Christ has so enlivened the thinking of which these souls are capable that human beings no longer have to die along with their bodies, as they would have had to do had the Mystery of Golgotha not taken place.

As the initiate looks up from his ego that has grown too strong and sees the pictures of the Mystery of Golgotha, he can to some degree now read in the spiritual world about the evolution of the human soul. Through his insight into this particular chapter of initiation science he knows that Christ brought human souls back to life through his resurrection. In this way modern initiation science in the anthroposophical sense leads to a living, inner understanding of the Mystery of Golgotha. It is a path towards Christ, not away from him. Through it Christ is found in a spiritual way.

Let me now conclude with a brief outline sketch of an evolution of humanity that arises out of modern initiation science in conjunction with knowledge about the Mystery of Golgotha.

Looking back into the very distant history of human evolution we discover that ordinary consciousness developed in the way I have described. Thinking was alive and human beings found themselves surrounded by creatures of nature all of which possessed a spiritual element within the physical. People's consciousness was dreamy when they perceived the spiritual element, but this dreamy consciousness, this instinctive clairvoyance, still had its original links with the spiritual world provided by thinking that was alive.

In those primeval times there were individuals who stood out from the crowd of ordinary humanity, just as eminent scientists do today. They possessed a degree of initiation science in the old sense, although indeed you could say that all the knowledge people had in those days was initiation science, since even ordinary human beings had some clairvoyance. They had not achieved what I have been describing, but they did have a degree of Imagination, Inspiration and Intuition. In Intuition of all kinds human beings experienced not only pictures of the spiritual world but the spiritual beings themselves. With their ego-being they streamed over into the spiritual. This is what was experienced through initiation science in the early days of human evolution; the beings who had come down to the human realm from the spiritual worlds were experienced. These were not physical beings and neither were they beings who could be perceived by means of physical senses, who used words, for example, that physical ears could hear. The only way of relating to them was through spiritual vision. Through immense spiritual seership the initiates in ancient times were in touch with beings who descended to them in spiritual bodies, not physical bodies. These beings taught them about a life in worlds of soul and spirit, something they could not reach through physical thinking.

The most essential aspect of this ancient knowledge is that the first great teachers of humanity were spiritual beings who communicated with the early initiates in a spiritual way. They taught them the Mysteries of the Birth of Man, the Mysteries of the living soul descending from supersensible, spiritual worlds before being born. In those ancient times, what came to be known through revelations from the spiritual world itself were the Mysteries of Birth. Human beings learnt to understand something they already knew through their instinctive clairvoyance: that they had life before birth. They learnt through ancient initiation science to look back to their destinies as souls in the spiritual world before they had descended to the physical.

The Mysteries of the Birth of Man were taught in ancient times. Certain external cultic ceremonies were no doubt performed in these Mysteries. But what was prophetically known would happen through the Mystery of Golgotha was still entirely different from what it was to become after the Mystery of Golgotha. Before the Mystery of Golgotha human beings did not look on death in the way they did thereafter. They knew they had life before birth, that they possessed a living soul just as they had done before descending into physical life. They counted on the fact that this living soul would live on through death. Death in all its tragedy was not yet something with which they were confronted. It did not occur to them to think that in death their soul might also die. They knew their soul was alive.

Then the time gradually approached when the power of thinking became less and less alive, and abstract thinking descended as a corpse from the spiritual world. Human beings experienced that their outer physical body died, which was increasingly significant for their inner life as well. They derived comfort from the ceremonies that were enacted, and which pointed to the Mystery of Golgotha. The gods, they reckoned, and therefore also divine human souls, would not die, they would be resurrected. However, this was no more than a consolation offered by the cultic ceremonies; it was not actual knowledge. Actual knowledge transcending death only came through the Mystery of Golgotha.

We looked back to those ancient spiritual teachers who had come down from spiritual worlds. Strange though it may sound to us today, we know from initiation science that those spiritual teachers who lived as spiritual beings in the supersensible worlds only came down when human souls were open to them. These spiritual teachers of humanity lived in the divine world and only came down to human beings as teachers; they did not participate in human destinies and were themselves not acquainted with the Mystery of Death.

This fact is in itself a profound and important mystery. Fundamentally speaking, human beings in ancient times only received teachings from higher worlds about the Mystery of Birth, but not about the Mystery of Death. They learnt about the Mystery of Life from souls who had themselves only experienced birth. When the first Christian initiates saw the Mystery of Golgotha in spirit, they discovered something no ancient Mystery wisdom could have told them. They discovered that in the worlds from which they received that wisdom there was no knowledge of death because not a single one of those beings had undergone a human destiny and experienced going through death. Those divine, spiritual teachers of humanity knew about birth but not about death.

Through a destiny outside the realm of the gods thinking became such that human beings had to live with the fear that death of the body would bring with it death of the soul. In the realm of the gods it was decided that a God should be sent down to earth so that as a God he might go through death and take the experience of death into divine wisdom. This is what is revealed through perception of the Mystery of Golgotha in Intuition: the Mystery of Golgotha achieved something not only for human beings but also for the gods. It was as though the gods—who in earlier times could speak to earthly human beings only of the Mystery of Birth—saw how the earth would gradually grow beyond the forces with which they themselves had endowed it, and how death would then take hold of the soul. They therefore sent Christ to the earth, so that a God should learn about human death and vanquish it with his divine power.

This was the divine aspect of the event. For the sake of their own destinies the gods introduced the Mystery of Golgotha as a divine event into the evolution of the universe so that they, too, might benefit from it. Prior to this all events took place in divine spiritual worlds; but now a God descended and a super-earthly event took place on the earth in an earthly form. What happened on Golgotha was a spiritual event transplanted to the earth. It is this important perception that modern anthroposophical spiritual science brings concerning Christianity.

When we direct our attention to the Mystery of Golgotha, where we see the divine playing a part in the evolution of the earth and bringing something about that is important for the earth's destiny, we are also looking at something that concerns the gods themselves. So long as we only live and work here on the earth we learn to develop solely what concerns the earth and ourselves. So long as this remains the case we can have only a small amount of strength which is insufficient to transcend the stronger ego. But when we have to go beyond this in order to understand and comprehend the Mystery of Golgotha, then we reach something that is super-earthly and which cannot be understood with our earthly understanding alone; now we need an understanding that transcends the earthly realm.

So it is only through the encouragement we receive from initiation science that we can reach an understanding of the Event of Golgotha as an event placed into the earthly realm as something both cosmic and earthly. By this we awaken in ourselves the strong powers of knowledge which can indeed lead us to say: 'Through ordinary earthly human powers I take in everything the earth gives me for my human ego; if I turn to the Mystery of Golgotha I take in something that removes me from this earth and kindles a life in me that could otherwise not be kindled; I take in something supersensible when I turn with devotion towards the Mystery of Golgotha. I recognize that humanity needs to have a new kind of inner supersensible feeling and knowing, different from the old kind where human beings still sensed a thinking that was alive. I recognize that human beings can receive such knowledge through the

Mystery of Golgotha, by which they experience their dead thinking which they consciously introduce into supersensible existence in a way that makes them able to say: Not I, but Christ in me makes me truly alive, now, since the Mystery of Golgotha.'

The lively stimulus provided by modern initiation science, modern anthroposophy, has the purpose of enabling human beings to say such a thing. When we receive such stimulus ourselves through modern initiation science we shall see the consequence to be not an anti-religious, irreligious life but a deepening of religious life because we consciously discard something that has come down to us from olden times. Through an understanding of the Mystery of Golgotha out of spiritual science we are led beyond all the doubts that are so powerful nowadays in religious life because of what we are taught by external science which, however, has nevertheless made us free. On the one hand it has achieved great triumphs, but on the other it has planted understandable doubt in our heart with regard to our religious life and any knowledge about supersensible existence.

Anthroposophy has set itself the task of sweeping human souls clean of those strong doubts that have been placed in them by external science. In a true scientific spirit, anthroposophical science has the task of overcoming what external science cannot overcome. It will be able to reintroduce genuine religious life into human souls. It will not contribute to the slaying of religious feeling but will reintroduce into human evolution a religious sense for everything. Human beings will gain a new understanding of Christianity when they turn towards the Mystery of Golgotha which anthroposophy alone can help people to understand and accept fully.

Since anthroposophy gives human beings not only a reawakening of old religious understanding but also a new religious sense through knowledge, it can most certainly not be said to be aiming for anything sectarian. It has as little intention in this direction as any other science. Anthroposophy does not strive to form sects. It wants to serve the religions that already exist, and in this sense it wants to bring new life into Christianity. It does not want to preserve old religious feelings and help religion press forward in the old way. It wants to contribute to a resurrection of religious life, for this religious life has suffered too much at the hands of modern civilization. Therefore anthroposophy wants to be a messenger of love. It does not want merely to bring new life to religion in the old sense; it wants to regenerate and reawaken the inner religious life of humanity.

3. FIRST STEPS IN SUPERSENSIBLE PERCEPTION

London, 17 November 1922

There is no doubt that at the present time very many people long to know something about spiritual, supersensible worlds. Even a good many scientists have begun to look for ways leading to knowledge of the supersensible. However, all endeavours to enter the supersensible world have been blocked for modern human beings by the manner of reaching conclusions that is fostered by science with all the authority it commands. Many of the sources from which people assume that knowledge of the supersensible world can be gleaned are viewed with prejudice because people consider that there can be no precise knowledge in the sense of modern science since none of the evidence put forward can be verified.

In contrast to this, the anthroposophical science I shall be speaking about today and over the next few days strives for truly precise knowledge of the supersensible world.[9] I mean precise not in the sense of the way experiments are conducted in ordinary science but in the sense that inner faculties of soul—otherwise asleep in us during our everyday life and our ordinary scientific work—are developed in such a way that the full clarity of consciousness implicit in precise science is maintained throughout. Whereas in the exact sciences we use the same consciousness as in ordinary life and employ precise methods in our investigations of the external world, in anthroposophical spiritual science we proceed by adopting an initial attitude of what I will call intellectual modesty. We remind ourselves that when we were children we had capabilities that fell far short of those we now possess as adults, which we have acquired through our education and through life itself. Obviously we have developed faculties since childhood that were not there originally, so we are justified in asking ourselves whether we perhaps possess further faculties that are still asleep in us, just as our present ones were asleep in us during childhood. By putting certain methods into practice we can indeed unfold such faculties in our soul.

In anthroposophical spiritual science these faculties must be unfolded by first applying exact methods to one's own development, before proceeding to the faculties themselves. We prepare ourselves for insight into the higher world by applying precise methods to ourselves. As I said in my previous lectures here in this hall,[10] this is how we then achieve exact clairvoyance. We acquire it by methods that are as precise and systematic as those employed when the facts of ordinary knowledge are being used in the investigation of nature.

Today I shall speak less about how this exact clairvoyance can be attained. I shall mention this merely in passing since those two previous lectures dealt with the methods through which exact clairvoyance can be attained; and information about these methods is also available from the book *Knowledge of the Higher Worlds*.

Instead I want to speak today about what it is that prevents human beings from penetrating into the higher worlds during their everyday life. The main obstacle lies in the fact that they can only ever perceive the immediate moment in the world. Our eyes only show us the world and its phenomena at the present moment. Our ears only let us hear sounds at the present moment, and the same goes for all our senses. We can only know the past of our earthly life in recollection, that is to say in pale, shadowy thoughts. You only have to compare how vital and real experiences undergone ten years ago were and how pale and shadowy are our thoughts with which we remember them today.

In our ordinary consciousness everything that lies outside the present moment can only live in shadowy remembrance. However, the flame of this shadowy remembrance can be fanned to light up as a higher reality through the methods which, as I have said, I do not propose to discuss in detail today, such as meditation in thinking, concentration on thoughts, inner training and the like.

Those who apply such methods to themselves, learning to live in their thoughts with all the intensity with which they otherwise live in their external sense impressions, acquire a faculty of observing the world not only in the immediate present. Depending on the aptitude of the individual concerned, exercises leading to this result must of course be practised for a long time in conscientious, systematic meditation and concentration. Some individuals, especially nowadays, already bring with them at birth the faculties that can be developed by these methods. Not that the faculty is immediately evident at birth, but at a certain moment in life it emerges from within the individual, who knows that had it not come with him or her at birth it would have been impossible to acquire it in the ordinary course of life. This faculty consists in being able to live within the thoughts themselves, just as through our body we live in the physical world.

Such a statement should not be taken lightly, for we must remember that human beings owe everything that gives them their sense of existing to the fact that they can experience the sense-perceptible world. When they reach the stage where, without depending on impressions received through their eyes, ears and other senses, they can unfold an inner life as active and intense as the life of these outer senses, an inner life consisting not merely of shadowy thoughts but of inwardly living thoughts experienced with all the intensity otherwise implicit only in sense impressions—then they know the reality of a second kind of existence, a different form of self-awareness. I will call it an awakening—an awakening to a life not outside the body but within the innermost core of being, while the physical body is as quiescent and as insensible to impressions from outside as is otherwise the case only during sleep.

If we think about our own inner life and being, we find that in ordinary existence we really only know what has been conveyed to us via the senses. We have no direct perception whatever about our inner life and being. Ordinary consciousness does not enable us to look into our own internal being. But when we achieve awareness of ourselves through pure thinking, then we learn to look inwards just as in ordinary existence we can look outwards to the external world.

We then feel something like the following. As we look into the external world, the sun or some source of light must be there to illumine the objects around us. Through the light that is outside us we perceive these objects. When we become aware of that second existence through the process of pure thinking—a process that is a matter of actually seeing as colourfully and intensely as we normally see what our senses show us—then we actually experience, spiritually, a light that we can shine into our inmost being as directly as we otherwise find outer objects illumined by outer lights.

That is why this condition of human experience can be called clairvoyance, 'clear seeing'. This clairvoyance in our newly awakened spiritual self-awareness engenders the faculty that enables us once again to be consciously present in every moment we have lived through during our life on earth.

It is, for example, perfectly possible to have the following experience. We see ourselves as an 18-year-old going through certain experiences. We not only remember these experiences, we actually live through them again more or less intensely. We become once more the human being we were at 18, or 15 or 10. One can transpose oneself into every moment of one's life and thereby unfold an inner, illumined perception of what we can call a 'time-body' in contrast to the spatial body that contains our sense organs and gives us an external appearance.

This 'time-body' is continuously present; we do not

experience it in a succession of separate moments but as a complete continuum. It is present in all its inner mobility. A vista appears before us of our whole earthly life up to that moment, whereas in ordinary circumstances we merely recollect our life in shadowy thoughts. We illumine the whole of our life on earth in such a way that we are right there in each single moment.

When this inner illumination arises we know that we carry not only a physical, spatial body but also a second, more subtle body, a body that is woven of pictures of what our life on earth has thus far brought us, pictures that nevertheless at the same time creatively shape this earthly life. They shape our organism and our activities, the organism in which we live, the activities we have carried out. In this way we get to know a second human being living within us.

This second human being is aware of itself as living within a subtle, etheric world of light, just as the spatial body experiences itself in the physical world. The world is there all over again, this time in its more subtle, delicate formations. The more delicate, etheric formations perceived in this way underlie everything physical.

We have the strange experience of only being able to hold on to this more subtle body for a short moment. Once we have attained this exact clairvoyance enabling us to penetrate our ether body or body of formative forces, as I might also call it, we are capable of seeing the etheric aspect of the world and of ourselves. At the same time we cannot help noticing how very rapidly the impressions disappear. We cannot retain them. We become anxious to return as quickly as possible to the perceptions of our physical body in order to be reassured by an inner sense of consolidation as a human being and a personality. We experience our own self in our ether body and also whatever is etheric in the higher world, but at the same time we see how fleeting all these impressions are; we cannot retain them for any length of time unless we resort to some kind of help.

As an example, let me now tell you how I help myself in order to prevent the impressions of this etheric vision from vanishing too rapidly. Whenever such impressions come, I try not only to perceive them but also to write them down. In this way the inner activity is carried out not only by abstract faculties of soul but is retained by the act of writing down the impressions. It is not so much a matter of reading what has been written down but rather of letting the more vigorous activity flow into the activity that is initially purely etheric.

By this means something that is immensely fluid and evanescent is poured into the more solid form of one's ordinary human faculties. This does not take place unconsciously as with a medium, but in full consciousness. Everything is poured into our ordinary bodily faculties so that we can retain it.

This enables us to understand something of great importance. It enables us to understand how we can keep hold, initially, of a supersensible, etheric world. (Later on we shall be speaking of other supersensible worlds as well.) We keep hold of a supersensible, etheric world that embraces the course of our life up to this moment and also the etheric aspect of external nature right up to the world of the stars. We get to know this etheric world. In this etheric world we learn to experience ourselves; and we know that without returning again to the physical body it is impossible to hold on to this etheric world for more than two or three days, even when our faculties have been developed to a very high degree. Certain powers of which I shall speak in a moment enable someone who is an initiate in the modern sense to perceive all this with clear vision; such an initiate also knows what it is that he is holding on to in his ether body, or body of formative forces, without the support of the physical bodily faculties. It is what we see when we step through the gate of death and depart from our physical body which then begins to decay. It is what we see at first through our higher awareness of self and what cannot remain in our self-awareness for more than two or three days after the death of the physical body.

Through the development of exact clairvoyance, therefore, we can experience the first conditions of existence through which we pass after death; they are experienced in advance, with conscious knowledge.

The conditions which the initiate is able to experience consciously, in advance, come to pass for every human being when the physical body is laid aside at death. However, in the ordinary way we can retain consciousness of these conditions for no longer than two or three days—that is to say, for as long as we are able, having developed higher knowledge, to hold fast to our ether body, our body of formative forces. (I shall explain later what it is that gives us consciousness after death.)

For two or three days after death the human being has in his ether body a consciousness of the etheric world. Then this consciousness is laid aside. Just as the physical body has fallen away, now the experience is of the ether body falling away, whereupon it becomes necessary to move on into a different consciousness in order to continue as a conscious human being after death.

The reality of what I am now describing to you as the first moments after death—they are the first moments measured against the cosmic existence to come—can be affirmed by one who has acquired the faculty of seeing into the higher world, since he experiences in advance the conditions which in the normal way only set in after death. Because he has developed the intensified consciousness of self that is no longer dependent on the body, he experiences in advance, in his present consciousness, those moments which immediately follow death.

The initiate is able to shed light on his own higher existence and to realize that he has within him the light which, during the first two or three days after death, will reveal to him a world quite different from the world our senses show us during earthly life between birth and death.

When this part of the lecture has been translated I shall go on to describe what happens after those few days.

★

The inner illumination I have described is needed so that we can survey the supersensible picture of the course of earthly life which lasts, as I have said, for a few days after death. Within yourself you have to kindle a spiritual light that shines inwards. You then get beyond being aware only of the present moment, which is all that the senses allow us.

If we are to attain further knowledge of the supersensible world, not only the state of our perception but also the state of our actual life has to change. In the ordinary living state we human beings are enclosed within our spatial, physical body; the boundary provided by our skin is at the same time the boundary of our life. Our life extends as far as our body. Within this state of experience we cannot get beyond the knowledge about the higher worlds that I have so far described. To go further in attaining knowledge about the higher worlds we have to transcend our ordinary experience by developing a way of experiencing that is not enclosed within the boundaries of our spatial body but participates in all the life of the surrounding world.

This extended consciousness, too, can be achieved, but as I have already said, I only want to mention a few points about the methods of the modern initiate by means of which he is able to gain exact knowledge of the higher worlds. The rest is to be found in the book already mentioned. The further stage is attained when we are capable not only of letting thoughts live with full intensity in our consciousness, but of eliminating them at will as the result of systematic exercises and practice. By this means consciousness arises of experiences outside the body. Let me show you a simple exercise.

Suppose you are looking at a crystal. It is there before your eyes. A person who is trying to make himself into a medium or to induce some kind of self-hypnosis stares fixedly at the crystal, and the impression it makes puts him into a state of confused consciousness. Anthroposophical science has nothing to do with such a method. The exercises it adopts are entirely different and can be characterized as follows. We look steadily at the crystal until we can entirely ignore it as an object physically perceived, and reorientate our attention in a way that we can otherwise only do with thoughts. The crystal is there before us and we learn gradually to look through it, not physically but with eyes of soul; the physical eyes are open but are not used for the purpose of looking at the physical crystal. In this act of inner cognition the crystal in front of us is eliminated, as a physical object, from our vision. The same procedure may be followed with a colour. It is there before us but we no longer look at it as a colour; we eliminate it from our physical vision.

This exercise can also be applied to thoughts that occur to us in the immediate present as the result of external circumstances, or to those which arise in the form of memories of earlier moments of earthly life. These thoughts are eliminated, emptied from consciousness, so that we are simply awake and in a state of consciousness from which the external world is altogether excluded.

When we do such exercises we can discover that it is possible for our life to extend beyond the boundaries of our spatial body. Then we share in the life of the whole surrounding world instead of perceiving its physical phenomena only.

Thereby, in complete clarity of consciousness, an experience arises which may be compared with recollection of the life passed through during sleep. Just as ordinary perception is limited to the immediate moment, so is our ordinary life limited to the experiences that have arisen in the hours of our waking consciousness.

When you think back over your life, the periods of sleep are always blanks as far as ordinary consciousness is concerned. Nothing that has been experienced by the soul during those periods of sleep is remembered; the stream of memory keeps being interrupted, but this fact is usually ignored.

By contrast, experiences of the soul during sleep arise like intensified memories in a consciousness that has awakened to such a degree that it enables us to live outside our body. This is the second stage in knowledge of the supersensible worlds. We begin to experience what we go through as beings of soul when our body, our physical body, is quiescent and asleep, when it has no perceptions, when the will is not functioning and when the soul has, so to speak, temporarily departed from the body. In this way we can to a degree recollect in ordinary waking life the experiences through which we have passed while outside the body during every period of sleep. But it is very important to assess these experiences correctly. The experiences of the soul from the moment of falling asleep to that of waking are, of course, experiences in the realm outside the body, and actual awareness of them is possible only when consciousness of life outside the body has awakened. Knowledge comes to us not only of something which, like the 'time body', is illumined by an inner light. In ordinary day-time memory that has progressed to this type of higher exact clairvoyance we now recognize what we have really experienced each time between falling asleep and waking up. This experience will astonish us at first. In ordinary consciousness during the day we live in our physical body with our lungs, heart and everything else inside us. But between going to sleep and waking up we have a cosmic consciousness, not a personal one. Strange though this may sound, we therefore feel in this clairvoyant vision as though we had reproductions of the worlds of planets and stars inside us. We feel ourselves to be within the all-pervading cosmic life and contemplate the world from this cosmic vantage-point.

Whenever we sleep we go in the reverse sequence of ordinary life through everything we have lived through in physical life, experiencing inwardly what is otherwise all around us. For example, when we go to sleep after a normal day, we live backwards over the experiences of the day—first the experiences of the evening, then those of the afternoon, then those of the morning. During sleep at night we live backwards in this way through all the experiences of the day.

Development of the exact clairvoyance about which I am speaking is connected with being able consciously to remember these night-time experiences. Just as in the ordinary way we can remember things experienced years ago in full waking consciousness, by means of this exact clairvoyance we can call up remembrances of this backward sequence of the day's experiences. So in actual fact exact clairvoyance is an extension of the ordinary faculty of recollection. We look back upon our experiences during sleep, knowing that in sleep we have been living outside the boundaries of the physical body in a cosmic existence which is a reflection of the whole life of the universe. During this cosmic existence we live backwards through the happenings of our own day. We discover that the time taken by this backward review is shorter than that taken by the experiences themselves in physical life. When we become genuine researchers in this matter through systematic practice and increasingly exact knowledge, we discover that this backward review takes place three times more quickly than the physical experiences in our ordinary consciousness. Assuming a person is awake for two thirds of his whole life and asleep for one third, it is during this one third spent in sleep that he lives backwards through the experiences which, in his everyday life, have occupied two thirds of his existence.

When exact clairvoyance enables us in waking consciousness to remember the life of sleep, we also realize that this backward review is not significant in itself, but merely as a foreshadowing. Ask yourselves what you think about a recollection of something that happened to you 20 years ago. You say: 'I experience it now in shadowy thoughts of remembrance; but this remembrance itself is the guarantee that I have not made it up but that it is a picture of an actual experience I had during this life on earth sometime in the past.' So a memory is a guarantee relating to something quite other, namely, an actual experience in the past. In the same way the conscious recollection of our experiences in sleep is meaningless in itself, but it is a foreshadowing of something belonging to the future.

Proof that a remembrance relates to something in the past is not needed. When exact clairvoyance has been acquired, it is equally unnecessary to prove that the recollection of those nightly experiences is not a figment of the present. It is obvious that it has to do with the individual's future, namely, that part of the future when he will actually have laid aside his physical body in death, just as now, in exact clairvoyance, it is only figuratively laid aside.

By this means knowledge arises of what the human being experiences after death, when the three days of which I have spoken have elapsed. The process resembling a remembering also enables us to understand the significance of those two or three days after death when the human being is aware of living in a cosmic consciousness, when from the vantage point of the cosmos he once again surveys the etheric picture of his life, looking back over the course of his earthly existence. We also come to recognize that these first days after death are followed by a life which runs its course three times more quickly than earthly existence. We met with this when we examined our night-time experiences.

The etheric vision which persists for only a short time after death is followed by a life lasting some 20 or 30 years, or perhaps less—depending on the age reached during life on earth. Everything is approximate, of course, but this life after death runs its course approximately three times more quickly than earthly life. If a person dies at the age of 30, then he will go through the life of which I am now speaking three times as fast, or in about 10 years. If someone reaches the age of 60 he will take 20 years to experience his life backwards after death—but these periods are approximate.

These things become known through exact clairvoyance, just as a past experience is known through an act of recollection or remembrance. Thus we learn to know that death is followed by a life in the supersensible world during which we live through the whole of our past earthly life in reverse. Every night we live backwards through the events of the preceding day; after death we live backwards over the whole of our earthly life. We experience it all once again in its spiritual aspect and thereby unfold a correct assessment of our own moral worth.

During the period after death we build into ourselves a consciousness of our personal, moral qualities, our moral worth, just as here on earth we are conscious of life in a body of flesh and blood. After death we live within what we were as a moral human being here on earth. By living through earthly life again in reverse and because we are not diverted from true moral judgement by instincts, natural urges and passions but survey our life from a purely spiritual standpoint, it is possible for us to form a true assessment of our own moral quality.

The forming of such an assessment requires the length of time of which I have just been speaking. When this period after death has come to an end, the backward-flowing remembrance of our moral life on earth fades and we must now pass onwards through the spiritual worlds with a different kind of consciousness. Knowledge of this different kind of consciousness, too, can be achieved by exact clairvoyance.

The attainment of such knowledge depends upon the capacity not only to live outside the confines of the spatial body but to unfold a kind of consciousness entirely different from the one we have here in the physical world. We discover what follows the period lasting about one third of the time during which we experience our moral qualities. What follows is a supersensible, purely spiritual state of experience. Before knowledge of it can be acquired, exact clairvoyance must have developed a still higher stage of pure consciousness and must, moreover, be capable of assessing this consciousness fully.

So far I have tried to describe two conditions that come into play after death. When the translation has been done I shall tell you about a third.

★

If you think about the experience undergone during sleep when you go backwards, you will realize that the human being does indeed lead a life outside his physical, spatial body, but he has no real freedom of movement in that life. He has to make his way through the experiences that have come to him during the hours of waking, but in reverse order. Even someone who has attained supersensible insight into these experiences through exact clairvoyance, even such a person feels as though he is confined to a world which he is able to call up into his clairvoyant vision but in which he cannot move, in which he is fettered. Freedom of movement in the spiritual world—this is what must be acquired as the third stage of supersensible knowledge and life. Without such freedom of movement it is not possible for spiritual consciousness in the real sense to arise.

In addition to exact clairvoyance, a power which I will call that of 'ideal magic' must be acquired. This must be distinguished from the unlawful form of magic which resorts to external means and is fraught with a great deal of charlatanism. A firm distinction must be made between such practices and what I now mean when I speak of 'ideal magic'.

I mean the following. When we survey our life in ordinary consciousness, we can see how in certain respects we have changed with the passing of every year or decade. Our habits have changed—slowly perhaps, but definitely nevertheless. Certain faculties have developed, others have disappeared. If we honestly observe the different faculties of our earthly life we can say that in many aspects we have changed. However, this change has been brought about by life. We have surrendered ourselves to life, and life educates us, trains us, and shapes our soul.

Someone who wants to find his way into the supersensible world as a real knower, in other words one who strives to acquire the power of ideal magic, must not only be able to make his thoughts so inwardly forceful and intense that he becomes aware of a second existence as described already, but he must be capable of freeing his will, also, from bondage to the physical body. In ordinary life we can only bring our will into operation by using our physical body, our legs, arms or organs of speech. The physical body provides the basis for the life of will. What we can do to go further in this has to be carried out very thoroughly and systematically by a spiritual researcher who wants to attain ideal magic in addition to exact clairvoyance. We must develop such strength of will that at a certain point in our life we can, at our own bidding, get rid of some habit of soul and acquire an altogether different one in its place.

Even with the most resolute will it may take several years to transform certain types of experience, but it can be done. Instead of allowing life in the physical body to be our teacher, we can take our education and inner training in hand ourselves.

Exercises of will like those described in *Knowledge of the Higher Worlds* mentioned earlier will lead someone who is striving to be an initiate in the modern sense to the stage where he is not only able to be conscious during sleep of what he has experienced by day. He will be able to induce a state of consciousness which is not that of sleep but is lived through in full awareness. In this he will be capable of movement and action even during sleep. He is not, as in ordinary consciousness, a merely passive being while outside his body, but he can act and do things in the spiritual world. If he is incapable of this he will make no progress during his sleep life. Someone who becomes a modern initiate in the true sense acquires the faculties by means of which he can also be active as a self-aware human being in the life which runs its course between the onset of sleep and the moment of waking. When his will becomes operative while he is actually living outside his body, he will be able gradually to unfold an altogether different kind of consciousness, namely, the consciousness that can actually perceive what the human being experiences during the period after death following the one I have already described.

With this more highly developed consciousness it becomes possible to see into the existence that follows after our life on earth as well as that which precedes it. We look into a life that runs its course through the spiritual world just as the physical life on earth runs its course through the physical world. We recognize ourselves as beings of pure spirit in the spiritual world just as here on earth we are physical beings in the physical world. Then we are able to ascertain how long the life will last that follows on after we have gone through the period of moral evaluation described earlier.

By integrating will into the life of soul in this way through ideal magic, we learn to understand the nature of the consciousness that awakens in us as adult human beings, and to compare it with the dim consciousness of earliest childhood and infancy.

As you know, ordinary consciousness has no remembrance of those earliest years of childhood. The consciousness of the human being in this period of his life is dull and dim; his entry into the world is wrapped in sleep. The ordinary consciousness of an adult human being is clear and intense in comparison with the dim, dull consciousness of the first years of earthly life. Someone who has acquired the power to put ideal magic into operation in the way described can understand the difference between his waking consciousness as an adult and the dim consciousness of early childhood; he knows that he steps on to a higher level as he passes from the dim consciousness of childhood into the clearer consciousness of adult years. Knowing the relative degree of consciousness in adulthood as compared with that in childhood, he can also judge the relative difference between his consciousness as an adult and that illumined awareness he attains when he has imbued his soul not only with exact clairvoyance but also with ideal magic, which makes him capable of moving freely in the spiritual world.

We learn to move freely in the spiritual world to the same degree that we learned to move freely with our body when we left the immobility of infancy behind us during physical earthly life. By understanding the relative degree of awareness we have in adulthood compared with that in childhood, we can come to understand the relative difference between adult consciousness and the highest, purely spiritual kind of consciousness.

Through this we come to realize that in the life after death we are a spiritual being living amongst spiritual beings. Over and above this we also learn to assess how long this spiritual life amongst spiritual beings is going to last. Again I must quote the example of recollecting an ordinary experience. Just as that recollection bears within it a reality belonging to the past, so this new experience bears within it the knowledge that the higher consciousness of the initiate is not significant in itself but that it anticipates existence after death as a spirit amongst spirits. We learn to recognize the relative position of this purely spiritual life in comparison with the life we have here between birth and death.

Looking back to childhood, an initiate realizes that the older he gets the easier it becomes to look into the spiritual world. There are of course those who while still comparatively young have the power to see into the spiritual world. But this increases in clarity and exactitude with every year they live. The ability to enter into this other state of consciousness grows constantly stronger, and with it comes clearer and clearer knowledge of the relative degree of one to the other.

For example: having reached the age of 40, one is only able, let us say, to remember back as far as one's third or fourth year. Having studied the length of the period of dreamlike consciousness in childhood relative to these 40 years, we come to realize that the life after death in the spiritual world will be longer than the span of one's earthly life by as many times as this earthly life as a whole is longer than the dreamy life of earliest childhood; hence the life after death lasts for many centuries. Thus the period during which the moral life is re-experienced and assessed after death is followed by a purely spiritual life during which the human being lives for many centuries as a spiritual being amongst spiritual beings. During this period of existence he has around him the tasks that belong to the spiritual world, just as here in earthly existence he has around him the tasks that belong to the physical world.

When exact clairvoyance and the power to move freely in the spiritual world brought about by ideal magic have been acquired, the nature of these tasks is revealed. All the forces that finally lead over to a new life on the earth have to be gathered from the spiritual world in which the human being lives after death. The future life on earth stands there as a goal from the very beginning of the life after death. This life on earth as a human being is truly a microcosm, and this microcosm is gathered together out of the mighty experiences in the spiritual world after death.

A seed in the physical world is minute, but nevertheless it will unfold and later on grow into a large plant or animal. I might also speak of a spirit-seed which the human being forms after death when his physical life on earth is over. In collaboration with spiritual beings he moulds out of the spiritual forces of the universe a spirit-seed for his coming life on earth. This process is not a recapitulation of the past earthly life but embraces modes of activity and realities of being far greater and mightier than can ever exist on earth. In his post-earthly existence, amid the experiences and realities of the spiritual world, the human being prepares his future earthly life.

I have spoken of the cosmic consciousness that arises in human beings after their death. This cosmic consciousness is, of course, present every night during sleep, although in such dimness that, to use a contradictory expression, it is really an 'unconscious consciousness'. Because they have this cosmic consciousness in their spiritual existence after death, human beings live together not only with other spiritual beings who never come down to the earth, having their abode in worlds of pure spirit, but paramountly with all the souls who are either incarnate in human physical bodies or, having themselves passed through the gate of death, have also entered into the cosmic consciousness that is common to all.

The relationships woven on earth between soul and soul, in the family, among individuals who have found one another through meeting while incarnated in physical bodies—all such ties in their earthly form are laid aside. What we experience as lovers, as friends, as associates of other human beings close to us in some way, in short, all experiences in the physical body—all are laid aside just as the physical body itself is laid aside. But because these ties of family, of friendship, of love and affection have been unfolded here on the earth, they are transmuted after death into those spiritual experiences which help to build a later life. Even during the period when the moral worth of the past life is being assessed we do not work alone but in collaboration with souls we have esteemed and loved while on the earth.

Through exact clairvoyance and through ideal magic these things become matters of actual knowledge, of direct vision, not of belief alone. It is true to say that in the physical world an abyss stretches between souls, for however much they love one another their meeting takes place in the body and the relationships between them can only be such as are determined by the conditions of bodily existence. But once a human being is in the spiritual world, the physical body belonging to a loved one left behind on earth is no longer an obstacle to living in communion with that loved one's soul.

Just as the faculty of 'seeing through' physical objects must be acquired before it is possible to look into the spiritual world, so the human being who has passed through the gate of death can penetrate through the bodies of those he has left behind and enter into communion with their souls while they are still living on the earth. Until they also die he goes on experiencing them as souls.

I wanted to speak to you in the first of these three lectures[11] about how perception of the supersensible life of man can be developed. I have tried to indicate that when we strive to unfold exact clairvoyance and the power of ideal magic, it is possible to speak with real knowledge of the higher worlds, just as exact science is able to speak about the physical world. As we learn to penetrate more and more deeply into these higher worlds—and undoubtedly there will be human beings who by developing their faculties will be capable of this—we shall find that no branch of science, however highly developed, can deter us from accepting the knowledge which can be revealed through exact clairvoyance and ideal magic concerning the human being's existence not only between birth and death on earth but also between death and the return to earthly life through a new birth.

In the lecture tomorrow I shall speak of the impulse brought into the life of man on earth by the Christ Event, the Event of Golgotha. It will be my task to show that the knowledge of which I have been speaking, in that it is the concern of every single human being, sheds light on the whole evolution of the human race on earth and can therefore also reveal what the entry of Christ into earthly existence signified for humanity.

The aim of these lectures is to show, on the one hand, that in speaking of supersensible knowledge there is no need to be at variance with exact scientific thinking. Our theme tomorrow will then be that the mightiest of all events in the life of humanity on earth, the Christ Event, is revealed in a new and even more radiant light to souls who are willing to receive knowledge of the supersensible world about which we have been speaking. My lecture will be about how anthroposophy relates to Christianity.

4. THE RELATION OF ANTHROPOSOPHY TO CHRISTIANITY

London, 18 November 1922

Opposition to what I call anthroposophical knowledge of the spirit is at present coming mainly from two sides. I alluded briefly in the lecture yesterday[12] to one of these, namely, the antagonism of scientific thinking which maintains that supersensible knowledge is beyond the reach of human faculties. From this angle, therefore, anthroposophy is regarded as an impossibility.

Today we shall be more concerned with opposition of a different character. It comes from people who feel that anthroposophy deprives them and a good many of their fellow-believers of their inward connection with Christ. In their own way such people are usually very devout Christians and it is from their very piety that their antagonism springs. They feel that people's relation to Christ ought to be the outcome of simple, naïve devotion of heart and soul and that this is disturbed and confused when scholarship is brought to bear on the Christ Being. Such people want to seek Christ in simplicity of heart and mind, without being disturbed by any attempt to speak of Christ in a scholarly way based on knowledge.

Due respect must, of course, be paid to such feelings. Nevertheless these people are entirely mistaken in their attitude to anthroposophy. If they realized the truth they would find that anthroposophy helps to smooth the sure path to Christ that they are seeking. They would find that all the longings drawing them to Christ in simplicity and devoutness of heart are inwardly strengthened by what anthroposophy has to say concerning him.

I shall illustrate this from different points of view, beginning with a consideration of what people in different epochs of human evolution felt constituted their religious life and consciousness.

Let us go back to ancient times. As we proceed you will see that a historical survey of this kind is not superfluous but will actually clear away many misunderstandings prevailing nowadays. Admittedly the very early beginnings of human evolution cannot be reached via external historical documentation but only through the methods of spiritual science of which I spoke yesterday, through the development of those faculties of inner perception I described as the means whereby the supersensible nature of the human being and our supersensible experience of destiny are revealed.

In those ancient times human beings listened to what they were taught by pupils of the Mysteries, cultural centres of humanity where art, religion and science were still one and the same thing. Any historical documents or relics we may still have concerning these places refer to much more recent times and provide almost no insight into the Mysteries themselves. In those very ancient Mysteries, the teachers or gurus were venerated to a superhuman degree by their pupils, and the pupils in turn then taught the rest of humanity, ordinary people, when they wanted to satisfy their religious needs. The pupils of the Mystery teachers passed on to ordinary human beings whatever insights into the world and its order they had achieved through their life of deep devotion and reverence. In order to illustrate what even today true piety, true veneration of Christ can be, I should like to speak briefly about the relationship of one of those pupils to the guru or teacher in the Mysteries.

We find, first of all, that these teachers were regarded by their pupils as being divinely inspired. When they spoke with the fire of enthusiasm that had been kindled in them in the Mysteries and through the sacred rites, their pupils felt that the words were not uttered by men but that the divine powers of the universe were speaking through their human lips.

This was not an inner picture given by the senses; for those pupils of the ancient Mysteries it was an actual experience. You can imagine the depth and intensity of veneration in such a pupil when he knew that a divine being, a god—not a human being—was speaking to him through the lips of his teacher. Strange as it seems to us today, the following was the typical attitude of the pupils of the ancient Mystery teachers. They held the view that in still earlier epochs of the evolution of mankind, in the initial stages of this evolution, divine-spiritual beings themselves had descended to the earth—in the spiritual sense, of course. These divine-spiritual beings, who did not incarnate in bodies of flesh but could nonetheless commune through spiritual knowledge with those who were the first gurus, the first Mystery teachers, gave the very earliest instruction concerning what must be taught to human beings in order that they may enter into real connection with the spiritual world. The view was held, therefore, that the wisdom originally given to human beings by the gods themselves was passed down through the generations to the pupils of the Mysteries in every age.

You will say that this amounts to an assertion that the origin of human wisdom lies in supersensible worlds. We are indeed here touching on a realm in which there is still great ignorance about the origins of things. You only have to consider the explanation usually given of the origin of language. People say that human language has evolved in the Darwinian sense from the sounds uttered by animals. Yet there are, or were until not all that long ago, individuals who attributed human language to a divine origin.

However, I shall not enlarge any further on this now, for it would take us away from today's main theme. The point I want to make is that what gave rise to those feelings of deep reverence in the pupils of the gurus was the conviction that the teachings received from their lips had once been imparted to humanity by the gods themselves.

What was the aim and goal of this kind of discipleship? The

pupils gave themselves to their guru in utter veneration and devotion; the guru was the link connecting them with the spiritual worlds; this teacher was the one and only channel through which the divine flowed to them. The pupils felt that whatever qualities they themselves possessed, whatever powers they unfolded, were due to their teacher; they felt they owed everything to their teacher.

Above all the teacher gave them instruction, first and foremost about how to conduct their thoughts. Their thoughts must be conducted in a way that enabled the pupils to learn thinking without looking at the sense-perceptible world. Through a power implanted in their soul by the guru using what were then legitimate methods of suggestion, the pupils directed all their thoughts, all their faculties of heart and mind, towards the supersensible. In ordinary sense-perception our thoughts come up against external objects. Thinking of a table involves our thoughts bumping into the table; thinking of a tree entails our thoughts being obstructed by the tree, bumping into the tree. But the influence of the guru in the Mysteries made the pupils' thoughts transparent, so that they saw nothing of the world itself but looked through a panorama of thoughts straight into those worlds which I described yesterday out of modern initiation science as being supersensible.

It was, in addition, essential for the pupils to experience the reality of these supersensible worlds, and to this end instruction was given to them concerning the use of language. When we speak in ordinary life we impart to someone else thoughts we either have ourselves or have received from elsewhere. Put briefly, what flows into our speech has its origin in the physical world. The guru gave his pupils mantric sayings to be part recited, part spoken by them. The purpose was to train them to live in the language and not only pay attention to the meaning of the words but also experience in the flow of the sentences the stream of divine wisdom in the world. A mantra was spoken in a way that disregarded the ordinary human content and instead brought in the flow of all the divine that lives in the world and in the human being. By making their thoughts transparent the pupils were to become capable of beholding the divine. When reciting the mantras they were not to heed the meaning of the words, but the divine power streaming through them was to flow over into the acts performed in the sacred rites. Their will, their whole human personality, was to be directed to the divine through the rites and ceremonies. Even today you can find an indication of this in the Buddha position. The position in which the limbs are held is quite unsuitable for earthly activities. By the very position of the limbs the human being is removed from the earthly world. By combining this with the acts of inner devotion one is led away in the direction of the divine.

What was the purpose of all this? The pupil's soul, directed in this threefold way to the divine, was to become capable of taking evil, sin and human transgression, and turning it round towards the direction of those supersensible worlds described to you yesterday. I told you that with modern initiation science, too, we can enter those worlds in which we live as beings of soul and spirit before entering earthly existence. We descend from those worlds in order to unite with a body provided by father and mother, and we return to them again after passing through the gate of death, so that we can there prepare a new life on earth, as I described yesterday.

The aim of those godlike teachers in the ancient Mysteries was not merely to turn the pupil's meditative glance towards the supersensible worlds, but to kindle in him a force of thinking akin to prayer, a force born of the divine power flowing in the mantric sayings, a force of deepest veneration while performing the sacred rites. Imbued with this great power the pupil was then able to turn the tide of sinfulness on the earth towards the supersensible worlds. These pupils in turn imparted to the other human beings what they had been taught in the Mysteries—and in this way the content of civilization in those ancient times took shape.

Upon what basic assumption did these teachings rest? The basic assumption was that the world in which human beings live here on earth does not, like the divine world, encompass their whole being. In those ancient times the guru taught his pupils: This world in which you live between birth and death encompasses the other kingdoms of nature which are entirely at home in it; but it does not fully encompass the deeper being of man. We can disregard the fact that in those days human activities between birth and death were considered to be fraught with sin. Apart from this, the pupils were taught to realize: None of my experiences here in the world between birth and death, none of the deeds I perform are an expression of my full humanity, for that belongs to supersensible worlds.

There were certain moments in the life of every pupil in those ancient times when he knew in complete clarity that before descending to the earth he had lived in a supersensible world and would return thither after death. This clarity of insight was due to a primary, dreamlike clairvoyance which he did not need to acquire by effort since it was a natural faculty in all human beings. The pupils knew that when their actions and life were concerned only with what exists on the physical earth their full humanity was not in operation. They knew they must guide the forces within them to the spiritual worlds where they truly belonged.

The aim of the ancient Mysteries was that by the ceremonial rites conducted with clairvoyant thought, and by the divine power flowing through the sounds of the mantras, the forces which human beings on the earth cannot turn to good account in their actions should be led upwards and away from the earthly world to the supersensible worlds, for it is there that such things can be made right again since that is where man lives in the fullness of his being.

The gurus brought home to their pupils in no uncertain terms that when human beings have passed through the gate of death they know that their actions and achievements on earth fall short of what their full human potential demands;

they know that compensation must be made in the spiritual world for actions which on the earth are full of imperfection and fraught with unwisdom.

Knowledge of the supersensible worlds includes the realization that what remains imperfect on the earth can be brought nearer to perfection in the supersensible worlds.

However, conditions in the days of the ancient Mysteries were quite different and, as we shall see, they must change now. The pupils in those olden days learnt from their teachers that when the human being has passed through the gate of death and has lived for a time in the supersensible world, a sublime being approaches him, a being whose outer expression is the sun and its forms of manifestation. Hence the sages of the ancient Mysteries spoke of the divine Sun Being. Just as we say that the soul of a human being expresses itself in his physiognomy and play of facial expressions, so did the gurus of old conceive the sun with its movements and forms of manifestation to be the physiognomic expression, the revelation of the sublime Sun Being who was hidden from their sight here on earth but who came before them after their death, helping them to make more perfect their shortcomings and imperfect achievements of earthly life. 'In deepest piety of heart, put your trust in the sublime Sun Being whom you cannot find on the earth, who will be found only in the spiritual worlds; put your trust in the mighty Sun Being in order that after your death he may help you take the right path through the spiritual world!' In such a manner did the gurus of ancient times speak of the Being by whom all human imperfections can be brought into harmony.

By the time the Mystery of Golgotha approached, the ancient Mystery wisdom was already falling into decay; little of it remained except traditions and vestiges here and there. There were still some initiates in the old sense. They clung with the same devotion and pious faith to the divine Father God by whom in days gone by the divine messengers, the teachers of the first gurus, had been sent down to the earth.

They were aware of the deep consolation that had been given to the pupils of the Mysteries when they were told how after death they would find the sublime Sun Being, the one who would help them transmute and make perfect all short-comings of earthly life, who would take away from them the bitter realization that they had fallen away from the divine world order. That same sublime Sun Being had to come down to the earth, had to take on human nature in the man Jesus of Nazareth; since the death of Jesus Christ on Golgotha he is no longer to be found in the spiritual worlds but must now be sought amongst human beings.

This was how the initiates spoke at the time of the Mystery of Golgotha and on into the third century of our era. To those who were willing to listen they were able to say: 'The being from whom true healing comes, and for whom you are longing, was within the reach of humanity in olden times; through a divine deed this being came down to the earth, into a human body, and has lived since then as a supersensible reality within the evolution of mankind.' Whereas the pupils in olden times had been obliged to go to the Mysteries and there be encouraged by the sacred rites to lift their eyes to the supersensible world, people today must learn to make direct connection on the earth itself with the Christ Being who descended to the earth and became a man like any other human being.

Such was the mood and attitude kindled amongst human beings by those who were contemporaries of the Mystery of Golgotha and also by many who were initiates in the first three centuries of Christendom. Historical records have little help to offer because all real evidence of the teaching was rooted out. But supersensible perception as it was described to you yesterday leads to the knowledge that in the first three centuries this was the Christian mood and feeling prevailing amongst those who were willing to listen to the initiates still living in those times. Then this feeling for Christ died away; and today it must be reawakened. I will speak about this in the second part of my talk, after the first part has been translated.

*

The veneration of the pupil for his guru in olden times had gradually taught humanity at large to look upwards to the divine. The teacher or guru himself was regarded as the channel by which the divine streamed down to the earth and as the one who, in turn, guided into the spiritual world the feelings of devotion and reverence in the human heart. The accumulation of these feelings and experiences passed along the stream of heredity from generation to generation and was directed, by those who became the first teachers of Christianity, not to gurus in the old sense but to the Christ who had descended from spiritual worlds and in the man Jesus of Nazareth had taken humanity, a body, upon himself. Few today realize the deep inwardness and intensity of devotion which characterized these early teachers of Christianity.

That accumulation of feelings continued on through the centuries, directed now towards the one who was proclaimed by outer Christian history to have gone through the Mystery of Golgotha, through death, for human beings so that from then onwards they would be able to find him on the earth.

The goal and aim of the modern initiation science about which I spoke yesterday is now once again to approach this Christ Mystery, this Mystery of Golgotha, with true understanding. Why should this be necessary?

Medieval Christianity was, it is true, pervaded by piety and religious devotion, but these were really like a continuation of the veneration paid to the gurus of old by their pupils. At the same time the dreamlike clairvoyance once possessed by human beings faded away. Anthroposophical spiritual science does not need the help of historical records to investigate what existed in human life so long ago. At certain times in their lives it was possible for human beings to pass into a state of dreamlike clairvoyance in which they became aware of the world from which they themselves had descended to their earthly existence. But this knowledge that the soul belongs to eternity had gradually been lost. If they had retained it, human beings would never have been able to gain a sense of their human freedom.

This consciousness of freedom, however, which is an integral part of true humanity, was destined to arise in human beings when the time was ripe. The epoch in history when this feeling of freedom dawned was that of the Middle Ages; this was the very time when the old consciousness, which could never have experienced the reality of freedom, was fading away. When human beings looked up to their existence as soul beings amongst spiritual beings in pre-earthly life they were aware only of dependence. They did not feel free. The ancient clairvoyant vision of the spiritual world grew dim, and in this twilight condition of consciousness over against the spiritual world humanity unfolded that feeling of freedom which in our modern civilization has reached some degree of culmination. In this condition it was not possible for human beings to penetrate into the supersensible worlds out of which Christ had descended into Jesus of Nazareth. Christian worship therefore became a matter of tradition. People relied on historical tradition and drew on the power that had come down through the generations from the veneration once paid to the gurus. The deep reverence for the divine that had once lived in human beings could now be directed to the being who had passed through the Mystery of Golgotha. But since that consciousness of the spiritual world was now dimmed, a science of physical nature was evolving such as ancient times had never possessed, and in consequence of this even the faintest inkling that a spiritual world is accessible to human cognition faded away.

The supersensible knowledge of which I spoke yesterday is a genuine extension of the science of nature. All the faculties we can develop through meditation and concentration in such a way that we penetrate into the spiritual world in full knowledge, all these faculties are immeasurably strengthened when, as modern individuals, we do not content ourselves with what science says about the external world, but wrestle inwardly with it, assimilating these exact, scientific thoughts while at the same time endeavouring to unite them with the innermost forces of our own being. A kind of attunement or attitude of soul then arises which is at first not easy to define. If we take into this mood our meditation and concentration in thought and in will, our soul is guided upwards into the spiritual worlds in the way I described yesterday. It becomes possible for us to understand what the supersensible really is. We learn to look away from the earth, about which science teaches us in a particular manner, and into a supersensible world that belongs to the earth and must be recognized as an integral part of the earth—above all when it is a matter of understanding the human being and human life on earth.

Questions with far-reaching implications then arise in those who are struggling to acquire anthroposophical knowledge; and when they seek answers to these questions they are led, in addition, towards an understanding of the Mystery of Golgotha.

On the one hand they have learned to see into the spiritual world through having raised their consciousness away from the earth, having unfolded a faculty of perception outside the physical body and even of action through the power of ideal magic as I described yesterday. In this state of being free of the body they have learnt to enter a spiritual world with knowledge and with will.

Once we have equipped ourselves with this inner understanding of the spiritual world, if we then turn our attention to Christ and to the Mystery of Golgotha as an event on the earth, our attention—unlike that of many modern theologians—will go beyond concern for the man Jesus of Nazareth alone. Having acquired the power of supersensible vision we no longer regard the Mystery of Golgotha in a materialistic way; we discover that within the man Jesus of

Nazareth we see the divine Christ Being. Anthroposophy, this modern theosophy, enables us once again to achieve direct knowledge of the divine spirit. Equipped with this knowledge of the spirit we can turn to Jesus of Nazareth and recognize in him the Christ who can only be known as a spiritual being. With the knowledge we have gained of the supersensible world we are led to Christ, beholding in him the super-earthly, divine principle, the God-Man.

Through a full understanding of the realities of the spiritual world, modern anthroposophy leads the way to Christ. The preparation provided by anthroposophy is especially suited to lead the way to Christ. In order to make this absolutely clear I want to mention the erroneous and the true ways by which human beings today may approach the spiritual world. Long ago there were those whose inspiration proceeded directly from the Mysteries. Then the spiritual consciousness of humanity grew dim, but even in this darkened consciousness people were still able to see into some conditions of pre-earthly existence; they strove to let a spiritual power stream from their sacred rites. However, the successors of those godly, pious individuals of old have become in modern times people who endeavour by rather questionable means to contact the spiritual world. The godly individuals of earlier times confined themselves to the realm of the soul, turning their eyes of soul to the supersensible worlds. This mood of holiness and piety persisted as a Christian feeling for those pious people I mentioned at the beginning of the lecture who desire to cling to their naïve, simple piety. Such piety is naïve today because in their natural consciousness human beings no longer have any vision of supersensible existence. This naïve piety no longer leads people upwards into the supersensible worlds—as it did the pupils of the gurus in ancient times; it makes them stay on the earth within their own physical body. Such naïve piety makes people cling to the feelings the soul has when it immerses itself in its own human nature. This does, though, lead to the knowledge that down there in the physical body there is more than merely flesh and blood, that there is also spirit in it. It is this spirit that a pious person wants to direct towards the divine. But those who today are the misguided successors of the pupils of the ancient gurus endeavour to kindle this spiritual force through mediumistic practices.

What kind of person is a medium? A medium is someone who lets the spirit speak out of the physical body, lets it write by means of the physical hands or manifest by some other physical agency. The very fact that mediums speak or write while their ordinary consciousness is dimmed indicates that the human body is not wholly physical, that a spiritual force issues from it, but of a mechanical, inferior kind. A medium desires not only to experience the spiritual in the body but strives to bring the spiritual to physical manifestation; and the spiritual force that is present in the body does indeed become articulate when the medium speaks or writes. The peculiarity about mediumistic people is, as you perhaps know, that they become extremely talkative, they love to talk and to write at tremendous length; but all these manifestations of the spiritual through the body contain a great deal that ordinary logic will regard as highly questionable. These mediums are themselves the proof that it is not right for modern human beings to fall back on ancient methods of establishing connection with the divine, spiritual world but that they must seek an altogether different way.

This different way of approach to the spiritual world is what anthroposophical spiritual science is seeking, and I would like to speak about this different approach for a particular reason. Those who take modern science seriously and accept its findings as truly great achievements of modern civilization will find, as they try to approach the spiritual world through anthroposophical spiritual science, that it is extraordinarily difficult to move their speech organs at all in order to speak about their experiences, let alone entertain thoughts about them or write them down in a mediumistic way. When meditation and concentration leads to an awareness of the spirit within, one initially prefers to keep silent.

Whereas a medium becomes talkative and allows his own organs of speech to articulate spiritual things, a person who is a conscientious, scientifically educated individual would prefer to remain silent when seized by the spirit. Such a person would rather not talk about the subtle and delicate experiences of which his soul becomes aware. He even prefers to forbid thoughts from intruding, because thoughts have been associated with earthly, physical things. He prefers not to let thoughts stream into his soul because he is anxious in case half-consciously he might apply to spiritual realities thoughts that are connected with outer, physical things; he is afraid that when thoughts are applied to spiritual reality, this spiritual reality will not merely slip away but that it will be profaned, distorted. Least of all will he take to writing, for he knows that in olden times, when the gods were worshipped in ceremonial rites that did make use of the human body, writing was not used. Writing first entered human civilization when intellect and reasoning faculties came to be directed to the material world of the senses; it goes very much against the grain for someone in the process of gaining awareness of spiritual reality. So when someone begins to become aware of the reality of the spiritual world, he stills his thoughts and, even more than that, he refrains from speaking and abstains from writing down anything to do with the divine.

I have said before that it is permissible for me to speak of these things because I have experienced them myself along the path of development which led on from ordinary science to a comprehension and actual perception of the spiritual worlds and of the Mystery of Golgotha through these spiritual worlds. But you will understand that someone approaching the Mystery of Golgotha through this modern, anthroposophical spiritual science will encounter difficulties. The Mystery of Golgotha as it reveals itself in the course of human history must be conceived in all its stupendous majesty and glory. You have to learn to comprehend the historical fact of the God passing through the death on Golgotha by means of the human being Jesus of Nazareth. You must learn to contemplate this greatest of all historical events in an entirely sense-free picture. But having achieved this it is then exceedingly difficult, as I have just described, to bring oneself to express this event in thoughts, let alone present it in words or even in writing.

What comes to us along this path is an inner reverence and awe as we contemplate the great Mystery enacted on Golgotha. This reverence pours through the soul of one who, in the way I have described, has silenced his thoughts and words, who wants to remain perfectly still when the power of the spirit within him draws him towards the Mystery of Golgotha. Feelings of profound reverence and awe pour through the soul of such an individual; it is as though he dare not approach so stupendous a Mystery. Thus the path of anthroposophical spiritual science leads not only to knowledge, although to begin with it is indeed knowledge, knowledge that directs our attention into the supersensible worlds. But it then streams into the life of feeling where it becomes holy reverence. It becomes something that lays hold of the human soul far more deeply than any other power, more deeply even than the veneration paid to the guru by his pupils in olden times. This feeling begins by being a profound longing to understand Christ Jesus on Golgotha. What was initially a supersensible vision in the life of soul is transformed through inner metamorphosis into feeling. This feeling seeks the God-Man on Golgotha; and it can find him through the vision of the spiritual already acquired. It does not speak of the man Jesus of Nazareth but learns to recognize that in this man the Christ as a divine, spiritual being can be seen as a reality within earthly existence. Thus anthroposophical science brings knowledge of the spiritual Christ Being, and at the same time a deep and true reverence for the divine which arises from this knowledge of the supersensible.

In the short third part of my lecture, after the translation, I shall describe what can lead to the fruition of Christianity.

★

When an individual first becomes aware of the power of supersensible knowledge he prefers to be silent in his thoughts and words and not to use any of his bodily faculties as an instrument for voicing his experiences. Nevertheless, having reached a transitional stage, when he resolves to speak of his inner life, he experiences something which justifies his speaking of the spiritual nature of Christ Jesus. At this transitional stage he makes the resolve to give the spiritual definite form in his thoughts, to speak and to write about the spiritual. The experience that then comes to him is that he feels as though lifted out of his physical body whenever he is speaking or thinking about the spiritual. The physical body is an essential instrument in ordinary thinking and speaking, but now, at this higher stage, one is aware of being removed in a certain way from one's physical body. Whereas a medium feels himself entirely within the physical body and even deadens his consciousness in order to remain within the physical while allowing the spiritual to manifest through the body, someone who has attained real knowledge of the supersensible lifts himself out of his physical body in an enhanced and more delicate state of consciousness. Because he is experiencing the reality of the spiritual world he finds it exceedingly difficult to take hold of the physical world; his faculty of speech and the natural flow of his thinking elude him; he cannot find the way to his limbs or the rest of his physical body. He now has to undergo the experience of trying to find his bearings in this physical world once again, and therewith the thoughts and language in which to express the realities of the supersensible world of which he has become aware. It is something that puts him in the position of having to enter life all over again, for a second time; it is like going through a self-induced birth process. Through this one learns about the profound depths of the being of man, for in having to take hold of this being of man for a second time, so as to make it into an instrument for thinking and speaking about the spiritual, one gets to know it properly.

Entering in this way with supersensible knowledge into one's own organism, one realizes that here, too, one will find the Christ who has passed through the Mystery of Golgotha. One then has some understanding not only of the Christ who once came down to the earth and passed through death in order to pour himself into all humanity; one comes to understand that Christ went through death so that henceforth human beings may find him in themselves if they really fathom the depths of their own being. This is experienced by someone who is taking hold of his body for a second time, more firmly now, through supersensible knowledge. He can then clothe the knowledge of Christ thus acquired in words which contain the true proclamation of Christ. He knows that Christ died on Golgotha, that through his death Christ entered the forces of human birth, that since then he has lived within the human being. The modern initiate knows that the words of Paul contain a profound truth: 'Not I, but Christ in me.' He knows he will find Christ within himself if he succeeds in fathoming the depths of his own humanity.

In order to make people into Christians in the real sense, the initiate then knows that he need not expect them all to have reached his own depths of initiation. Equipped with this understanding and knowledge of Christ, he can also discover new paths for simple-hearted piety. This simple piety, too, can indeed find Christ, but the paths along which it does so cannot be quite the same as those that led in ancient days to the adoration poured out at the feet of the guru. Piety that is fitting for the modern age must be an inward piety, for human beings are no longer called upon to send their feelings of reverence for the divine up into a supersensible world; they must enter into their own being in order there to find Christ who, since the Mystery of Golgotha, has been alive on earth.

Anthroposophical spiritual science can say to someone whose heart is filled with simple piety: If you enter deeply enough into your own being you will find Christ; this is no illusion because by his death on Golgotha Christ did indeed descend into the depths of your own innermost self. Someone schooled in spiritual science knows that by speaking in this way to those of simple piety he is saying what is true; he knows that he is not playing upon the emotions of the other but pointing to a goal within his reach. It is perfectly possible for simple, godly individuals to tread the path that leads in the modern age to supersensible knowledge.

Whereas in earlier times, reverence and veneration for the guru made the thoughts of the pupil transparent, enabled the divine power to resound in the mantras and the rites to become potent deeds, someone desiring to find the true path to Christ in our modern age must, above all else, inwardly deepen his soul. He must learn to look within himself in order that he may find and become aware of inner reality when he turns his attention away from the world of sense impressions. Within himself he will find the power that leads him through the gate of death because he learns about it here on earth through devotion to Christ and to the Mystery of Golgotha.

The guru of olden times said to his pupils and through them to all human beings: When you pass through the gate of death you will find the sublime Sun Being who brings harmony into the imperfections of earth existence. The teacher in our time says: If here on earth, with inner reverence and deep devotion of heart, you establish connection with Christ who has descended, and with the Mystery of Golgotha, you will be inwardly filled with a power which does not die with you, but which you carry through death and which will work together with you towards the fulfilment of what cannot be wholly fulfilled on earth while you are living in a physical body. What the sublime Sun Being did with the human being in ancient times, the Christ Power will do with you once death has freed you of your body. The power of Christ in the earth will work on what is still imperfect in human beings, and they will be drawn together in the social life through their recognition of him. For the power that streams from Christ, the power upon which anthroposophical spiritual science is able to shed the light of understanding, can enter into the actions and the will of human beings and thereby flow into their social life. The powers of Christ can flow into social life.

There is much talk today of social reform and social progress. Who will be the great Reformer of the social life when people's actions are performed in the name of Christ Jesus so that the world may become truly Christian? Who will be the great Reformer, having the power to establish peace amid the social strife on earth? Christ alone will be the one, when people lead a social life that can become for them at certain moments an act of consecration, when they look up to Christ and do not say 'I', but when they say: 'Where two or three, or many, are gathered together in the name of Christ, then he is in the midst of them.' Work in the sphere of social life will become an act of consecration, a continuation of the sacred acts and rites. Christ himself will be the great social Reformer, since he works as a living reality within the being of man today.

The social life must be filled with the Christ Impulse. People of simple piety long to find Christ's power within their soul so that what they do in the social life may be done in Christ's name. These people with their simple piety can still be sure of their ground when a modern initiate says to them: The power you can find through your simple piety of soul when you meditate on your own being and upon the Christ who lives within you, this power streamed from the death on Golgotha, from Christ himself. It works as the Christ Impulse in the deeds you perform in social life, because Christ is present among human beings as a living reality when they find their way to him. They find him through themselves, through taking social life into themselves, just as they find genuine, devoted love that builds a bridge from human heart to human heart and brings a supersensible element into feeling, in the same way that light kindled within the human being brings a supersensible element into thinking.

In this way individuals of simple piety need no longer say that their path is disturbed by the knowledge imparted through anthroposophical spiritual science. If science were to continue along purely external lines, this simple piety would die out altogether in the course of time. But if science itself were able to lead on to knowledge of the supersensible and thereby knowledge of the Christ as a supersensible being, then all pious individuals would indeed be able to find what they are longing for: assurance in their life of soul, certainty that their deeds and actions, lovingly performed, are in harmony with the Christ Impulse. What pious and godly individuals are longing for can be given the certainty of knowledge by anthroposophical spiritual science. This spiritual science therefore has the right to insist that it does not impede the path of simple godliness or lead people away from Christ. Seeking as it does to lead the way to the spiritual world by working with and not against modern science, anthroposophy has this message to give: Humanity must not go forward into the future without Christ but with him—with Christ as a being who is known and recognized, whose reality is felt and whose impulse human beings resolve to make effective in the world.

5. MAN AS A PICTURE OF THE LIVING SPIRIT

London, 2 September 1923

After the two very satisfactory events at Ilkley and Pen-maenmawr,[13] this opportunity to speak to you here at our branch in London gives me the greatest pleasure.

I would like to begin by reminding you of what I said in former lectures here.[14] In carrying on their daily tasks day by day and year by year, human beings work by means of the physical body they have been given, which links them physically with all life on the earth. When we consider our surroundings in earthly life here in the physical world and think about what the work we do contributes to this earthly world, our attention is of course in the main turned towards the periods of each day during which we are awake. But as I said in those earlier lectures, what happens to us while we are asleep is even more important for our whole existence and indeed specifically for what we do on the earth.

Whenever we look back in memory, we always exclude the times we spent asleep; we join together what we have done and undergone by day while we were awake, forming this into a coherent sequence. Yet none of this would be possible without the intervening periods of sleep. If we really want to know the true human being it is to these periods of sleep that we must pay attention. It is easy to maintain that we know nothing about what goes on while we sleep. Although this may appear true for ordinary consciousness, it is not true in fact, for if we were to look back over a life uninterrupted by periods of sleep we should be automatons. True, we should still be spiritual beings, but we should be automatons.

Even more important than the daily periods of sleep throughout our life are the times we spent in sleep as very little children. We retain the effects of those early periods of sleep all through our life; in a sense, we only add to them what we later gain spiritually night by night throughout the rest of our life. We should be automatons if we came into the world as little children wide awake, if we never slept. In fact we should not only be automatons; in this automatic state we should be incapable of doing anything consciously. We should not even recognize what came about as a result of our own actions to be our own concern.

Although we believe we have no memory at all of those periods we have slept through, this is actually not quite correct. When we look back, the periods when we were asleep always evade our memory. But when we look back at the nothingness of the periods in time when we have been asleep, what we actually see, in one way or another, are the events we experienced while we were awake. On the face of it, we see nothingness at the places where we have slept. If you had a white wall and there was a patch where the white paint was missing so that there was nothing except a black disc, then you would also be seeing nothingness there. You see the darkness; perhaps there is not even a black disc but an actual hole with nothing lit up behind it. You see darkness behind the hole. This is like the darkness you see when you look back over your life. The periods when you were asleep appear like darknesses of life, and these darknesses of life are what you call 'I'. You would have no awareness of the ego if you did not see these darknesses. You owe your ability to say 'I' to yourself not to the circumstance of always having been busy from morning to night but to the circumstance that you have slept. For our 'I', our ego as we can address it during life on earth, is initially a darkness of life, an emptiness, a non-existence. Looking at our life in the right way we cannot say that we owe our consciousness of self to the daytime, for we owe it to the nighttime. It is the night that makes us real human beings rather than automatons.

Looking back to earlier epochs of human evolution on earth we find that, once there came to be some difference between waking and sleeping, human beings were no longer full automatons, yet because their states of sleep were more or less there also during their daytime consciousness a great deal of what they did in all the aspects of their earthly life was much more automatic than is the case with human beings now.

What this implies is that we never bring our real and inmost ego with us from the spiritual world into the physical world of the earth. We leave it in the spiritual world. It was in the spiritual world before we descended to our earthly life, and it is there again between falling asleep and waking up. It stays there always. When we call ourselves an 'I' during the ordinary daytime consciousness of today, we are using the word to point to something that does not exist in this physical world at all; it only has its picture in this world.

We are not seeing ourselves in the right way if we say: 'I am this sturdy human being, I stand here on the earth with my true being.' We see ourselves properly if we say: 'My true being is in the spiritual world; what exists here on the earth is a picture, a real image of my true being.' It is entirely true if we regard what is here on earth not as the true human being but as the picture of the true human being.

This picture character becomes even clearer when you consider the following. Imagine yourself asleep. Your ego is gone from your physical and ether bodies, your astral body is gone from your physical and ether bodies. Yet we know that the ego works in our blood and our movements. The latter cease when the ego goes away in sleep, but whatever goes on in the blood continues even when the ego is not there. So what is in our physical body when we sleep? There must be something weaving in our blood, just as the ego weaves in it during the day when we are awake. Our astral body, too, is present in the whole process of breathing, yet when it departs during the night our breathing continues. Again, there must be something working in us in the way our astral body works in us during the daytime.

Every time we go to sleep we withdraw our astral body from

our organs of respiration, and we withdraw our ego from the pulsation of our blood. So what becomes of them during the night? When we lie in bed asleep and our ego has departed from the pulsation of our blood, beings of the adjacent Hierarchy enter into the pulsation; Angeloi, Archangeloi and Archai now live in the organs in which our ego lives during the day when we are awake. And when our astral body departs from our organs of respiration, beings of the next higher Hierarchy—Exusiai, Dynamis and Kyriotetes—work there during the night.

So when we fall asleep in the evening and depart from our daytime body with our ego and our astral body, then angels, archangels and yet higher beings enter into us and while we are absent give life to our organs from the moment we fall asleep to when we wake up again. As to our ether body, we are incapable even during our daytime consciousness of doing what needs to be done in it. Even while we are awake it has to be filled by beings of the highest Hierarchy—Seraphim, Cherubim and Thrones. They remain permanently in our ether body.

Finally we come to our physical body. If we had to take care of all the great and wonderful processes in it, we would not merely do this very badly, we would be incapable of doing anything at all, for we are entirely helpless in this respect. What ordinary anatomy ascribes to the physical body would be incapable of moving as much as a single atom of it. Powers of quite another order are required here, namely, none other than those that have been known since primeval times as the supreme Trinity—the powers of the Father, Son and Holy Spirit. They—the essential Trinity—indwell our physical body.

In truth, for the whole duration of our life on earth our physical body is not our own. If it depended on us it would not go through its proper development. Our body, as was said in ancient times, is the true temple of the Godhead, of the divine threefold Being. Our ether body is the dwelling place of the Hierarchy of Seraphim, Cherubim and Thrones; they have to help care for the organs assigned to the ether body. The Second Hierarchy, Kyriotetes, Dynamis and Exusiai, have to care for the physical and etheric organs deserted by the astral body during the night. And the organs deserted by the ego have to be cared for during the night by the Third Hierarchy, Angeloi, Archangeloi and Archai.

There is constant activity in us, and it is not carried out by ourselves. While we are awake we are merely sub-tenants in our organism, for our organism is also the temple and dwelling place of spirits from the higher Hierarchies.

Bearing this in mind, we have to admit that we are only seeing the external human form correctly if we see it as a picture, a picture of the work of all the Hierarchies. They are within it. If I look at the form of the human head in all its details, and also the rest of the human body, I do not see it correctly if I maintain that it is a being in its own right. I see it correctly if I say that it is a picture of the invisible, super-sensible work of all the Hierarchies. When we can look at these things in this way we shall be able to speak correctly about what is otherwise always explained in an extremely abstract way.

It is all very well to say that the physical world is not reality but *maya*, and that reality lies behind the physical world. But by itself such a statement does not get us very far. It is a generalization, like saying there are flowers growing in the meadow. Just as this statement will only be of use if you know what kind of flowers are growing in the meadow, so can we only make use of knowledge about the higher world if we can show in detail how this higher world works in what appears to us as the outer picture, *maya*, the reflection, which is its physical, sense-perceptible manifestation.

*

Seen as a totality both in earthly life by day and in earthly life by night, the human being is connected not only with the sense-perceptible, physical earth but also with the world of higher spirituality. A kind of lower spirituality is at work in the kingdoms of nature here on earth—the mineral, plant and animal kingdoms. In the same way a higher spirituality influencing human beings is working through the world of the stars. Seen in his totality, the human being is related to plants, animals, water, air here on earth through his physical existence. In the same way he is related in his totality to the world of the stars, which in itself is also only a picture, a manifestation of what is really there. It is the beings of the higher Hierarchies who are really there. When we look up to the stars we are in reality looking up to the spiritual beings of the higher Hierarchies who only send down a symbolic light in what shines towards us so that in our physical existence we may have a hint of the spirit that fills the universe all around us.

Here on earth we long to know mountains, rivers, animals plants, and we ought to feel a similar longing to get to know the starry world as it really is. In its true being it is spiritual. In Penmaenmawr I gave a few indications about the spiritual nature of the moon in the way it shines from the universe in the present phase of earthly evolution.

When we look up to it we never really see the moon itself. At most we see a scant indication of where the illuminated crescent is continued. All we see is reflected sunlight, not the moon itself. We are reached on earth by cosmic forces reflected down to us by the moon, but never by what lives within the moon itself. That it reflects the sun's light to the earth is only a small part, indeed the smallest part of all that pertains to the moon. It also reflects back to us like a mirror all the physical and spiritual impulses that reach it from the universe. Just as we never see the other side of a mirror, so do we never see the interior of the moon, yet in this interior there is a real population of spirits with exalted guiding beings. These exalted guiding beings and the rest of the lunar population once lived on the earth. They withdrew to the moon more than 15,000 years ago. Prior to that the moon also looked physically different. In reflecting the sunlight down to the earth it also mingled something of its own essence in the sunlight. This is not our concern just now, however. But what does interest us is the fact that the moon today is like a fortress in the universe, in which there lives a population that fulfilled its human destiny over 15,000 years ago, after which it withdrew to the moon together with the spiritual guides of humanity.

Very advanced beings once lived on earth. They did not take on a physical body in the way we do, but lived more in an etheric body. Nevertheless, they were the great teachers of human beings at that time. These great teachers of humanity who once brought primeval wisdom to human beings on earth—that wonderful primeval wisdom of which Veda and Vedanta are only echoes—now live inside the moon and only reflect back to the earth what lives in the universe outside the moon.

One aspect of the moon forces did remain on the earth, and that is the force of physical reproduction in human beings and animals. Only the most extremely physical element remained behind when the great teachers of humanity migrated to the moon, which itself had withdrawn from the earth long before.

When we look up to the moon we only see its whole reality if we understand that high spiritual beings who were once linked with the earth now make it their task there to reflect back to the earth not what they bear within themselves but the physical and spiritual forces that come to them from the universe. Those who seek initiation wisdom today must also above all things strive to receive into this initiation wisdom what the beings of the moon with their sublime spiritual forces have to tell.

This is only one of the 'cities' in the universe, one colony, one settlement among many. Others are no less important, notably those belonging to our planetary system. As far as what concerns ourselves, as humanity on earth, the other pole, the opposite extreme to the moon is the population of Saturn.

As you may gather from my book *Occult Science*,[15] the Saturn population, too, was once united with the earth, but in a different way from the population of the moon. The Saturn beings are connected with the earth in quite a different way. They do not reflect anything back from cosmic space. Even physical sunlight is barely reflected back to the earth by Saturn. Like a solitary hermit Saturn wanders slowly round the sun, shedding very little light. What outer astronomy can tell us about Saturn is a very small portion of the truth, but actually the significance of Saturn for humanity on earth is made manifest every night, though only as a picture. It is realized more fully between death and a new birth when the human being passes through the spiritual world and therefore also through the world of the stars, as I explained in a lecture here not long ago.[16]

Although in the present phase of their evolution human beings do not encounter Saturn directly, they do encounter the Saturn beings indirectly by a roundabout way which I shall not go into now. These beings on Saturn are of the highest perfection, immensely sublime; they are in near relation to Seraphim, Cherubim and Thrones; Seraphim, Cherubim and Thrones are the beings closest to them, nearest amongst the Hierarchies.

The beings who populate Saturn do not radiate anything down from Saturn to the earth; they do not give anything to human beings that can be found in the external, physical world. But they preserve the cosmic memory, the cosmic record. The Saturn beings faithfully preserve in memory all facts and all events, both physical and spiritual, which the planetary system has undergone, all that the beings within our planetary system have experienced. They are forever looking back in recollection over the entire life of the planetary system. Just as we look back in memory over the limited range of our earthly life, so do the Saturn beings—in their collective activity—cherish the memory of what the planetary system as a whole and all the beings in it have undergone.

For human beings, the spiritual forces living in this cosmic memory are present through the fact that they enter into a relationship with the Saturn beings between death and a new birth, and indeed—more in picture form—every night. In this sense the forces emanating from the Saturn beings, which actually represent the deepest depths of the planetary system, are at work in human beings. Just as memory is our own deepest inner life on earth, so is what lives on Saturn the deepest inner 'cosmic I' of the whole planetary system.

Processes go on in our lives as a result of the way these influences are also present in us, processes the significance of which for the most part remains entirely hidden from us although they play the greatest imaginable part in our lives. What we are conscious of is, after all, only a very small portion of our life.

Think of an incisive moment, an all-important event in your life. For example you met the person with whom you were to go through life, or perhaps there was some other very incisive event. If you look back in time from that event you will be struck by the way there seems to be something like a plan that had been leading you towards this event for a long time. You can sometimes trace back the causes of an event that happened between the ages of 30 and 50 to the time when you were 10 or 12 years old; from that early age everything that happened led towards that event.

Elderly people looking back over their life in inner con-templation will find that everything has worked out. They will be able to confirm the presence of a subconscious thread. Forces of which we are not aware impel us to the decisive events of our lives. These are the Saturn forces that have been implanted in us through our relation with the inner popula-tion of Saturn.

On the one hand, then, the physical forces of reproduction are all that is present on the earth from the moon; they are what was left behind when the moon departed. On the other hand the very highest forces, the cosmic, moral forces, are present on the earth through Saturn. Saturn is the greatest bringer of balancing adjustment in all earthly events. While the moon forces now present on the earth have to do only with heredity, with what comes to us through father, mother and so on, the Saturn forces bring into human life all that lives in karma and goes from incarnation to incarnation. In this respect the other planets are intermediate between the two. They mediate between the physical on the one hand and the highest morality on the other.

Jupiter, Mars and so on are there between the moon and Saturn. In their various ways they mediate what at either extreme the moon and Saturn bring into human life—the moon inasmuch as its spiritual beings have withdrawn leaving behind in the earthly realm only the physical aspect, the physical forces of reproduction, and Saturn inasmuch as it represents the moral justice of the universe in its highest aspect. These two work together, with between them the other planets linking and intermingling the one with the other. Karma through Saturn, physical heredity through the moon: these in their interrelation show how human beings on their path from earthly life to earthly life are linked with the earth itself and with the great universe beyond the earth.

It is easy to understand that science today, concentrating exclusively on earthly life, has very little to say about the human being. It knows a great deal about the forces of heredity while failing to realize that these are moon forces left behind on the earth, so it cannot relate them to the way they transcend the earth. And it knows nothing at all about karma, the destiny that leads from earthly life to earthly life. Yet in reality, just as the physical human being is filled with the pulsation of the blood, so is karma filled with the pulsation of beings who bear within them the vast memory of the planetary system with all its cosmic happenings. Looking into our own inner life we must admit: We are true human beings only inasmuch as we have memory. Looking out into the planetary system with all its physical and spiritual happenings, we must, if we want to make an approach to initiation wisdom, equally admit: This planetary system would have no inner quality if the inhabitants of Saturn did not always preserve the memory of its cosmic past, and if they did not constantly pour this into humanity so that all the individual human beings can be immersed in a living spiritual and moral nexus of causes and effects leading from earthly life to earthly life.

★

On earth, in our conscious actions, we are confined within narrow limits in our relations with other human beings. But looking at what we undergo between death and a new birth, we find that there our relations with other human beings, who are also not in physical bodies, encompass far wider circles. Of course in the period between death and a new birth we are for some of the time closer to the lunar influences and, at other times, we are closer to Saturn or Mars or other influences, and so on. Yet each kind of planetary force interpenetrates all the others throughout the cosmic spaces. Just as on earth we work from one individual to another across the narrow confines of terrestrial space, so between death and a new birth there is a working from planet to planet. The universe then becomes the scene of human activity and of the interrelationships between human beings. There between death and a new birth one human soul is perhaps in the realm of Venus while the other is in the realm of Jupiter. Yet the interplay between the two is far more intimate than is possible in the narrow confines of earthly life. Just as the cosmic distances are called into play to be the scene of action of the relations between human souls between death and a new birth, so too the beings of the Hierarchies are there, working throughout the cosmic spaces. We have to tell not only of the working of the several kinds of beings, for example the inhabitants of Venus or the inhabitants of Mars. We can also tell of the relationship between the Venus population and the Mars population, a never-ending interaction, a constant to and fro of spiritual forces between the population of Mars and the population of Venus in the universe.

What goes on in the universe between the population of Mars and the population of Venus, all that lives in the constant interplay in the universe, all the mutually fruitful deeds of Mars and Venus, all this also relates to the human being. Just as the Saturn memory is related to human karma, and just as the physical lunar forces, left behind on the earth, relate to the external forces of reproduction, so is the hidden spiritual interaction between Mars and Venus related to what appears in earthly life as human speech. Physical forces alone would not enable us to speak. It is the eternal being of man, going on from earthly life to earthly life, living between death and a new birth, which radiates into this outer world the gift of speech. During our life as a spiritual being between death and a new birth we also become involved in the sphere of action of the mutually fertilizing life that goes on between Mars and Venus, between the populations of Mars and Venus. These spiritual forces raying back and forth, this collaboration works on us in our life between death and a new birth. It then becomes visible in a physical picture, for it is this that emerges from the inmost realm of human becoming and enters into the organs of speech and song. We should never be capable of speaking with our organs of speech and song if they were not physically stimulated by forces we receive into the depths of our being between death and a new birth from all that is forever streaming back and forth between Mars and Venus in the cosmos.

Thus in all we do in everyday life we are under the influence of spiritual forces to the outward signs of which we raise our eyes in wonder when we look into the starry heavens. We can only look up to the stars in the right way if we know that the stars shining down to us from cosmic space are no more than characters of the cosmic script. They are the script of the universe, of the universal spiritual processes that live in us and of which we are merely an image.

Long ago human beings were able to see all these things in an instinctive atavistic clairvoyance, but this vision gradually faded. If they had retained it they would have been incapable of achieving freedom. So it gradually darkened, and in compensation the Mystery of Golgotha entered into the life of the earth. A sublime being from the population of the sun brought to human beings a consciousness not immediately of what is going on out there in the world of the stars, but of the powers that would be needed so that this consciousness could gradually be attained.

Initially, while the Mystery of Golgotha was taking place, there was an ancient Gnostic wisdom inherited from the past that was still able to comprehend the Mystery of Golgotha. That disappeared as early on as the fourth century after Christ. But the power brought to the earth by Christ has remained. We can now call this power to life within ourselves if we open our eyes to the reality of spiritual worlds through the communications of present-day spiritual science.

This ability to open our eyes to the spiritual worlds will bring many things to humanity in modern times. Actually there are a number of individuals who have preserved some relics of the ancient, instinctive wisdom which is, in the best meant sense of the word, no longer appropriate for our time because it ought to be replaced by a more conscious wisdom. In consequence we have a curious situation in which learned scholars in various parts of the Orient, who have preserved the ancient wisdom, look down in disdain on Europe and America. They are convinced that their ancient oriental wisdom even in its present decadent form, no more than rags and tatters in fact, is still superior to everything of which western civilization is so inordinately proud. So it is interesting to see a book recently published by a Sinhalese author, entitled *The Culture of the Soul among Western Nations*,[17] in which this Indian from Ceylon says to Europeans, in effect: 'Your knowledge about Christ has been dying out since the Middle Ages. You no longer have any real knowledge about

Christ for only those who are capable of looking into the spiritual world can have such knowledge. Therefore you ought to call upon teachers from India or Asia to come to you and teach you about Christianity.' This is what is said to Europeans in that book by an Indian from Ceylon: 'Let teachers come to you from Asia; they will be able to tell you what Christ really is. Your European teachers no longer know this. Since the decline of the Middle Ages you have lost your knowledge of Christ.'

Yet in reality it is up to Europeans and Americans themselves once more to summon up the courage to look into the spiritual worlds from which knowledge of Christ, the wisdom of Christ, can be regained. For Christ is the being who came down from spiritual worlds into life on earth. Only by grasping him spiritually can this being be comprehended in his true inwardness.

For this to be possible, it is necessary that human beings learn to regard themselves truly as the image of spiritual beings, of spiritual realities and activities here on earth. This can best be done when they fill themselves with ideas and perceptions such as those I put to you at the beginning of this lecture. Amid their conscious experiences in the stream of time they look into emptiness. Then they discover how their true ego never comes down from the spiritual world, how in the physical world they are merely a picture because their ego is not present in the physical world. They see what looks like a hole in time, a dark-looking hole. It is to this that they can say 'I'.

Human beings must become aware of this deeply significant fact that when they look back over their life in memory they have to say: 'In memory I see the experiences I underwent day by day, but in the midst of these there is always a dark gap, like a hole. In my ordinary consciousness it is to this dark hole that I say "I". But I must now become conscious of something more than this.'

I have summed up this 'something more' in a few words, a kind of meditation reaching out to the true 'I', that can be

inscribed in the soul of every human being in our time if we
bring it to life more and more often:

I look into the darkness.
In it there arises Light,
Living Light.
Who is this Light in the darkness?
It is I myself in my reality.
This reality of the 'I'
Enters not into my earthly life;
I am but a picture of it.
But I shall find it again
When with good will for the Spirit
I shall have stepped through the gate of death.

Ich schaue in die Finsternis.
In ihr erstehet Licht,
Lebendes Licht.
Wer ist dies Licht in der Finsternis?
Ich bin es selbst in meiner Wirklichkeit.
Diese Wirklichkeit des Ich
Tritt nicht ein in mein Erdendasein,
Ich bin nur Bild davon.
Ich werde es aber wiederfinden
Wenn ich, guten Willens für den Geist,
Durch des Todes Pforte geschritten.

By entering ever and again into meditative words of this kind
we can confront the darkness. We can reach an understanding
of how here on earth we are only a picture of our true being
which never comes down into earth existence. Yet in the
midst of the darkness, through our good will towards the
spirit, a Light can dawn for us of which we may truly admit:
'This Light I am myself in my reality.'[18]

★

Last time I was able to speak to you here I had to conclude by telling you about a great worry that was oppressing my soul [see page 278]. It was the worry about how we could continue with the building of the Goetheanum which was to be an indication here on earth of what would come into the world through anthroposophical spiritual science. The concerns I expressed met with understanding.

Meanwhile an event has occurred, an inexpressible pain which is deeply inscribed in the history of the anthroposophical movement. There was no way of avoiding this pain. It has been inscribed in the depths of the anthroposophical movement's book of history by hostile powers who are opposed to the movement. Since then all the things it has been my task to speak about have been overshadowed by this pain. So now the worries I have to speak about are not only those I mentioned on the last occasion, but they are also spoken now out of the utmost pain that came to us all during the night of New Year's Eve 1922 to 1923. Your representatives, together with those of other countries who attended the delegates' meeting in Dornach in July this year, have resolved to do whatever is possible to bring about the rebuilding of the Goetheanum. We shall of course have to try and make the new Goetheanum worthy of what it stands for, even if for this second building a different material will have to be used, one that is less likely to be destroyed by fire.

So at the end of my talk today I want once again to commend the Goetheanum to your hearts now that out of such deep pain it must become the concern of all those who loved it and who love what can be brought into the world.

Let us act, dear friends, as we must act out of the pain and out of our awareness that spiritual life must be enabled to enter our cultural life. Let us remain bound together in this awareness even when we cannot be physically together for a while. What can stream from anthroposophy and indeed from a spiritual movement like it is something that belongs to humanity in general which can bring souls together in the spirit. Even when they are spatially separated they will always find one another. Not only will they find one another but they will always be together, in the true reality of the spirit we are seeking, in a movement like ours.

PART TWO

OXFORD

Rudolf Steiner gave three lectures on the social question during a congress on 'Spiritual Values in Education and Social Life' at Manchester College, Oxford.[19] Patrons of the congress were the Minister for Education, Dr H. A. Fisher, the Principal of the college, L. P. Jacks, and other public figures. Rudolf Steiner had been invited to participate by Mrs H. M. Mackenzie, MA, Professor of Education at University College, Cardiff.[20] Representatives from 20 nations were present, including about 200 students as well as several persons connected with the anthroposophical movement who had travelled to England with Rudolf Steiner.

PRELIMINARY NOTICE.

HOLIDAY CONFERENCE AT OXFORD 1922.
"Spiritual Values in Education and Social Life."
AUGUST 15th. to 29th.

THE Programme for this Conference is not yet complete, but it can already be announced that Dr. RUDOLF STEINER will give 12 Lectures, — 6 on Education, and 6 on Social and other questions of the day.

It is hoped that:-

Professor H. WILDON CARR, Mr. EDMOND HOLMES, Principal L. P. JACKS, Professor J. S. MACKENZIE, and other Educationists and social workers will be able to take part in the Conference. The Programme is likely to include Eurhythmy Performances both by artists and children, Plays by The Sheffield Repertory Company, and those who wish to do so will have the opportunity of taking a course of Lessons in Eurhythmy.

CONFERENCE FEE ... ... TWO GUINEAS.
One guinea to be paid in advance as booking fee. Early booking desirable.

Board Residence has been arranged for, in two or three of the Colleges. For Terms and particulars apply to:-

MRS. MACKENZIE,
56, Bassett Road, London, W.10.

1. THE EVOLUTION OF HUMAN SOCIAL LIFE: THE THREE SPHERES OF SOCIETY

Oxford, 26 August 1922

Ladies and gentlemen, it has today become a matter of universal concern to study the social question and find answers capable of generating actions that can guide our social situation in a direction for the future which many people have hazy notions about but concerning which there cannot as yet be any clear concepts—and I mean 'cannot be' rather than 'are not'.

If I have the temerity to speak about this social question in three brief lectures you will, I am sure, understand that the time at my disposal will only allow me to give the vaguest outline, an outline that will have to take shape in what you, my respected audience, will make of what I have to say. Please regard the content of these lectures as the merest hints which may serve you as suggestions.

What can we make of the social question nowadays? If we look squarely at human life as it is today we certainly do not find a clear picture with any obvious solutions. What we see is a huge number of differentiated conditions of life spread across the face of the earth, conditions that have created great gulfs and abysses within humanity between internal human experiences and the external life of commerce and industry. The tremendous variety of differentiations becomes all too obvious when you look at the difference between life prior to the terrible World War and life now. If you look at any larger region of the earth you will find that the differentiations in social life prior to and following the War are entirely different from those that pertained even only 50 years ago in the same region.

Today—thank goodness, we should add—we tend to look

on these conditions of life with our heart, we feel their tragedy. But our intellect, well trained though it has become over the course of recent centuries, cannot keep up. This is the strange thing about all social matters now, that real questions, questions of life itself, are so very pressing and yet human understanding cannot keep pace with them.

It is hard to find ideas that can truthfully be called genuinely fruitful. The thoughts people have tend to fail when they are applied to social life.

The direction social development has taken makes it necessary to link the question of social life with another question in which only factual knowledge can be decisive, only a direct, concrete understanding.

It is easy, ladies and gentlemen, to think about a paradise on earth in which human beings can live a good life and be contented; such a thing appears to be a matter of course. However, to state how an existence worthy of the human being is supposed to arise out of today's economic life, out of the concrete facts that nature and human labour and our inventive spirit present us with requires a profounder knowledge of the matter than any branch of science can provide. Compared with the complicated facts of social, economic life, what we see under the microscope or in the sky through the telescope is exceedingly simple.

As a matter of fact, everyone has something to say about the social question although hardly anyone has the patience or tenacity, or even the opportunity, to acquire an expert knowledge of the actual facts. As far as the social question is concerned, we have just come through a period with regard to which we should thank God that it is behind us. This was the period of Utopia, the period when people imagined the kind of paradise on earth in which human beings should live in the future like characters in some kind of novel. Whether these Utopias have been written about or whether someone has tried to establish them in reality, as Owen[21] did in Scotland or Oppenheimer[22] has been doing in Germany, is irrelevant. As far as present-day social life is concerned, it is irrelevant whether a Utopia is described in a book—in which case it becomes obvious that it cannot be realized—or whether someone founds a little settlement like an economic parasite which can only exist because the rest of the world is there around it, which can only exist so long as it can maintain itself as a parasite on the commercial world and then perishes.

The important thing to be considered with regard to the social question is the need to develop an awareness of the social waves pulsating beneath the surface of humanity, an awareness of what existed in the past, what is there now in the present and what wants to work on into the future—for what is preparing to work on into the future already exists everywhere to a great extent in the subconscious part of human beings. It will therefore be necessary in these lectures to point very firmly to what is there in the human unconscious. Above all, though, we must gain a broad conception of social life as it has developed historically.

Ladies and gentlemen, what once existed long ago is still with us now in the form of tradition, a remnant, but we can only understand what is here amongst us if we understand what existed long ago. Similarly, future tendencies are already mingling with what is here now in the present, and we must understand those seeds of the future that are already planted in our present time. We must not regard the past solely as something that happened centuries ago; we must see it as something still widespread amongst us, something effective that we can only comprehend as a past in the present or a present from the past if we learn to assess its significance correctly. We can only gain some insight if we trace the external symptoms back to their deeper foundations.

Please do not misunderstand me, ladies and gentlemen. In describing things like this one sometimes has to emphasize them rather forcefully, so that one appears to criticize when one merely intends to characterize. I do not mean it as a criticism when I say that the past is still a part of the present.

In fact I can admire this past and find it extremely attractive as it makes a place for itself in the present, but if I want to think socially I must recognize that it is the past and that as such it must find its proper place in the present. This is how I have to gain a feeling for social life as it really is.

Let me give you an example, and please forgive me for quoting something from the immediate present, for I mention this somewhat strange symptom without intending any slight whatsoever. Yesterday we met your respected chairman on the street wearing his cap and gown.[23] He looked remarkably handsome and I admired him very much. Nevertheless, what I beheld before my eyes was not only entirely medieval but I even thought someone from the ancient oriental theocracies was approaching us in the midst of the present day.

Underneath the gown there was, of course, an entirely modern soul, an anthroposophist actually, who possibly even saw himself as embodying something of the future into the bargain. Yet the symptom, the actual face of what I saw was history, history in the present time.

If we want to understand social life, if we want to understand the economic interrelationships that have their effect on our breakfast table every morning and determine how much we have to take out of our purse in order to make it possible for our breakfast to be there, then we need to have an overall view of humanity's social evolution. Yet this social evolution of humanity, especially with regard to the social question, is today almost exclusively approached from the materialistic point of view.

What we must do first is look back to those quite different conditions that once obtained in human history and pre-history. We must look back to those social communities that were the social theocracies of the Orient, although to this day they still exercise a strong influence in the West.

These were very different social communities. They were communities in which social relationships were structured through the Inspiration received by priests who remained aloof from ordinary conditions in the world. From the spiritual impulses that came upon them people derived the impulses for the external world. If you look at ancient Greece or Rome you see a social structure involving an immense army of slaves with above them a self-satisfied, wealthy upper class—relatively speaking. It is impossible to understand this social structure without taking account of its theocratic origins in which people believed in it as something given by God, or by the gods; they believed this not only with their heads but also with their hearts and with their whole being. So the slaves felt they were occupying their rightful place in the divine scheme of things. Human social life in ancient times is only comprehensible if you take into account the way in which external, physical structures were filled with commandments received through Inspiration.

These commandments, received from beyond the world by priests who remained aloof from the world, determined not only what human beings needed for the salvation of their souls, not only what they thought and felt about birth and death, but also how they should relate to one another. From the distant Orient we hear resounding not only the words 'Love God above all things', but also 'and thy neighbour as thyself'.[24] Today we take a phrase such as 'thy neighbour as thyself' very abstractly. It was not so abstract when it rang out to the crowds from the inspired priest. It was something that worked from individual to individual, something that later came to be replaced by all those concrete conditions we now summarize by the name of law and morality. These conditions of law and morality that only came to be a part of human evolution later were originally contained in the divine commandment 'Love thy neighbour as thyself' through the very way in which they were brought into the world by the inspired priests of theocracy.

In the same way the duties of the economic life, what human beings were supposed to do with their cattle, with their land and soil, these things were also determined by divine

Inspirations. You can find echoes of this in the Mosaic laws.[25] With regard to their culture and spiritual life, with regard to their life of law and morality, and with regard to their economic life, human beings felt themselves placed into the earthly world by divine powers. Theocracy was a unified structure in which the various members worked together because they were all filled with a single impulse. The three members: the life of culture and spirit, the life of law—what we today call the life of the state—and the economic life, these were combined in a unified organism filled with impulses that were not to be found on the earth.

As human life evolved further these three impulses, spiritual/cultural life, state/legal/moral life, and economic life pulled apart from one another and became differentiated. The single stream flowing in the form of unified human life in the theocracies gradually divided into two, as I shall show next, and then into three. It is with these three streams that we are confronted today.

*

Ladies and gentlemen, theocracy in olden times rested on the Inspiration received by the Mystery priests which flowed into the social life, including the legal-moral life and also the economic life. Rules of conduct in the form of commandments could be derived from those Inspirations so long as economic life was based mainly on the soil, agriculture, animal husbandry and so on. Based on their special relationship with the land, human beings bore in their hearts something that went out to meet what came towards them from theocracy.

Once trade and commerce began to play a greater role in human evolution this changed. We can only understand the oldest theocracies if we know that essentially all economic life rests on the human being's sense of belonging to the land and the soil, and that trade and commerce are merely superimposed on top of this. They existed, of course, but in the way they developed they followed on from what related to the soil, to agriculture. Looking at human evolution we can see how trade and commerce emancipated themselves from agriculture, initially in ancient Greece and much more so in the days of the old Roman Empire. Roman life as a whole received its characteristic configuration from the way the activities of trade and commerce became an independent element in the social structure.

The significance of this emancipation for people in the Roman Empire deeply touched the hearts of the Gracchi, Tiberius Sempronius and Gaius Sempronius,[26] and the words they found with which to express what was in their hearts led to the great social struggles of Roman times. In fact the first social movement leading to strikes had taken place in ancient Rome when the plebeians streamed out to the 'sacred mountain' to demand their rights.[27] That was when the urge arose to push for new social forms for the future.

Then for the first time it was noticed that something independent had arisen, something that had up to then been an integral part of the whole social structure, and this was the human being's labour, which brings into being a specific relationship between one individual and another. When an individual is told by the commandments that he is more lowly than another, he does not ask how he ought to arrange his work since this arises naturally from the relationship between the two. But when labour manifests as something that has emancipated itself and become independent the question arises: How do I relate to my fellow human beings in a way that enables my labour to be integrated within the social structure in the right way? Trade, commerce and labour are the three economic factors that stimulate human beings to bring to birth their legal rights and also an independent morality, a morality that has been separated off from religion. So human beings felt the need to let two streams flow from the single stream of theocracy. Theocracy was allowed to continue, and a second stream, the stream of the military life and specifically of the law, then flowed along beside it.

So as eastern culture spread towards Europe we see how under the influence of trade, commerce and labour the ancient theocratic ideas moved over into legalistic thinking. We see how in place of old situations that were not legalistic at all legalistic conditions developed to regulate questions of ownership and other matters that express the relationship between one individual and another. (You must try to understand what this means in relation to ancient Mosaic legislation.)

The seeds for this were sown at the time of the Gracchi, and these germinated later in Diocletian's day.[28] You can see how the second stream gradually established itself alongside the first and how this expressed itself in human life as a whole.

In the ancient theocracies over in the East the spiritual knowledge human beings were to have about the super-sensible worlds was self-evident theosophy. Theo-Sophia is the concrete wisdom that was received through Inspiration.

Then, when the stream moved on towards Europe, jurisprudence came to join it. Jurisprudence cannot be a 'sophia' for it is not something that is received through Inspiration; it is something that human beings have to work out for themselves through the way one individual relates to another. The capacity to form judgements is what counts. So 'sophia' was replaced by logic, and the jurisprudence that was then poured into the whole social structure became predominantly logical. Logic and dialectic triumphed not so much in science as in the life of the law, and the whole of human life became squeezed into this second stream, this logic. The concept of ownership, the concept of personal rights, all such concepts were realized as logical categories.

This second stream was so powerful that it began to colour the first, thus turning 'theo-sophia' into 'theo-logia'. The first stream came to be influenced by the second. So then, side by side with a well-tried 'theo-sophia'—who, a little less lively and somewhat skinnier than she had been in her youth, had turned into a 'theo-logia'—there came into being a 'jurisprudentia' as well. This jurisprudence encompassed every-thing that emerged in various disguises right up to the fif-teenth, sixteenth, seventeenth century, and it is still at work in the whole of economic life.

It was at work in Adam Smith, even though his concern was the economic life.[29] Read Adam Smith while retaining your sense of how legalistic thinking continues to rumble on. The economic life was beginning to arise, but it was into the old concepts of jurisprudence—obviously these concepts were old by then—that he tried to squeeze the economic life and its complications arising out of the way scientific thinking had taken hold of technology and so on.

So for a while in the civilized world two streams developed. There was 'theo-logia', which on the one hand flowed into science; it is easily proved how the later sciences developed out of 'theo-logia'. But meanwhile human beings had learnt to think dialectically and logically, and this, too, they poured into science. This is how modern times have come into being. Social and economic conditions are developing an over-whelming complexity. People are still accustomed to thinking theologically and legalistically, and this they are now applying to science on top of everything else. The scientists have failed to notice this. When they put their eye to a microscope or study the starry heavens through a telescope, or when they dissect a lower animal in order to study its organism, it does not occur to them that they are applying a historical phase of human thinking rather than anything absolute. In recent times this scientific thinking has most certainly been taking over human civilization. One is expected to think scientifically about everything, and this has become a habit not only amongst the well-educated, for it is rife in the whole of humanity down to the simplest people.

I hope you will not misunderstand me when I make the following observation. When we discuss things in the way I have been doing over the past few days with regard to edu-cation one must include spiritual aspects that can illumine the scientific aspect. But people educated in science react by presuming that there can be no truth in things that are not written down in a book on physiology or pronounced from the rostrum in the physiology department. They do not assume that things that cannot be pronounced in this way, things that I have said with regard to scientific matters, have in fact all been checked and that full account has been taken of what the physiology books and the professor on the rostrum tell us. But people today cannot discern how one thing develops from another. As a result today's science which is so brilliant and which is fully recognized by anthroposophy becomes a hindrance not because of what it says but as a result of the way people see it. In fact you can use the latest developments in human evolution to demonstrate clearly the way in which it has become a hindrance.

Karl Marx is well known to you by name.[30] In recent times he has spoken about social life in a way that has impressed millions and millions of people. How did he speak? He spoke in a way that a representative of the scientific age is bound to speak on social matters.

Let us imagine how this representative of the age is bound to speak. The scientist has thoughts in his head, but he is not too concerned with them. He only begins to take them into account when they have been verified by what he sees under the microscope or by some other experiment or observation. What he observes must be kept entirely separate from himself, it must not be linked with himself in any way but must come from outside. So someone who thinks scientifically is bound to see an abyss between his own thinking and whatever comes to him from outside.

Karl Marx learnt this way of thinking that one wants to keep separate from the outside world not quite from the newest science but in a somewhat older form, namely, Hegelian dialectics. In fact this is only a slightly different colouring of scientific thinking. While he was learning this scientific way of thinking he was living within his own surroundings. But as a representative of the scientific age he could make nothing of it. As a German he was at home within the German way of thinking logically and dialectically. But he was unable to make anything of his thoughts, just as the scientist cannot make anything of his thoughts but has to wait and see what the microscope or telescope will show him, namely, something from outside. Karl Marx was incapable of doing anything with his thoughts, and as he was unable to escape from inside his own skin he escaped from Germany instead and came to England. Here he found himself confronted with external social conditions just as the scientist is confronted by the microscope or telescope. Now he had a world outside of himself. This enabled him to speak and establish a social theory in a scientific way, just as the scientist establishes his theory—and since people are totally immersed in this way of thinking he became immensely popular.

When one talks about human beings in terms of external nature—as Karl Marx did—then human beings, including the social conditions in which they live, are made to look as though they were in fact nature. I can say what I have to say about Jupiter, about the violet, about the earthworm equally well in Iceland, in New Zealand, in England, in Russia or anywhere else. There is no need for me to speak in concrete terms, for everything must be kept general.

So if you establish a social theory along scientific lines it seems that this is something that has validity all over the world and can be applied anywhere. In fact the main characteristic of the legalistic political way of thinking—of which Marxism is merely the culmination—is that it wants to take general abstractions and apply them anywhere. You will find this even where there is as yet no sign of socialist thought, but only a legalistic, logical way of thinking, as in Kant with his categorical imperative which is also perhaps known to you as something from beyond your shores.

Ladies and gentlemen, this categorical imperative states: Act in such a way that the maxim of your action can be valid for all people.[31] Such a thing has no application in real life, for you cannot say to someone: Get the tailor to make you a jacket that will fit anyone. This is the logical model on which old-fashioned legalistic, political thinking is founded, and it has reached its culmination in Marxist social thought.

So you see how what Marx observed scientifically by applying his German thinking to the English economic situation was initially realized. This he then transported back to Central Europe where it lived in people's will impulses. Subsequently it was also carried further eastwards where the ground had even been prepared for this application of something totally abstract to real human situations. In the east Peter the Great had even prepared the ground for Marx.[32] Peter had already inserted western thinking into Russian life. Even though Russia bore many oriental traits in its soul while its people were still steeped in theocracy he brought in legalistic, political thinking and side by side with Moscow set up St Petersburg further to the west.

People overlooked the fact that here were two worlds, that St Petersburg was Europe and Moscow was Russia where pure oriental theocracy still had a profound role to play. So when Soloviev[33] created a philosophy it was theosophical rather than dialectic and scientific like that of Herbert Spencer.[34] Soloviev belonged to Moscow, not St Petersburg. Not that things in Russia can be divided neatly in accordance with geography. However much he remains attached to Moscow, however far eastwards he might travel, Dostoevski belongs to St Petersburg.[35] Experiences in Russia take account of the interplay between St Petersburg and Moscow. Theocratically speaking, Moscow is Asia, even today, while St Petersburg is Europe.

St Petersburg had been prepared in a legalistic, political way for what Leninism perpetrated in Russia when something that was the final outcome of the Western European soul was impressed upon the Russian soul, to which it was completely foreign. It was so abstract, so foreign that what Lenin[36] did in

Russia might just as well have been done on the moon. He could have chosen anywhere else, but he happened to want to rule Russia.

So conditions have arisen that we entirely fail to understand in a concrete way if we only look at the social situation. We must make an effort to understand them in a concrete way, ladies and gentlemen. We must understand that in human evolution the spiritual, cultural life came before legalistic, political life which established itself as a second stream beside the first one. We must understand that the time has perhaps now arrived for something new to happen, something that goes beyond the way the legalistic life has coloured 'theo-sophia' and transformed it into 'theo-logia'. Perhaps it is time for spiritual, cultural life to reawaken in a new form.

The fact is that in human evolution many aspects of the spiritual, cultural life have retained the forms they had in olden times. Not only cap and gown but also thought forms have remained. These thought forms no longer fit in with a world in which trade, commerce and labour have emancipated themselves in a way that has left the spiritual, cultural life behind as a separate aspect alongside the rest of life. This is more the case the further west one travels.

It is least of all the case in the Russia of Moscow. In Central Europe all the struggles, including the social ones, concern the fact that people cannot find a proper way of relating the dialectical, legalistic, political element with the theocratic element. They cannot work out whether cap and gown should be retained when the judge takes his seat or whether they should be discarded. Lawyers are already rather embarrassed by having to wear gowns, while judges still find they enhance their dignity. People cannot decide. There is a fierce struggle going on about this in Central Europe. In Western Europe the theocratic element has become strongly preserved in thought forms.

Nevertheless, there is no getting away from the fact that the second stream has established itself in human evolution. On

the one hand there are those who—symptomatically speaking—have retained the ancient ways including cap and gown.
But now people want to see them take these off in order to
find out what they are wearing underneath. Whether it be a
king's mantle or a soldier's cloak it will have to be something
that does justice to a legalistic situation, a political situation.
When we meet such people in the street we want to remove
their cap and gown in order to see them as complete individuals; underneath we want to find a kind of soldier's cloak or
some garment that would be appropriate for a solicitor's
office. Then we should see before us both the streams living
side by side within the person.

I must confess—in jest, of course, although I mean it quite
seriously—that when I meet someone in the street wearing a
cap and gown I cannot help asking myself whether such a
person would know whether the next letter he writes should
bear the date of 768 BC or—if perhaps the gown conceals a
legal scholar—AD 1265. It is difficult to decide on a date, since
the distant past and the medium past appear side by side in
two streams. The last to occur to me would be today's date,
for there is no question of taking the present time into consideration just yet. The two different pasts relate to one
another as does Moscow to St Petersburg.

We are faced with the question of how the aspects that
proceed side by side today can be brought into a meaningful
organizational structure. We shall see how the twofoldness
about which I have been speaking leads on to a threefolding in
modern times, a threefolding in which the three elements also
proceed side by side.

When I speak of threefolding, ladies and gentlemen, I do
not mean that there is at present a beautiful unity in social life
which we are to cut into three pieces so that three elements
can evolve side by side. I mean that a threefoldness already
exists, just as it does in the human being who has a system of
head and nerves, a rhythmic system, and a system of
metabolism.[37] The three must function properly together,

however, and to each must be assigned what belongs to it. If the digestive system works too little, leaving too much for the head to do, the result is all kinds of migraine-like disorders. If the spiritual, cultural element—which is the head in the social organism—does not function well, leaving too much to the economic element, then all kinds of social ills will ensue.

To observe social life in depth we have to see such things in the context of human evolution, for this is the best way of avoiding superficiality. We must succeed in putting cap and gown into a context that enables us to conceive of two different historical dates as being one inside the other. This then becomes the present time. Otherwise the past remains the past with its two streams flowing side by side and continuing to be the fundamental cause of the social ills present in the world today, even though people do not wish to see it like this. There will be some more to say in the third part of my lecture.

*

Ladies and gentlemen, as it has grown rather late I will be brief in what I still have to tell you today. This will bring us up to the present time and I shall save the greater part for the next lecture.

From the beginning of the fifteenth to sixteenth century, but most clearly from the nineteenth century onwards, the two streams I have been describing came to be accompanied more and more by a third one. This has become increasingly apparent the further civilization and culture have moved westwards. To what was originally theocratic and adapted to the land and the soil, to agriculture, there was added in the middle regions the legalistic element adapted to trade, commerce and labour. And now in the West a further element has come to join these, the element that later came to be termed industry, everything industrial including all the technical things this involves.

Consider what the introduction of the actual industrial element into human evolution has meant. It would be an easy calculation to adapt what I am about to say to present-day conditions, but I shall refer to an earlier point in time, roughly the 1880s. At that time it was said that the population of the world amounted to 1,500 million human beings. But this was not a correct calculation of the earth's population. It would have been correct for the most ancient antiquity when virtually every individual laboured manually in some way, or with something closely connected to human life such as guiding the plough or leading the horse and so on. But by the nineteenth century another entirely new population had entered the world, namely, the machines that relieved human beings of a part of their labour. Even for the 1880s if you calculate the amount of labour from which human beings had been relieved by machines you arrive at a world population of 2,000 million, about a quarter more. Today—and this was much more so before the War—if we count the number of human beings on the earth purely physically, we arrive at a completely erroneous total. To accord with the amount of work done we have to add another 500 million human beings.

This has indeed added an entirely new element to the ancient theocratic and legalistic streams, an entirely new stream, in fact, for instead of bringing human beings closer to their environment it has thrown them back upon themselves. In the Middle Ages one part of the human being was, let's say, the key he had just crafted, or even the entire lock. What a human being did passed over into his work. But when a person is operating a machine he does not much care what kind of a relationship he has with that machine—relatively speaking, of course. So he is turned more and more in upon himself. He experiences his humanity. The human being now enters evolution as an entirely new being, for he is detaching himself from what he does externally.

This is the democratic element that has been arising in the West over the last few centuries, but so far it is only a requirement, a postulate, and not something that has been fully realized. These conditions are overwhelming people, for they are only capable of thinking in a theocratic or a legalistic manner. Yet life is becoming more and more industrialized and commercialized and confronting human beings with overwhelming demands. They have not penetrated this with their thoughts. Even someone like Marx thought only legalistically, and the manner in which millions and millions of people have come to understand him is merely legalistic.

In this way, then, a third stream, about which we shall speak tomorrow, has come to join the other two. The proletarian human being is born, and what rumbles in the inner being of this proletarian comes to life in a particular conception of capitalism, of labour. Life itself is forcing human beings to come to grips with these problems and only now can we really say that human evolution has reached the present time.

There stands the man in his cap and gown, handsome and lordly, radiating towards us from the far past. And there stands the man with his soldier's cloak and sword as an embodiment of the legalistic element—for the soldierly aspect is only another side of the legalistic—belonging to the more recent past but not yet to the present. We might even take the man in cap and gown for a good lawyer as well, since this is the image he has been presenting to humanity for centuries, and the uncomfortable fit is therefore not yet too noticeable for us. But if he were to plant himself into economic life— well, unless he is able to enter this fully despite his cap and gown, then I fear his only achievement will be to lose his money. People have in general not yet succeeded in entering upon what this third stream means in life, and neither has humanity as a whole. That is why the social question confronts us as a question for all humanity. The human being finds himself placed beside the machine. We must grasp the social question not as an economic problem, but as one concerning humanity as a whole, and we must understand that it is within the human sphere that we have to solve it.

As yet we lack the necessary thought impulses such as existed for the theocratic and the legalistic streams. We do not yet have such thought impulses for the economic stream. Today's struggles are all about finding thought impulses for the economic stream such as existed for the theocratic and the legalistic stream. This is the main content of the social question today, and large-scale beneficial solutions are proving even more difficult to come by than are small-scale ones. States that have suddenly been confronted with having to take on an industrial economic life tried to encompass it within the old legalistic forms. Having failed to do this they have now found a kind of safety-valve that is enabling them to avoid allowing the economic life to develop in a real way alongside the life of the state. This safety-valve is colonization. Having failed to find vigorous social ideas within, they sought evasive action in founding colonies.

This worked for England but not for Germany. Germany undoubtedly failed to encompass its industrialization because it was unsuccessful in founding colonies. The great question facing humanity today is: How is the human being to cope with industrialization in the way he once coped with theocratic life and then with legalistic life?

People today think that a purely materialistic solution can be found for this great problem. Everyone wants to solve it on the basis of economic life. I intend to show the modest beginnings of a spiritual way in which it can be solved. This is what I shall speak about in the next two lectures.

2. SOCIAL IMPULSES

Oxford, 28 August 1922

In thinking about the social question these days we must remember more than anything else that in the real world effects arise from causes that we do not even notice if we only look at things in a superficial way. By merely skimming the surface we only see the external aspects of reality, and not the real causes and reasons, which lie at a deeper level. That is why there have been and still are so many well-meaning Utopian ideas about how to meet the demands of social life today. At a very significant moment in history between the end of the war and the Versailles attempt at a peace settlement I endeavoured to sketch out a way of developing an organic structure for our present social organism[38] in accordance with the three parts of social life that I ventured to describe in the lecture two days ago.

In that lecture I drew attention to the fact that in the course of humanity's historical evolution three very different streams emerged from the original theocratic stream. I also showed that in our time the social organism contains the cultural-spiritual life, the politico-legal life and the economic life side by side. I stated expressly that I was not seeking to establish a theory about these three elements into which the social organism is divided. I said that looked at realistically and not theoretically this would be like someone wondering how to divide the human being into head, breast and limbs. The division of the social organism is a historical given. It exists, and there is therefore no need to puzzle out how to divide up the social organism into three parts. What we need to do is find the links that unite the three elements that exist anyway.

To consider this question as the basic question of our time we must think in ways that are entirely commensurate with reality, taking only actual facts into account. To be realistic in this way means to consider a specific point in time and a specific place. I wrote my book *Towards Social Renewal*[39] at the request of friends in Stuttgart in the southern part of Germany, and this book deals with the specific period of spring 1919 and the specific place, southern Germany.[40] I imagined that if people were to find the will to do something, then at that time and in that place this will would be such that there would be an understanding for the things suggested by this book not so much as points in a political programme but as directions of will.

The question dealt with in the book is different for the eastern part of the civilized world, for Russia and Asia; it is different for Central Europe, and different again for the western world, for England and America. You can reach this conclusion if you think realistically. I described in the lecture two days ago how the industrial world order emerged from the two earlier orders and now exists side by side with them as a separate stream. It is something that evolved chiefly under the influence of western countries. It evolved under the influence of customs, habits and the social order of the eighteenth century in western countries and adapted itself to all these things. A more concrete and precise way of describing this would be to say that during recent historical times England became the great trading nation of the world. Every third word in discussions of the proletarian question in socialist circles is 'capital'. Under the influence of the great trading links capital has come to mean commercial capital in Western Europe.

Such things give a particular slant to situations, in this case one arising from the fact that the commercial system of recent times has evolved organically out of the habits and customs of life in western countries. What Karl Marx saw here in England was not the same as the situation he had observed in Germany. From Germany he brought with him only his ideas and dialectic, but here in England he found a social structure that was foreign to him. The way industrialism came to be structured is an evolutionary continuation, the next link in the chain of commercial development in the West. Industry evolved organically out of trade.

This was not the case in Central Europe or its representative country, Germany. Right until the middle of the nineteenth century Germany remained essentially agrarian, a country in which agriculture dominated. What modern industry there was—that third stream that came to join the other two streams—was more or less a function of the state and tended to become more and more absorbed by the state structure and integrated in it.

Make a realistic comparison between pre-war Central Europe and pre-war Western Europe. In Western Europe the economic sphere of commerce and industry managed to remain separate from the state, as did the cultural life to an even greater degree in the way it retained its independence from the other two strands.

In Central Europe there was a compact amalgam of cultural life, legal-political life and economic life. So in Germany there was a need to tease the three strands apart before they could be brought to work together in an organic way; they needed to be side by side for collaboration to be possible and so that the links between them could be established.

Here in the West the three strands sit side by side, clearly separated from one another. Even spatially the cultural life is separated off to such an extent that you can get the feeling, for example here in Oxford, that culture and learning lead a life of their own in splendid isolation from any state or economic life going on elsewhere. Consequently there is also a sense of this isolated cultural life no longer having the strength to work outwards into the other two strands. It seems to live within itself and have no organic links through which to interweave with the other two.

In Germany you feel that cultural life is so interwoven with the life of the state that it will need a good deal of help before being able to stand on its own feet. Here in England, on the other hand, cultural life is so independent that it takes no notice at all of the other two strands. If you think realistically about the whole social aspect today and the fundamental impulses that sustain it, you will find that such differences give the situation in each country its own quite distinct colouring.

I therefore find it quite natural that my book *Towards Social Renewal*, which was widely read in Germany in 1919, should now be almost, although perhaps not quite, forgotten there. The moment in time when the suggestions made in it might have been realized has now passed as far as Central Europe is concerned. It had passed as soon as the galloping inflation set in that now so completely binds the hands of the German economy.

When *Towards Social Renewal* was published, many people said that it was all well and good, but surely the important thing at the moment was to get that galloping inflation under control. Yet at the time the situation was relatively stable compared with the disastrous situation today. All I could say was that they would be able to find out from the book how the inflation situation might be alleviated. But they failed to see it. They could not find the place where the answer is given. They looked for obvious statements on the surface and couldn't find the answer in the depths. People did not understand that the book itself was the answer they were looking for.

This very attitude is one of the fundamental impulses in social life today. When you try to think realistically and provide answers based on reality, people do not understand what you are saying. They counter with theories; their heads are stuffed with 'capital' and 'value added' and 'class struggle' and all kinds of things, including all the old prejudices. They approach matters with all their old habits of thought intact. In practical life today reality is killed stone dead by theory. This is the puzzling thing about our time. Practical people have become theoreticians with ideas in their heads like objects forged in a factory; and these theoretical ideas are what they try to use to solve all the problems of social life.

I therefore believe that *Towards Social Renewal* should in future be read more in the West and in Russia, for in Germany there seems to be no possibility of putting any of the suggestions it makes into practice. In the West, for instance, people will find there is much that can be learnt from the book. Without being Utopian it clearly describes how the three strands ought to run side by side and yet interweave with one another. In the West the point in time is irrelevant for here, too, there remains much to be done with regard to the proper interlinking of the three strands of cultural life, economic life and the political-legal life of the state.

Above all we shall have to learn to think in a really modern way so as to achieve the capacity to form judgements about social matters that are relevant to modern times. Please do not take this superficially. What I mean is that we need to acquire social judgements that are relevant today, and we can only do this if we look into the depths that lie beneath the surface of social phenomena. In this connection we are faced with a remarkable fact. It is impossible for an individual alone, however intelligent or idealistic or practical—and I should like to underline 'practical' three times!—to arrive at a social judgement at all. It is a social mystery that any social judgement reached by someone in isolation is wrong.

Look at the immensely clever judgements made when the gold standard was to be set up in Europe. Immensely clever things were said in the trade associations and parliaments— and I say this with conviction and do not mean it ironically. If you study these things you gain a profound respect for all that was said by those immensely clever individuals, from the middle of the nineteenth century onwards, about the influence of the gold standard on the social structure of the world. Above all else they proved without a shadow of doubt—in the most logical manner for which we ought to have the greatest respect—that free trade would flourish once the gold standard had been introduced.

Yet the opposite happened. The gold standard even necessitated the re-establishment of tariff barriers. In other words, the cleverest individuals talked nonsense when looking towards the future. This is not meant as a reproach. It happened because even the cleverest people talk nonsense—perhaps the more so the cleverer they are—if they talk about social matters as lone individuals, if they form their judgements only on the basis of insights a single human individual can bring forward.

Today there is no point in letting ourselves be moved emotionally by social wretchedness. Individuals cannot form judgements about the connection between cause and effect in social life. We shall have to dig deeper than that. We shall have to examine the very way that humanity as a whole is structured. We must ask ourselves how a truly social judgement can be achieved.

In ancient times social judgements were formed unconsciously. We do not want to return to this way of doing things, for it belongs to the past, to the age of the theocracies. Social judgements in those times came about through groups of human beings.

It is quite untrue to say that the family was the first kind of social order to arise, for in fact the family is a latecomer on the social scene. Primeval human beings did not ponder about what social judgement they ought to make; they accepted the Inspirations of their priests and absorbed these into their unconscious. These unconscious communal judgements only arose amongst people who belonged to a social group, whether that group was one of consanguinity or based on some other order. Social groups had a mutual understanding, not individuals—social groups of people living together. The right kind of social order arose out of the way the people in those groups lived with one another. The right social form developed out of the whole group in the spirit of human beings. This was the case with democracy also, and thus with the idea of democracy. A culmination was only reached after long periods of time. Then the individual human being appeared on the scene of world history. Such individuals still brought with them what the groups had built up and this lived on in the form of tradition. It still helped to form the political, legal sphere of the social order. But it could not persist further and enter also into the aspect that has become mechanical and entirely detached from the human being, namely, the industrial order. What the groups originally created no longer has the power to enter into this realm.

So you see, the time has come to create something new within the commercial and economic order, something resembling those original social groups, but now in full human consciousness. These are what I termed 'associations' in my book *Towards Social Renewal*. In the associations the social judgement would not come from individuals but from all that lives in the communal life of each association of consumers, producers and traders. Then we should have new social groups in which judgements would be formed in full consciousness, judgements of a kind that individuals would be incapable of forming in isolation. However long you spend trying to work out a solution to the social question, your efforts will be fruitless. The only sensible thing to do is form social groups which can be expected to come up with partial solutions to the social question, groups in which people who form judgements in common create something that is a partial solution to the social question for a particular place at a particular time and can thus be properly integrated within humanity.

This is what is so essential for today but is so little understood. I came across it myself in connection with a particular aspect of the social question when my book *The Philosophy of Freedom* was published in the 1890s.[41]

I had to touch briefly on the question of women's emancipation which was a part of the social question at that time—

30 years ago. I did not make a statement about how to solve the women's question since what any particular individual thinks about this is irrelevant. It can be the subject of a newspaper article, or a novel perhaps, but neither of these touch on reality. What I said, therefore, was: 'First find out what the women themselves are actually thinking about this question, then we shall gain some sort of realistic basis for action.'

Women had in fact not been genuinely asked about this at all, for the few who had spoken thus far had reached only male judgements. They had merely adopted men's ways which had, of course, always predominated, from the lowest primary school right up to the universities. Those women did not even want to bring their social judgement to bear on social reality. They did not ask whether social life adapts to the kind of clothes you wear. Pardon me for mentioning such garments if it is not polite to do so in England, but these women simply wanted to put on trousers like men and become the same sort of doctors, lawyers, clergy and schoolteachers as men. They did not want to bring the feminine element into the social organism. Instead of taking reality for what it was, they made a theory their point of departure. But nowadays theories are the most unfruitful thing imaginable. So you have to realize that in the question of women's emancipation, too, you must first listen to real women. It is with reality that we must concern ourselves.

It is the same with the overall social question. There is no point in answering theoretical questions such as: 'What attitudes must employer and employee adopt? How should a factory be socially structured?' Proper associations, groups of actual people must be established. From these the answers will come in due time. Questions must be correctly formulated and then one must wait for the answers to emerge from the groups of real people.

If we want to write books they must be books that do not give definitive answers. They must show how groups of human beings will give the answers if they have been brought together in the right way. If a book is to touch fruitfully on the social impulses of our time it must be written out of a social way of thinking and out of a social attitude.

*

It is extraordinarily difficult at present to talk about practical thinking. People imagine they are realists when in fact all you find everywhere is confused theories which, unfortunately, do have an effect on real life. Allow me to make a personal observation in order to clarify what I still mean to say.

I believe that what can be said today about social three-folding can certainly be found in my book *Towards Social Renewal*, particularly outside Germany. But when I wrote the same things down for a Swiss magazine, for a country outside Germany, practical and realistic thinking made it imperative to express the matter differently. This article has now appeared in *The Hibbert Journal*.[42] I wrote it in an inter-national way because from the outset it was intended for everyone. But this is not the way people see this now, which is why I felt I had to make this personal observation so as to ensure that what I want to say now will not be misunderstood, since these things are important for an understanding of social life at the present time.

To me theories as such are irrelevant, so any formulation of ideas or concepts is simply a language in which to commu-nicate about reality. If I find the language of materialism suitable to express certain realities, then I use the language of materialism. If the idealists appear to have concepts more suitable to express some aspect of reality, then I use the language of idealism. Materialism, idealism, realism are all the same to me; I see them as languages by means of which realities can be formulated. There was a time when I used the style of Ernst Haeckel to express what I wanted to say, and this earned me the reputation of being a materialist.[43] Looked at in this way my work will be found to be full of contradictions.

But such is life, especially with all the complexities modern times have brought. If we want to think in a practical way about society today we have to take into account that all today's 'isms' derive from a legalistic, logical way of thinking that is no longer appropriate for our time. Naturalism, idealism, materialism or spiritualism are all equally inappropriate, as are also industrialism, communism, or socialism. They are fine when it is a matter of expressing some particular aspect, but used as theories, slogans or propaganda to stir up agitation they are all antiquated. That is why it is so difficult to choose a title. For instance I very much dislike the title I have chosen for tomorrow's lecture because it is based on outdated slogans that have no validity today.

What we have to do now is immerse ourselves in real life. Life is not ideal, it is real and needs to be looked at from a great variety of angles. As I have said before: if you photograph a tree from one angle you get materialism; if you photograph it from another you get idealism; and from a third angle you get naturalism. Photograph social life from one angle and you get socialism, from another autocracy, and from a third communism. But none of these terms is appropriate today. We lack a reliable instinct that could help us find concepts that should be won from modern life, which is everywhere steeped in industrialism.

Only consider how intense life was in bygone ages of human history. Theocracy was once so strongly imposed on the whole of social life that even the economic aspects were derived from theocratic directives, as I pointed out the day before yesterday. However, this only went as far as agriculture. Agriculture is easily encompassed by a theocratic social order, for human hearts are glad to combine the land and the soil with theocratic ideas. Ask someone who is closely bound up with land and soil what bread means to him. He will tell you that it is a gift from God. In the very way the words are used you can see the link between food on the table and theocratic ideas in society.

After this came the social orderings that I described the day before yesterday, founded on trade and the crafts. The question of labour appeared on the scene. The other day I tried to describe the way it first arose in Roman times. It brought with it a whole new way of thinking. All the concepts we have today such as ownership, human right versus human right, acquired a legal, dialectical, logical colouring. 'God wills it so', was the social motto of theocratic times. 'Human beings must come to appropriate arrangements', was the social motto of a legal, political state.

Such things are so strong that they put a stamp on the whole way people live together. It was not merely that the wisdom about God became theology, as I pointed out the day before yesterday; things entered into life much more deeply than that. Look, for example, at the magnificent painting by Michelangelo in the Sistine Chapel in Rome.[44] Here you have Christ the Judge of the World, painted in a way that befits an age that was intensely legalistic and political. A religious mystery was to be shown on that wall in a place that was at the centre of religious activity.

Do you imagine that if Christ had been painted out of the ancient eastern theocratic view he would have appeared as Michelangelo painted him? Never! He would have been depicted as one who bestows heavenly gifts of grace on human beings, reaching down with hands of benediction; he would have become the cosmic deity who, blessing, gives to human beings.

Who is Christ in Michelangelo's painting? He is the great cosmic upholder of the law, the world judge who rewards the good and punishes the wicked. The whole painting is legalistic, steeped in the age out of which it was born. Through the medium of art it depicts the overall social impulse of the age that created it. The ancient view of the divine world, where God was God and nothing else, had changed to one in which the world was seen as a cosmic jurisprudence. In Michelangelo's painting God is the great judge. Jurisprudence entered into the most subtle threads of thought, even those of religion. Religion became a feeling for what is just or unjust, good or bad, deserving reward or punishment. The world no longer leaned towards something to which it tended in ancient oriental times: reunification of humanity with the divine substance. The world ended as a great assize where judges decided its destiny.

That is how Michelangelo painted. That is how Adam Smith thought, although his ideas went in the opposite direction.[45] Michelangelo's painting tended towards theocracy, but in his artistic work the theocratic order slipped into a legalistic mode. Adam Smith's thinking was entirely legalistic, as was that of Ricardo,[46] and of Karl Marx too. They strove to impose this legalistic thinking on the new industrial order which no longer accords to human beings the position once accorded to them in earlier social structures.

In the theocratic order the human being related to the land, to the soil; he became one with the soil. With the theocratic order at his back he felt he could unite with the soil. The centre of society, its middle point, was the place where those who received Inspiration passed it on to others. Later this became the village with its surrounding land and its church. Then humanity evolved further and the town came into being. The town arose out of the legalistic social order. The polarity was no longer that of peasant and priest, but of town and country.

Everything was securely woven into legalistic categories, and even those who began to see the social organism of town and country as the state still thought in terms of legalistic categories, people like Adam Smith and John Stuart Mill,[47] right up to Karl Marx. In their thinking, abstract legalistic categories abounded, although Karl Marx did treat them critically. Whereas Adam Smith had been positive about them, Karl Marx was negative, yet he worked entirely with legalistic concepts. These legalistic concepts have now become the general currency of a humanity that is no longer linked with anything.

The peasant was linked with the soil. The trader in his commercial dealings was linked with other human beings. We no longer appreciate properly how one individual valued another when he bought something from him or sold him something he had made himself and which therefore meant something to him. The measure of such a transaction was a legalistic one. The measure that determined the just price was something that flowed from one human being to another, from town to country and vice versa. It was the reciprocity of what human beings mutually agree on.

In the time that followed this, human beings were confronted with the machine, with the world of technology. Human beings who are now immersed in the world of machines have been wrested from all earlier links. They are no longer bound to the land and the soil; they no longer live in the interplay that existed between one individual and another during the age when trade and the crafts dominated society. They are now thrown back on their own humanity.

Social structure is evolving into something immensely abstract. All an entrepreneur can do is take note of his balance sheet and the results of his enterprise, for every other factor escapes his observation. He no longer has any direct relationship with human beings, but only with what people have written in books. That is why it is so very difficult to make oneself understood by people who regard themselves as practical individuals if one bases what one says on genuine, proper thinking.

This became very obvious when we tried to found something practical that would work back into everyday life, something in which managers would not only manage in accordance with theories obtained from books but where they would use their own thinking in a concrete situation. But very little was forthcoming from those involved, the majority of whom distanced themselves by saying that theoreticians think things out in their head whereas the practical person knows what he is doing. We are the practical ones, they said. But what did they have in their heads? Nothing but a few entirely theoretical concepts on the basis of which they imagined they knew what needed doing. They were philosophers all right, philosophers with a few concepts derived from the angle of economic life, who drew themselves up to their full height and said: 'Here are the theoretical concepts and here is practical reality, and if anyone has anything else to say he doesn't know what he is talking about.'

So you see how very difficult it is to do anything based on really practical thinking, for the so-called practical people are all theoreticians, and extremely abstract theoreticians at that.

Today we are faced with human beings pure and simple, regardless of their station in life, for concepts such as 'bourgeoisie', 'proletariat', 'the medical profession', the 'priesthood' are all equally invalid now. These traditional classifications no longer lead anywhere. For if we assess things realistically—forgive me if I keep harping on the same theme, but when I met our esteemed co-chairman in the street the other day wearing his cap and gown, I was quite unable to distinguish whether he was a priest or anyone else. We fail to make distinctions because we are applying fixed concepts to real life.

It is time to get everything moving again; we must immerse ourselves in life and see what industrialism has become and how it has separated off from human beings. In earlier times every lock made by a locksmith had an element of humanity in it, just as did a Gothic cathedral. Social impulses streamed out from these things.

Nowadays nothing human emanates from the articles made by factory workers in a factory or from the hideousness of a department store put up by an architect; indeed you could say that the department store style of architecture is very suited to our time for this very reason.

Spirituality used to radiate from the land and the soil in a way that made human beings say: 'The bread given to us by the soil is a gift from God.' In fact theocracy did not only grow downwards from heaven to earth; it also grew upwards from the soil with every stalk of wheat. Such a thing lived in human souls. In later times, when human beings gave to others what they had acquired or achieved, this engendered human interrelationships founded on trade and commerce. To form a human relationship with a machine, however, is impossible. A machine is cold, it has a cold existence. So we fail to achieve social judgements and opinions because we cannot understand how to find a content for the human being elsewhere, a content that cannot emanate from a machine in the way it once emanated from the land and the soil. Stalks of wheat that were a gift from God grew up out of the soil; interpersonal relationships came from trade and commerce, giving people a sense of needing to behave decently to others. But no gift of God comes forth from a machine; and behaving decently to a machine is rather a futile undertaking. Therefore an age that is immersed in industry needs a human content that is not derived from this earth, a content that comes from the spiritual world to fill human souls.

So long as the earth gave spirituality to human beings there was no need to strive for a free unfolding of the human spirit. Equally, so long as there was still a strong warmth of feeling amongst human beings there was no need to strive for a free unfolding of the human spirit. But now that nature, which gives gifts from God, has largely been transformed into means of production created abstractly by human beings as a kind of second realm of nature, we need to add to the means of production the world of free spiritual unfolding that will give us an inner content.

With this content one can approach those with whom one wants to form associations. I have been gathering new experiences in Dornach where, as you know, a small army of workers is busy. These workers want more than work; they want something human as well. So the idea arose to give them something human. But what they were given were talks on all kinds of economic subjects, touching on capitalism, socialism, the bourgeoisie, communism and so forth. People assumed that these subjects would interest the workers, and most of all it was the workers' leaders themselves who thought that these were the kind of subjects that would interest them. In the end I had to take the matter in hand myself, and I too began by talking about economic subjects. But now I do not choose the subject myself, but let the gathering choose it at the beginning of the session. So one day a man got up, pulled a copy of our magazine *Die Drei* out of his pocket and said he wanted to know what it was like when the earth was still a moon, in other words when it was in an entirely different phase of evolution. Since then I have spoken about the nature of the human being, about how human beings are embedded in the cosmos, in ways that are fully understood by all those men. So-called proletarians find it perfectly normal to hear about the influence of the signs of the zodiac.[48]

If we want to join together with other people in associations we first have to find a way of ascertaining what qualities of soul and spirit those others have in them and what is in ourselves, too. We must bridge the chasms that have opened between us. This is the first challenge.

Hence the social question in its most profound sense is first of all a cultural question: How can we spread a homogeneous spirit of culture amongst our fellow human beings? Then we shall be able to come together in associations in the economic sphere. Such associations will be able to formulate the question in a realistic way and—partially, I have to say—find some solutions to it.

As yet we are still thinking in the old forms of thought. We think legalistically but not yet economically for—strange though it may seem—to think economically means to think in freedom. In an age when a second kingdom of nature has appeared in the means of production, in an age when the spirit has departed entirely from the means of production, we need a spirituality that is not drawn from nature in the way it was drawn during the time of the theocracies from what lived more physically in human beings; we need a spirituality that is freely achieved and that has its own content.

I am aware that people think this sounds extremely Utopian, but in fact it is extremely practical. However many social communities you found, however many trade unions or co-operatives, if you stick with concepts and ways of thinking that have crept into our time from the Middle Ages you will not succeed in bringing even a little movement into the social question, let alone finding partial solutions. The social question is a global question today.

So what has come to join the kind of thinking that judges the social organism in terms of legalistic, dialectic and habitual morality? Charity has appeared on the scene, wonderful, heart-warming human compassion. Now that the social question has become a burning question all over the world we see collecting tins for the East appearing everywhere in Western Europe. It is wonderful that people collect and I do not wish to decry it in the least. In fact the more we are in a position to contribute to these collections the more we ought to do so. Nevertheless, what happens in consequence of these collections belongs to the past and not the future. All this compassion and charity arises out of a kind of thinking appropriate for the Middle Ages.

I see two pictures in my mind's eye. On the one hand there is the medieval cathedral in which the prelates stored their gorgeous vestments while they sat together in their houses doing something that was remarkably revealed a few months ago by a Swiss newspaper when it published the menu of the Christmas feast enjoyed by those prelates in a Swiss cathedral. You would be astonished at the number of pigs consumed by those prelates at Christmas time. Around these cathedrals, on the other hand, armies of paupers were encamped to whom alms were distributed. This was how things were done in the Middle Ages; there was no other way. It was the obvious thing to do at that time. Whether we now think it good or bad is irrelevant, for in those times it was taken for granted.

So is it not the same thing to see the misery in Russia on the one hand—the paupers encamped around the cathedrals—while on the other hand people set about collecting alms for them? Such collections are good and praiseworthy. But they fail entirely even to touch the social question, let alone partially solve it. We should not forget that because of the uselessness of our social thinking voices are everywhere becoming audible that do not say: 'We are grateful for the alms given to us.' What those voices say is: 'It is an absolute disgrace that we are given alms, for it shows that there are still people in the world who are in a position to give alms; there ought to be no such people any longer!'

This is what we should wholeheartedly endorse as the fundamental impulse of the social organism in our time, which is actually already a global organism, although it is still only perceived nationally. What people everywhere ought to realize today is that above all else we need something that can bridge the chasms that exist in the social order.

Why do we talk so much about the social question nowadays? It is because we have become antisocial through and through. As a rule people theorize most about things that are lacking in their feelings and instincts but not about things that genuinely exist in their feelings and instincts. If genuine social sensitivity existed amongst human beings there would be hardly any social theories or social unrest. People theorize about things when they lack a sense for them. Theories are always about things that are unreal. But what we have to do today is search out what is there in real life, something that is much harder to do than theorize. Human beings will not make progress unless they can find their way properly into real life, for it is the theorizing spirit that has chopped up our world and brought our civilization to the brink of chaos. The only thing that can lead us forward is a full awareness of real life.

I cannot help repeating yet again that this is what we should be feeling in the depths of our hearts to be the fundamental impulse of today's social question. Once we have understood how human beings can once again find one another we shall be able to tackle the social question along the right lines.

What have the upper classes done in this field? They have stuck their noses into proletarian misery and shaped it into works of art. At least you got some kind of a clear impression of a theocratic god when Michelangelo painted Christ as the judge of the world. What Christ will look like in a depiction that fits in with today's industrial social order is what we are trying to work on in Dornach now.[49] So far there is little understanding of these things because we do not know how to relate the spiritual world to the cold world of machines. Unlike the days when a legalistic or a theocratic way of thinking could be modelled on reality, we have so far not yet discovered a way of thinking that can relate to and enter fully into a reality that has grown cold. So the upper classes stuck their noses into the misery of the poor and made it into what present-day poets, sculptors and painters have created out of it: art with a social conscience. The result is a dreadful sentimentality because people are not yet filled with any truly spiritual freedom that can stand side by side with today's human reality. We have yet to find the strength with which to work out of industrialism, but now enriched by a free spirituality, a strength like that possessed by people of earlier times when they were able to shape agriculture through theocracy, and trade and commerce through jurisprudence. We must achieve a social way of thinking, social understanding and concepts that cannot be achieved unless abstractions such as 'capital' and 'value added' are thrown overboard. But social concepts can only come about if we bring the revealing warmth of spirituality to the cold world of the machine. Although they may not be aware of it, the very people who now lead their lives surrounded by machines are the ones who long for genuine spirituality so as to escape from the grip of outdated materialism with which they are otherwise forced to fill their hearts.

The village with its church was joined by the country with its town. These were social structures that could be encompassed by social ideas. The factory is no longer part of the town; it is a new social structure. It is removed from the universal order like a kind of solitary demon. The factory has no spiritual content. So we need to bring spirituality to it from the other side. That is why today's social question is first and foremost a spiritual question. We must find ways of doing better than merely sticking our noses into proletarian misery. We must find a spirituality that comes quite naturally from our own heart but also from the hearts of those, however lowly, with whom we speak. Just as the sun shines on all of us, so does genuine spirituality shine on every human being regardless of position or class and without concern for any kind of social or class struggle. We have reached a momentous point in world history, for the demand now is that all human beings should be able to step on to the stage of history as individuals.

In earlier times society consisted of ranks and classes. Today and in the future we shall be concerned with the human being, with the individual who gives birth to a new world. This is what we must help to bring about, not by perpetuating old ways or muddling along as before, but by going down into the profound depths of the human being in order to find there, spiritually, the widest spaces of the universe. This will be a sure way of making a contribution to solving the social question.

This is what I was aiming for in my book *Towards Social Renewal*, because now is the time when people can surely be expected to understand such things not merely theoretically with their heads, but with their hearts and with their will. Those who see *Towards Social Renewal* as an intellectual book will not understand it. Only those will understand it who see it as a book of the will, a book of the heart spoken out of life itself and out of what must be accepted as the most important social impulses of the present time that can be found everywhere beneath the surface of existence.

Tomorrow I shall round off what I wanted to say about the social question.

3. ON FOUNDING AN ASSOCIATION FOR FURTHER WORK ALONG THE LINES OF THESE LECTURES[50]

Oxford, 28 August 1922

Ladies and gentlemen, from the way I have been presenting these lectures you will have gathered how much importance I attach to the sum-total of impulses amongst which a particular education method is only, you might say, a partial expression—a partial expression of what, in my opinion, ought to come about at the present moment in human evolution through a deeper understanding of life, an understanding of life founded on reality. Having noted the fundamental tone I believe I have managed to sustain during these lectures, you will believe me when I thank you most warmly—not so much in my own name as in the name of this matter as a whole for which, as you know, I would like to pledge my whole existence—when I thank you most warmly for your decision to take the matter in hand for this part of the world.

We can only hope that in the association you intend to create as the result of intentions that have ripened here there will be a number of persons who will have the strength to carry what you hope will arise out of the meetings we have had today.

For matters of this kind, ladies and gentlemen, it is important that there should be persons capable of carrying the impulse. The anthroposophical movement, as we call it, can only make progress in the world if it is carried by individual human beings. Of course there have to be associations or societies, but the most important thing is that personalities emerge from such societies who with their own individual strength can carry whatever it is that comes to be regarded as important.

If we consider the very important position in which the population of this country, in particular, finds itself in the present historical situation, and if we take seriously the responsibility arising out of this position, we have to say that something exceptionally important could arise out of the decision you have taken today. The number of those who say that the world needs a push towards the spirit is small as yet. On the degree to which this small number becomes an ever-growing crowd will depend whether world evolution can make any progress at all through new impulses.

As I said in the lecture this morning, the old impulses have more or less come to a standstill. We still use the old words; numbers and strong parties talk in old-fashioned terms. Let us endeavour to talk in new-fashioned terms, and let us strive to take these things into the real world. But do not let us become over-enthusiastic about our intention of bringing spiritual values into evolution. Let us not get over-excited! 'Bringing spiritual values into reality' can become a slogan just like any other.

The most important thing is that with our whole heart, in the fullness of our being, we can stand for what can be guided, thought and willed from real life, through real life and for real life. It is this that is essential.

Perhaps your association will initially bring to fruition things that can and, I believe, must be directed towards education. Whatever the case may be, something extra-ordinarily positive, something connected with the evolution of humanity in our present age, will come from your decisions.

I wanted to say these few words of warmest gratitude to you for attaching your hearts to what has been expressed in these lectures in the form of ideas, something with serious intent that needs to be elicited from human evolution by human beings with true feelings in order to become an impulse for evolution on into the future.

4. THE HUMAN BEING WITHIN THE SOCIAL ORDER: INDIVIDUAL AND SOCIETY

Oxford, 29 August 1922

Today I hope to conclude my remarks about human society in the present time and the social demands it makes on us, but I am only too aware that all I have been able to say and still intend to say here can amount to nothing more than a very scanty guideline. The social question in our time is extremely wide-ranging, and there are two main aspects that need taking into account if we are to reach some clarity about it. These are firstly the present historical moment in human evolution and secondly the immediate external circumstances in the world.

The present historical moment in human evolution needs to be approached with the utmost impartiality. Our understanding is all too easily clouded by preconceptions and an emotional approach that leads us to skate over the surface of what is going on in the depths not so much of the human soul as of the very nature of the human being as such.

We are easily misunderstood when we say that we are living in an age of transition, for this has been said in almost every age. Obviously we always live in a time of transition from past to future, but the point is to discern the nature of the particular transition in question. To do this it is necessary to realize that 'the present' does not mean this year or even this decade but a much longer period of time. The present time has been in preparation since the fifteenth century, and the nineteenth century was its culmination. Although we are now right in the midst of this age, people in general have little appreciation of the particular character of this particular moment in world history.

To put it plainly, to gain any kind of insight into social life today we have to investigate the way human beings are straining to extricate themselves from old social forms because they long to be free, independent human beings pure and simple.

To use a German term, we need a *Weltanschauung der Freiheit*, a universal conception of freedom or—since 'freedom' in this country has other connotations—a universal conception of spiritual activity in deed, in thought and feeling deriving from the spiritual individuality of the human being.

Early in the 1890s in my book *Philosophy of Spiritual Activity* I endeavoured to paint a picture of what human beings are now striving for not so much in their conscious as in their subconscious activity.[51] In former times human beings were bound within a social context as far as their thoughts and actions were concerned. Look at someone in the Middle Ages: he was not an individual in the sense we mean today, but rather a member of a class or a particular station in life; he was a Christian, or a nobleman or a citizen. All his thoughts were bourgeois or aristocratic or priestly. It is only in recent centuries that individuals have extricated themselves from these structures. If one wanted to fit into society in a social way in former times one had to ask oneself: 'What is priestly behaviour? How should a priest behave towards others? How should a citizen behave towards others? How should a nobleman behave towards others?' Nowadays we ask: 'How should one behave in a way that is in keeping with one's worth as a human being and one's rights as a human being?'

To find the answer one has to look for something within oneself. We now have to seek within ourselves the impulses that formerly showed us how to behave in society in consequence of being a citizen, a nobleman or a priest. These impulses are not in our body but in our spirit which is impressed into our soul. That is why in my *Philosophy of Spiritual Activity* I described the moral impulse that is at the same time the most profound social impulse guiding the human being as 'moral intuition'.[52] Something needs to come to fruition in us that can guide us even in the most concrete situations and tell us: This is what you must do now.

Then, you see, everything depends on the individual. Then you have to look at the individuality of each human being with the presupposition that moral intuitions reside in his or her heart and soul. All education must be aimed at awakening these moral intuitions, so that every individual can express the sense: 'I belong not only to this earth, I am not solely a product of physical heredity; I have come down to the earth from spiritual worlds and as this particular individual I have a specific task to do here on earth.'

But to know that we have a task is not enough; we also need to find out what that task is. In each concrete situation we must find within ourselves what it is that we have to do. Our soul must tell us. Vague pricks of conscience must develop into individual moral intuition. This is what it means to become free as a human being; it means to build only on what we can discover within ourselves.

A good many people have taken strong exception to this because they imagine it would lead to placing the whole moral sphere in society at the mercy of individual caprice. But this is not the case. The moral sphere then rests on the only basis suitable for society, which is, on the one hand, the basis of mutual trust. We must learn to acquire this mutual trust in the larger concerns of life, just as we already have it in small things. If I come up against Mr K. in the doorway as I leave, I instinctively trust that he will not come straight for me and knock me down. I myself act in accordance with the same trust and we both make way so as not to knock into each other. We already do this in the lesser events of life, but it is something that can be applied in all our affairs if we learn to see ourselves rightly as free beings. There has to be trust between individuals—what a golden word this is! In educating ourselves and others to trust and believe in the individual human being, rather than just the nation or humanity as a whole, in working towards trust in the individual we are doing the only thing that can generate an impulse for social life in the future, for only such trust can create community among individuals. This is the one aspect. The other is that when there is no longer anyone telling us what to do or compelling us to do it, we shall have to find the necessary impetus within ourselves not only to act but also to respond to situations with feeling, to be active in our soul. What does this mean? If someone was a priest in former times he knew his station in society. Without having to look it up in a book he knew how to behave when he wore the habit of a religious order, and that certain obligations were connected with this. Likewise if he wore the sword of the nobility he knew that his place in human society was based on being a nobleman. He had his specific place in the social order, and the same applied to the citizen.

Whether we like it or not, this is something that is no longer appropriate in human society. Of course there are plenty of people who want to go back to those days, but world history is telling us otherwise. There is absolutely no point in establishing abstract programmes for all kinds of social set-ups. The only useful thing we can do is look at what current history is telling us.

So now we have to ask ourselves what the emotive impulse for our social actions can be when we are no longer pushed along by virtue of being a priest, a citizen, a nobleman or a member of the fourth estate. Only this: we must have as much trust in our dealings with other people as we have in a person whom we love. To be free means to realize oneself in actions carried out with love.

One golden word that must rule social life in the future is 'trust'. The other is 'love' for the task we have to do. In future, actions will be good for society as a whole if they arise out of love for the whole of humanity.

But first we have to learn what love for the whole of humanity means. It is no good jumping to the conclusion that it already exists. It does not, and the more we tell ourselves that it does not yet exist the better it will be. Love for the whole of humanity must be a love of deeds, it must become active and must realize itself in freedom. Then it will gradually move on from the domestic hearth or the local pulpit and become a universal, world-wide appraisal.

From this point of view I now want to ask how you think a worldwide appraisal of this kind can be applied, for example, to that most dreadful and heartbreaking example of social chaos now taking hold in Eastern Europe, in Russia.

In such a situation it is important to ask the right question, and the right question is: 'Is there too little food on the earth for the whole of mankind?' We have to refer to the whole globe, for since the last third of the nineteenth century we have a world economy, not national economies, and it is important to take this into account in the social context. No one will reply that there is too little food on the earth for the whole of humanity. Such a time may come, and then people will have to use their ingenuity to solve the problem. But for now we can still be sure that if countless people are going hungry in any corner of the earth, it is because human arrangements in recent decades have brought this about. It is these human arrangements that are preventing the right food supplies from reaching the starving corner of the earth in time. It is a question of distributing the food supplies in the right way at the right time.

What has happened? At a specific moment in history Russia has isolated a huge territory from the rest of the world by instituting a continuation of Tsarism on the basis of a purely intellectual abstraction. A feeling of nationalism extending over a large territory has locked Russia away from the rest of the world, thus preventing global social arrangements from enabling human hands to let nature from one part of the world help out generously in another where nature has failed for once.

When we can find the right angle from which to view these things, the sight of such social distress will lead each of us to cry: 'Mea culpa.' For although we feel we are all individuals, this does not deprive us of a sense of unity with the whole of humanity. In our human evolution we have no right to feel ourselves as individuals unless we also have a sense of belonging to humanity as a whole.

I should like to call this the fundamental ground from which any 'philosophy of freedom' must spring, for such a philosophy must place each individual human being in the social context in an entirely new way. Our questions, too, will then become quite new.

Very many questions have been asked about society in recent centuries, and especially in the nineteenth century; and what have the proletarian millions made of these questions which arose first among members of the higher classes? Why is there such a widespread view that the proletarian millions are on the wrong track? It is because they have taken erroneous doctrines on board from the higher classes. They have become the pupils of the higher classes; the doctrines are not their own.

We must learn to see things clearly. Some maintain that human beings are the product of their environment, that they are produced by the social circumstances and arrangements all around them. Others say that social circumstances are what people have made them. All such views are just about as clever as asking: Is the human physical body the product of the head or of the stomach? The physical human being is the product of neither but rather of a continuous interaction between the two. The two have to work together; the head is both cause and effect, and the stomach is both cause and effect. Indeed, if you look a little deeper you will find that the stomach is made by the head, for in the embryo the head is created before the stomach is formed; but on the other hand it is the stomach that forms the organism.

So we must not ask whether human beings have been created by circumstances or circumstances by human beings. It is essential to understand that each is both cause and effect, that everything affects everything else. The foremost question to ask is: 'What social arrangements will enable people to have the right thoughts on matters of social concern, and what kind of thoughts must exist so that these right social arrangements can arise?'

In practical life people tend to think in terms of doing one thing after another. But this leads nowhere. We can only make progress if we think in circles, but many people do not feel up to doing this because it would be like having a mill-wheel turning in their head. It is essential to think in circles. Looking at external circumstances we must admit that they have been created by people but also that people are affected by them. And looking at the things people do we must realize that these actions bring about the external circumstances but also that they are sustained by these same external circumstances. To arrive at reality we must skip back and forth in our thoughts, but people do not like doing this. They want to set up a procedure and make a programme: Point 1, Point 2, Point 3, right up to, let us say, Point 12, with Point 1 coming first and Point 12 last. But there is no life in this. Any programme should be reversible, so that we can begin with Point 12 and work back to Point 1, just as the stomach nourishes the organism, and if the nerves situated underneath the cerebellum are not in good order we cannot breathe properly. Just as things can be reversed in life, so must we also see to it that they can be reversed in social life.

In the same vein, when I wrote my book *Towards Social Renewal* I had to assume, on the basis of the social situation at the time, that it would find readers who would be capable of going both forwards and backwards in their ideas. But people do not want this. They prefer to begin at the beginning and read through to the end, at which point they know that they have finished. They are not interested in being told that the end is also the beginning. The worst misunderstanding connected with this book with its social intentions was that people read it the wrong way; and they continue to do so. They do not want to adapt their thoughts to life; they want life to adapt to their thoughts. This, however, is not at all the precondition for social arrangements with which we are dealing here. I shall continue with this theme after the translation.

★

When people began to discuss the idea of a threefold social organism I heard about an interesting opinion. The idea of a threefold society draws attention to the three streams in social life that I have been describing over the last few days. Firstly there is the cultural, spiritual stream which is today the heritage of the old theocracies, for all cultural life can ultimately be traced back to the origins of theocracy. Secondly there is what I have called the sphere of political, legal affairs, and thirdly what can be termed economic life. When attention was focused on the threefolding impulse, on these three ideas, there were people of good standing in the world, manufacturers perhaps, or clergymen, people with a specific position in society, who came and pronounced on the matter: 'How delightful to discover a new suggestion emerging that will once again validate Plato's grand ideas.' These people thought I had breathed new life into Plato's division of society into the order of agricultural producers, the order of soldiers and the order of statesmen and scholars.

All I could say was that perhaps this might seem so to those who rush to the libraries to ascertain the origins of any new idea. But for those who understand what I mean by a three-folding of social life it will be obvious that it is the opposite of what Plato meant by his three orders, for Plato lived a good many years prior to the Mystery of Golgotha. His three orders were appropriate in his time, but to bring them back to life now would be absurd. The idea of a threefold organism is not concerned with dividing individuals into groups with some being producers, others soldiers and yet others statesmen. What we want to do now is create arrangements, institutions in which every individual can partake in turn, for today we are concerned with human individuals and not with orders or categories. There will be arrangements in which the cultural, spiritual life of humanity can be cultivated, this being built solely on people's individual capabilities. Secondly there will be independent arrangements that govern political and legal life without wanting to swallow up the other two elements of the social organism. And thirdly there will be arrangements dealing solely with economic affairs.

The political, legal life will deal with agreements people have to make with one another, with things that are determined between individuals.

In the cultural, spiritual sphere not everyone will be able to make judgements, for in this sphere only those can judge who have the necessary competence in a particular subject. Here everything emanates from the individual human being. There is a wholeness in the cultural life; it has to be a coherent, uniform body. You will object that this is not so, but I shall come to this in a moment.

The political, legal sphere requires individuals to work together in the sense of present-day democracy in matters that require no specialist knowledge, so that every individual is competent to form judgements. Such a sphere exists; it is the legal and political life.

Thirdly there is the sphere of economics. Here individuals do not make judgements; indeed, an individual opinion is irrelevant, for it can never be correct. In associations or communities of individuals judgements arise when opinions merge in a common judgement.

The whole point in all of this is not the division of the state, or for that matter any other community, into three parts. The important thing is that each of the three aspects is in a position to make its own contribution to the health of the overall social organism.

The way of thinking I have represented here is capable of holding its own in the midst of life. Suppose someone wants to apply his capabilities and do something, using the necessary skills or techniques. What this person does is then carried forward by others. It is important that I should do something, but it is not the main thing. The main thing is that a second, third, fourth person or any number of people carry my action further in an appropriate manner. For this to happen the social organism must be so managed that traces of my activity do not disappear. Otherwise I might do something here in Oxford that is carried on further for a while, but by the time it reaches Whitechapel there is no trace of it. All that remains visible are the external symptoms of the hardship prevalent there. Hardship will inevitably arise if human forces cannot enter into the social organism in the right way.

Look at the misery in Russia. What causes it? It is there because social forces cannot come to grips properly with the social organism, because the social organism is not structured in the right way according to its natural three parts. The actions of individual human beings will be able to percolate through the whole social organism like blood through the human body only if that social organism is so arranged that the cultural life depends freely on individuals, if there is a legal and political life that orders all the business that falls within the competence of every individual regardless of each person's level of education, and if, thirdly, there is an independent economic sphere concerned solely with production, consumption and distribution.

Such a thing can indeed result from a true and realistic insight into the world so long as people really do come to grips with it on the basis of a realistic understanding. But if such things, once stated, are merely explained away by Marxist theories and doctrinaire intellectualism, then of course they remain incomprehensible. No one then knows what is meant by someone who does not look at hardship superficially but who delves down more deeply, saying: 'You cannot improve matters in this way. First you must create social inter-relationships of a kind that enables the hardship to be sent packing.' That is where the problem lies.

We must begin to realize how far what was once theocracy

has retreated from real life. The original theocrats did not need libraries; their science was not neatly stored in libraries. To study a science there was no need to sit down and pore over old books, for what they did was go and dwell with living human beings. They paid attention to human beings. They asked how best to do what was right for human beings. The real world was their library. Instead of studying books they looked into human faces, they took account of them; instead of reading books they read the souls of human beings. Today all our science has been swallowed up by libraries or stored by other means, well away from human beings.

We need a sphere of spirit and culture firmly rooted in the real world; we need a sphere of spirit and culture in which books are written from life and for life, full of ideas for life and ways and means of living. Especially in the sphere of spirit and culture we must emerge from our libraries and go out into life. We need education for our children based on the children present in the classroom, not on rules. Our education must be derived from knowledge of the human being; what should be done each day, each week, each year must derive from the children themselves.

We need a legal and political sphere in which human being encounters human being, where the only basis for decisions is the legitimate competence of each individual, as I have already pointed out, regardless of profession or whatever other situation each is in. The legal and political sphere exists for all the situations in which human beings meet one another as equals.

What else will belong to the sphere of spirit and culture if this sphere is accepted in the form I have described? Little by little the administration of capital will move of its own accord from the economic to the spiritual, cultural sphere.

However much we may rail against capitalism there is nothing we can do about it, for we need it. What matters about capital and capitalism is not that they exist but what the social forces are that work in them. Capital has come into being through the intellectual ingenuity of human beings; it came into being out of the cultural, spiritual sphere through the division of labour and intellectual knowledge. Merely as a way of illustrating the possibilities, and not to make a Utopian statement, I described in my book *Towards Social Renewal* how capital might stream towards the spiritual, cultural sphere of the social organism. Just as the copyright on books lapses after 30 years, so that their content becomes common property, so, I suggested, might someone—having amassed capital and had capital working for him while he was himself engaged in the work which his capital generated—transfer his capital to the common good after 30 years or so. I did not state this as a Utopia but merely as a possibility of how, instead of stagnating everywhere, capital might begin to flow and enter the bloodstream of social life. All the things I wrote were illustrations, not dogmas or Utopian ideas. I merely wanted to hint at what might be brought about by the associations.

What actually happens may turn out to be something quite different. When one has brought life into one's thinking one does not set down dogmas to be adopted, one counts on human beings. Once they are embraced in the right way by the social organism they themselves will discover what is meaningful and useful socially in the environment in which they find themselves. In everything I say I count on people, not dogmas. Unfortunately it has been my experience that what I really meant in my book *Towards Social Renewal* is never discussed. Instead people ask questions such as: 'Is it really possible for capital to be inherited by the most capable after the passage of a specific number of years?' People do not want realities, they want Utopias. This is what militates against an unprejudiced reception of the threefolding impulse.

Once the legal, political sphere is able to function properly people will notice that it will involve itself with questions of labour. Today labour is entirely enmeshed in the economic life and is not treated as something to do with how people relate with one another. In 1905 I wrote an article on the social question in which I demonstrated that with today's division of labour, labour is reduced to a commodity as it flows into the rest of the social organism.[53] Our own labour only has an apparent value for us. What others do for us has real value, and what we do for them also has value. This has been achieved by technology, but our moral outlook has not kept pace with it. Within the social order as it is today one can, technically speaking, make nothing for oneself, not even a jacket. If you make it yourself it still costs as much, taking the whole social structure into account, as if it had been made by someone else. The economic aspect of the jacket is universal in the sense that it is determined by the community at large. It is an illusion to imagine that the jacket made for you by a tailor is cheaper. If you work it out in figures it might appear cheaper. But if you were to calculate its price as part of the overall balance sheet you would see that by making your own clothes you can no more jump out of your own skin than you can remove the process from the economic sphere or change that sphere in any way. The price of the garment you make for yourself remains an item in the total balance sheet. Labour is what one person does for another. It cannot be measured by the number of man/hours required in a factory setting. The value put on labour is a supreme example of something belonging in the realm of law, the legal, political sphere.

You can tell that this is not an outdated idea by the way labour is everywhere protected and safeguarded by laws. But these regulations are not even half-measures, they are quarter-measures. No regulations will be properly effective until there is a proper threefolding of the social organism. Only when this has happened will human beings meet each other as equals. Only then will labour be rightly regulated when human worth meets human worth in that sphere where all are competent to speak.

You might want to object: 'Perhaps there will sometimes not be enough work to go round if work is determined in this way in a democratic state.' This is indeed one of the areas where the social life is affected by history, by the evolution of humanity as a whole. The economic sphere must not be allowed to determine the amount of work available. The economic sphere must be bounded on the one hand by nature and on the other by the amount of labour determined by the legal, political sphere. You cannot get a committee to decide in advance how many rainy days there are to be in 1923 so as to enable the economy to run on course in that year. Just as you have to accept the limitations set by nature, so in an independent economic organism will you have to reckon with the amount of labour available being determined by the legal, political organism. I can only mention this in general terms here, as an example.

Within the economic sphere of the social organism there will be associations in which consumers, producers and distributors will together reach an associative judgement based on practical experience—not an individual judgement that can only be irrelevant in this sphere. The small beginnings being tried today show that this is not yet possible, but the fact that these small beginnings are being tried shows that unconsciously humanity does have the intention to form associations. Co-operatives, trade unions, all kinds of communities show that this intention exists. But when co-operatives are founded side by side with ordinary social life as it exists today they will perish unless they conform to this social life by charging the same prices and using the same marketing practices. In working towards a threefold social organism we should not be trying to create new realities based on Utopian concepts; we should be coming to grips with what is already there. Institutions already in existence, consumers, producers, the entrepreneur, everything already in existence needs to come together in associations. There is no need to ask how to create associations. The question to ask is: 'How can existing economic organizations and institutions be integrated in associations?'

If such associations can be achieved, commercial experience will enable something to arise that can indeed lead to a genuine social ordering, just as a healthy human organism leads to a healthy life. There will be circulation in the economy, circulation of production money, loan money and gift money. There can be no social organism without these three. We may want to rail against gifts and donations, but they are a necessary part. You deceive yourself if you say that a healthy social organism should make gifts unnecessary. Yet you pay tax, and taxes are merely a roundabout way of making donations to schools and other facilities.

People deserve to have a social order in which they can always see how things flow without having to make suppositions. When social life has been extricated from today's general muddle, in which everything is mixed up together, we shall begin to see—just as we can already observe the blood circulating in the human organism—how money circulates in the form of production money, loan money and gift money. We shall see the different way human beings relate on the one hand to money they invest—money for trading, production and purchase—which goes back into production because of the way it earns interest, and on the other hand to the money they give as donations, which must flow into an independent cultural sphere.

People can only participate in social life as a whole through associations which make visible how the life of society flows. Then the social organism will be healthy. Abstract thinking is incompatible with the idea of a threefolding of the social order; only living thinking can encompass it.

Yet even in the economic sphere our thinking is no longer alive. Everywhere we have abstraction. Where is there any life in the economic sphere today? How did it begin in the days when people jotted down their income and expenditure on odd scraps of paper? As things grew more complicated clerics were employed to do the job; they became the clerks. They ran external life to the best of their ability. And who are the successors of those clerks taken from the church to record the economic affairs of princes? They are today's bookkeepers. In some districts you still occasionally come across a small reminder of those early times. If you turn to the first page in their ledgers—is this the case in your country also?—you see the inscription: 'With God'. But there is little in subsequent pages that is 'with God'. What you find there is an abstraction of something that ought to be full of life, something that ought to be present as life in the associations and not stored up in ledgers.

In working towards a threefolding of society we certainly do not aim to juggle about in old ways with concepts such as cultural life, political life, economic life, mixing them up perhaps in slightly different ways, as has been done in recent times. Our main concern is to comprehend what an organism really is, and then to bring back into real life those things that have become such total abstractions. The most important task is to rescue things from abstraction and bring them back to life. Every individual will belong to the associations of the economic sphere, including representatives of the cultural sphere, for they, too, have to eat, as do the representatives of the legal, political sphere. Conversely, too, every individual also belongs to each of the other spheres as well.

There is a necessary consequence of all this that shocks people a good deal when the subject is brought up, especially when the examples one uses are somewhat exaggerated so as to be more explicit. I once told an industrialist, an excellent man at his job, what was needed in order to bring things back to life: 'Suppose you have an employee who is fully integrated in the life of your factory. Then along comes a technical college and snaps this man up, not someone recently trained but someone who is fully immersed in the life of the factory. For five or ten years this man can talk to the youngsters about what the life of a factory really is. Then, when he gets a bit stale, he can return to the factory.' Well, such things will make life complicated, but they are what our time requires. There is no getting away from it.

Just as new life must continually flow through the social organism if it is not to decay, so must people either become full human beings, which means that they must be able to circulate through all the spheres of the social organism, or we shall fall into decadence. Of course we can choose decadence if we like, by standing still with our old points of view. But evolution will not allow us to stand still. This is the salient fact.

★

In conclusion I should like to add that I have developed the subject of my lectures more from a feeling angle. It should not be taken one-sidedly as being purely spiritual except in the sense that it arises out of the spirit of real life. I have only been able to give you a kind of feeling for the impulses that are to arise out of these social ideas. More is not possible in only three lectures.

However, as I bring these lectures to a close I want to thank you in the warmest possible way for allowing me to speak to you about these things. I especially want to thank Mrs Mackenzie who has chaired the committee, for without her efforts this whole Oxford enterprise would not have taken place.[54] I also thank the committee for all they have done to assist her. Another thing I am especially grateful for is the opportunity given us here in Oxford during this meeting to bring in the artistic endeavours, eurythmy specifically, which we are trying to send out into the world from Dornach. Thank you all for your endeavours!

You will sense how seriously I want to express my thanks when I remind you that everything we are starting in Dornach is only a beginning that cannot become reality without such efforts as have taken place here in Oxford. The understanding and stoutness of heart we need in Dornach is expressed in a fact which I also want to mention to you, although this is not in any way at all intended as a hint. It is likely that by November we shall have to break off our building work in

Dornach because by then we shall have run out of funds. These funds do exist in the world, I believe, but somewhere there is a blockage in this connection. If things were to proceed as they ought in a rightly functioning social organism, then ... The fact that this work has begun but may well have to be interrupted because of the unfavourable times if an understanding for the need to continue does not emerge in time—this is something that oppresses us greatly in Dornach. I have mentioned this to show you how very heartfelt and cordial are the thanks I have expressed to you.

I have endeavoured to speak to you about education on the one hand, and about social matters on the other. From Dornach these things will be cultivated in a general way. When the anthroposophical movement was founded the point of departure initially was that of a world view and a theoretical understanding. Then people began to see and feel what strong forces of decline exist in our time, whereupon they realized that something needed doing in education and in social life. That was when they began to approach me with the question: 'What has anthroposophy got to offer with regard to the establishment of schools that take the fullness of real life into account, and with regard to a future that needs to emerge from the deeper layers of humanity?' For there is not much to be gained for the future from the more superficial layers of human existence.

The education movement did not arise out of some fad or abstract idea. It came about because people began to enquire what anthroposophy had to offer on the basis of real life rather than out of some kind of sectarian effort.

This was even more strongly the case with the social question. Here, too, people whose hearts were filled with dismay at today's signs of decay came to ask what anthroposophy might say out of its encounter with genuine reality about impulses that could be sent towards the future.

I am immensely grateful to have been met with understanding here, for what needs saying must go forth into the fullness of life; from this college it must send its effects out into the world where real human beings are at work. I am grateful that it is not antiquated knowledge, for the centres of cultural life must send out impulses to ensure that the right people are in position in the factories, the people who know how to administer capital that generates life. You will not take it amiss that I endeavoured to demonstrate this by means of such examples as came to hand, for on the other side I want to repeat what I have already said before: I have been most happy to explain these impulses here in Oxford where every step you take outside in the street brings inspiration from ancient times and where such strong influences come to the aid of someone wanting to speak out of the spirit.

The spirit that lived in former times was not the one that is needed now to work on into the future. But it was a living spirit that can still inspire. Therefore it has been deeply satisfying to give these lectures and suggestions for the future here in Oxford surrounded by impressions of ancient, venerable learning.

Finally, yet more thanks remain to be expressed. I am sure you will all understand how grateful I am to Mr Kaufmann who has done all the translating with such great love.[55] When you know how much effort goes into translating quite complicated texts and how much this effort can deplete a person's strength in quite a short time you can appreciate the work Mr Kaufmann has done here during this holiday conference over the past weeks. I want to express my sincere thanks to him, and I hope that many of you will also do so. I now ask him to translate these final words as accurately and faithfully as he has translated all the previous things I have said.

PART THREE

ILKLEY AND PENMAENMAWR

Much was experienced during the visit to England in 1923, which begin with the education lectures given in Ilkley, Yorkshire, from 4 to 17 August 1923.[56] Rudolf Steiner gave a report on this visit after his return to Dornach in which he also described the atmosphere of the region, where soul-destroying industry rampaged in smoke blackened towns interspersed with high moorlands in the green solitude of which traces of ancient spirituality would suddenly take one by surprise.

Having moved on to Penmaenmawr in Wales where he stayed from 18 to 31 August 1923, Rudolf Steiner gave 13 purely anthroposophical lectures at a Summer School there.[57] He also gave a number of addresses, which are reproduced below, the first being his reply to the welcome expressed by the organizers of the Summer School.

Marie Steiner

1. WALDORF EDUCATION

Ilkley, 10 August 1923

May I begin by apologizing for not speaking to you in your language. As I am unable to do so I shall have to speak my own, and the lecture will be translated afterwards.

I have been asked to tell you about the general principles of the education method used in the Waldorf School,[58] which has evolved out of the confluence of two spiritual factors. The Waldorf School in Stuttgart was founded in Germany during the turbulent aftermath of the War at a time when people hoped it would be possible to initiate a number of social arrangements. The industrialist Emil Molt was initially concerned to found a school for the children of his factory workers.[59] He wanted it to be a school where children could be educated in ways that would enable them gradually to enter social life in a sensible and entirely human way, so that social initiatives would no longer be entirely swayed by political propaganda. That was the one factor, which was joined by the other.

Emil Molt had already been a long-standing member of the anthroposophical movement, which seeks to bring spiritual knowledge into the social life of today, spiritual knowledge in all its reality, founded on the true principles of the human being just as firmly as is the case with the sciences that have been coming more and more to the fore over many centuries. As the bearer of this anthroposophical movement, I was asked by Emil Molt to introduce appropriate didactic and educational methods into this Waldorf School.

This school therefore differs from those arising out of all kinds of educational reform movements that are under way nowadays. It is a school built entirely on the foundations of the kind of educational methods and practice that arise from genuine, deeply penetrating knowledge about the human being.

As our civilization has proceeded to develop we have gradually lost what used to be our genuine knowledge about the human being. Instead we tend to turn our attention to external nature and can therefore only see the part of the human being that belongs to nature and the physical world. Of course this physical and natural basis must not be neglected by education, but human beings have a soul and a spirit as well as a body, and the full knowledge of the human being can only be gained when spirit, soul and body are all understood in equal measure.

The educational principles of the Waldorf School are based on the true knowledge of the human being and therefore also the growing human being. They are not principles that apply to a specific locality, to schools in the countryside or in towns, to boarding schools or day schools. The Waldorf School is founded strictly on an educational and practical principle that can be adapted to suit any external situation and any circumstances provided by whatever social forms are present.

That is why the Waldorf School, initially founded for the children of Emil Molt's factory employees, now has pupils from all social classes or positions. Humanly it is a genuine comprehensive school. Educational ideas and methods derived from true knowledge of the human being are suitable for all human beings everywhere, for all children no matter what their class or caste.

There is not enough time here for me to give you a systematic description of all the principles of the Waldorf School, and anyway it is not a school in which the education is programmed down to the last detail. The way it works arises out of the day-to-day practical situation and the teachers' immediate work with the children and their essential nature. I shall therefore only be able to give you hints about the principles of the Waldorf School, and I beg you to take into account that all I shall be able to do here is give you a very sketchy description of what the whole thing is about.

A most important facet of genuine knowledge about man is the fact that the growing human being is subject to developmental phases. This is much more strongly the case than is generally supposed. Of course these phases of development have been taken into account to some extent in all ages of history, but they are to be brought to the fore much more strongly in Waldorf education.

The first absolutely clear indication to be made is that around the seventh year—approximately, of course—when children change their teeth, a complete transformation and metamorphosis takes place in the life of the child. In a certain sense the child becomes a different being by getting a new set of teeth. What is the nature of this transformation? Up to about the seventh year forces have been at work in the child, organic forces helping the body to develop, giving impetus to breathing, blood circulation, and generally building up the organism through growth and nutrition. But at this point only a small portion of these forces continues to work in the organic development of the child. The remainder is withdrawn and now begins to metamorphose and transform the soul life of the child.

Recently there have been a good many psychological investigations about how the soul works into the body, into the child's organism. A true science of the spirit does not float in a mystical mist; it looks at the world in a practical way, gaining direct experience of life and the world. So such a science does not ask abstract questions about soul and body but investigates what can be directly experienced in real life about how soul and body are related.

When you look at things in this way you discover that the soul forces of the child work in the physical organism during the period between birth and the change of teeth. What takes place in the body during that period is the same as what later comes about between the change of teeth and puberty through the child's thinking, through memory and the like, when those soul forces have become more emancipated and are used psychologically instead of in the body.

For all of us, but especially for the teacher, the first thing that must become a part of our inner attitude and indeed of our very nature is a sharper eye for this metamorphosis in human life around the seventh year, and beyond that an understanding of the tremendous change that occurs around the fourteenth or fifteenth year when puberty is accomplished.

Those who approach children with an attitude like this will know that up to its seventh year a child is a kind of universal sense organ, so that its whole organism relates to its environment in a manner that resembles the way an eye or an ear relates to its environment. A sense organ absorbs impressions from its surroundings and imitates them in picture form. Until the age of seven a child is filled with pulsating, intensive elements, absorbing whatever goes on in its surroundings just as though it were one great sense organ. A child is a being entirely given over to imitation. If you study children you will see, in the way they relate to the world around them through their physical organism up to their seventh year, a relationship that later develops into something spiritual, or indeed religious. Our understanding of a child up to the time of the change of teeth is only correct if we see that child as being *homo religiosus* because of the forces and impulses that emerge from its physical and psychological make-up. Therefore all of us in the child's environment ought to behave in an appropriate manner. We must do in the vicinity of the child whatever it is fitting for it to imitate through its direct senses.

Let me give the example of a child who was said to steal. His parents approached me in considerable agitation saying: 'Our son steals!' I replied immediately that we would have to see whether the boy was really stealing. What had he been doing? He had been giving coins taken from his mother's dresser to other children. In fact he had been doing a friendly deed! Each day he had observed his mother taking money out of the dresser. He thought that what his mother did was the right thing to do. So he copied her. He was imitating his mother, not stealing.

So we must make quite sure that all the things children see happening in their environment are things they are allowed to imitate; and the most important aspect of this is that it even applies to our feelings, and indeed our thoughts as well. Those adults who are the best of all at bringing up children to their seventh year are the ones who not only act in a way that children are allowed to imitate but who also do not permit themselves any feelings or thoughts other than those suitable for children to imitate.

We must observe correctly how all aspects of the way we bring children up have a spiritual effect on them. During the first seven years everything affects the child organically. The way we live according to our nature has an effect on the child, for example if someone is given to angry outbursts. Children are vulnerable to such manifestations; they experience the shock inwardly. It affects not only their psychological state but also their breathing and blood circulation, right down to the way the blood vessels develop. Those who really understand human nature and observe an individual by taking into account not only a particular moment but the whole of that individual's life on earth, from birth to death, know that psychological, spiritual and physical impressions received from the environment affect the blood vessels, the blood circulation and the intimate breathing processes in such a way that the effects will become apparent in later life, up to the fortieth or fiftieth year. An individual who is torn hither and thither between conflicting impressions as a child will later on develop weaknesses in the way breathing and circulation function together.

These are not necessarily effects that a generalized medical examination would detect; they are something very delicate connected with the circulatory system which those educating children ought to know about.

The change of teeth that takes place around the seventh year represents a kind of full stop. We only change our teeth once. Thereafter the forces that bring about the change of teeth become free for the individual to use later; they move into the sphere of the soul. In children of junior school age the forces that worked in a structuring way up to the age of seven now work musically in the organism up to the age of puberty. Up to the age of seven it is the head organization that works in the whole of the human organism. The head is the great sculptor, shaping blood vessels, guiding the blood circulation, and so on. From the seventh to the fifteenth year the rhythmic system becomes the dominant one at work in the human organism. If we succeed in introducing rhythm, musical timing, indeed an overall musical shape into our lessons and the whole way we educate and even run the school, then we shall be supporting the human nature of the children.

The lessons we give to children between the change of teeth and puberty must be such that essentially they appeal to the artistic element in the children.

This artistic element does indeed pervade the whole of the education at the Waldorf School between the ages of seven and 14. The children should be led to the content of the lessons by means of pictures. We do not immediately teach them the abstract letters of the alphabet, for this would not give them a human relationship to those abstract scribbles that civilization calls the letters of the alphabet. These letters are abstract. At the Waldorf School we work through pictures. First we get the children to paint and draw, before approaching the shapes of the letters out of what flows from human nature in painting and drawing. Then, only when the whole organism of the child in body, soul and spirit has been taken hold of by writing that has been derived out of art, do we proceed to reading, which involves only a part of the human being. Reading only involves a part but not the whole of the human being, whereas writing can be derived from the totality. If we proceed in this way we are looking at the human being in the right way and taking body, soul and spirit into account.

Something extraordinary begins to come about if we bring things to the children in an artistic way, if the teachers are artists in education in the whole way they work in the lessons. Nowadays people worry a lot about how not to make children too tired. They draw graphs depicting which subjects and which actions, whether physical or mental, tire the children most. The lessons in the Waldorf School, however, draw most strongly on that part of the human being that does not get tired at all. Human beings get tired when they use their head in thinking and when they live the life of the will in movement. But whether you are awake or asleep, or tired or not tired, your rhythmic system—your system of breathing and heart function, which is what really artistic work is founded on— continues to work from the moment you are born to the moment you die. The healthiest of all education systems is the one that draws on the never-tiring rhythmic system of the human being.

From a sound understanding of the human being we therefore try to make sure that all the lessons in our education are founded on and draw on the human rhythmic system.

If you bring movement and music into everything, if you make pictures, rhythms, melodies your point of departure, you will notice something remarkable. You will find that as the children progress onwards from their artistic activities a kind of demand will develop in them, a demand arising out of the pictures you have given them and the musical way in which you have helped them take hold of the world. This demand will show that this way of dealing with the world is too rich for human beings to enjoy constantly. In their tenth or eleventh year the children will show that the artistic realm is too rich for the human being to be constantly involved in, and they will begin to develop a desire for simplification. This desire for simplification is a natural, elementary desire arising in the children.

The point when the desire for simplification arises out of their artistic activities is the point when artistic work can be taken forward into intellectual work. Having given the children the wealth of what the artistic element has to offer, we may then permit ourselves to introduce them to the poverty of the intellect without harming their physical or psychological development. What we are doing is elaborating everything intellectual on the foundation of the artistic element.

On the other hand, by getting the children to move their bodies in an artistic way, by getting them to let their limbs move in a musical way—as is the case in eurythmy which, by the way, can be seen over in Ilkley just now[60]—by helping the children to enter into moulded, musical movements that take hold of their whole body, we cause a strange hunger to arise in them, a hunger encompassing spirit and soul as well as body. Their whole organization then longs for quite specific bodily exercises, a quite specific kind of bodily culture. Physical care of the body is only healthy for the development of the human organism when it harmonizes with a mysterious hunger for the kind of movement, like those of health gymnastics, which are such that the desire to be active in the intellect and the desire to be active in the will are both drawn from the desire for the artistic element.

By working in this way we arrive at a type of education and a way of giving lessons that is directed not to a particular portion of the human being but to the human being as a whole. By doing this it is possible to develop the memory, for example, in such a way that it has a positive effect on the human organism as a whole. This sounds paradoxical today, but in the future it will become an integral part of physiology. Everything that works mentally and spiritually in the child also goes deeply into the physical organism; and that is where it remains. There are individuals who get all kinds of metabolic illnesses, such as rheumatism, in their fifties. If you observe human beings with regard to education not only while they are children but also when they are adults, taking into account the fact that, like the seed of a plant, childhood is the seed for the whole of life, you will realize that excessive demands made on the child's memory will bury themselves in its organism in such a way that at 40 or 50 metabolic illnesses will set in which cannot be controlled by the organism.

I am telling you this to show why in the Waldorf School everything we do is aimed at making sure that mental and spiritual work is done in a way that has the right effect on the physical organism. Every lesson is geared to promoting health because we see how the human spirit works right into the physical organism.

By building our education and teaching on the foundation of our knowledge of the human being we are thus able to derive the educational aims for each school year from what the child actually is in each year of childhood. We take our cue exclusively from what the children tell us. Our education is nothing other than knowledge of the human being.

We consider that the way we educate the children takes account not only of their childhood but of the whole span of their life on earth. There are views and methods that are entirely justifiable from other standpoints, but they must not be exaggerated. For example, it is a mistake to imagine that children should only be taught what they can understand through their own observation at a particular age. Those who maintain that this is so have no understanding of one of the most valuable factors in childhood. This is that between the ages of seven and puberty it is of the utmost benefit if children can be taught by someone whose authority they respect as a matter of course. Just as the principle of imitation reigns up to the seventh year, so must the principle of authority reign between the seventh and fourteenth years. When this is the case many things that the children do not quite understand can be taken into their soul through love simply on the authority of the teacher they love—for love is the most important educational principle of all. Then, when these individuals reach the age of 30 or 40 they think back to something they took in on the authority of a beloved teacher when they were eight or nine. It rises up out of their soul and enters their consciousness now that they are mature. Something that was taken in at the age of eight or nine on the authority of a beloved teacher is now understood through the individual's own humanity.

When something happens in this way it is a source of refreshment for the individual's human resources; it provides a kind of revitalization for the whole of later life when after decades a person reaches an understanding of something he originally accepted out of love for a respected individual in authority. This is the way we take the whole of a human being's life into account, without focusing in a one-sided way solely on what is immediately obvious naturally.

I also want to show how this applies in the moral sphere as well. We derive the religious education of the children from the primeval religious impulse living in them. You have surely observed how there are individuals who after they have reached a certain age radiate a kind of blessing towards their fellow human beings simply by being amongst them. When a person like this enters a room with a group of people in it, it is not so much what he says as the way he says it, the modulation of his voice and the kind of gestures he makes, indeed the very fact of simply being present there, which is like a benediction poured out over the gathering. By looking back into the childhood of such people we can discover how it has come about that they bestow grace in this way as though giving a blessing. It is the result of having been given the opportunity in childhood to revere and look up to a beloved person in authority in an almost religious way. No one can disseminate blessing in old age who has not as a child looked up with reverence to a beloved person in authority. In pictorial form you could say that you cannot in later life hold out your hands in benediction if you have not as a child folded them in prayer in the most inward way imaginable. The prayerfully folded hands of childhood work on in later life as the hands that give out blessing.

What we have to do is look towards the wholeness of the human being, sowing during childhood the seed of a morality that is inwardly grasped in a religious way, the seed of a human being who is fully capable of dealing with life.

This can be done if we endeavour to derive our education out of a full knowledge of what the human being is, out of a knowledge gained from observation of the human being from birth to the grave. Educational reform is such a burning issue today because in our time the question of education amounts in fact to the most urgent social question as well.

This is what glows in the education of the Waldorf School—about which I have spoken only briefly today—as its fundamental attitude, as a love of human beings everywhere. Weak and inadequate though our endeavours are, we allow ourselves to hope that an education founded on knowledge of the human being will be an education best suited to bringing up human beings. We hope that by observing human life we shall be able to work in schools in a way that will enable the schools to work on in life. And this, surely, is the fundamental question facing all the many efforts currently seeking to bring about a reform in education.

2. INTRODUCTORY ADDRESS AT THE SUMMER SCHOOL

Penmaenmawr, 18 August 1923

The most kind and friendly welcome extended to Frau Steiner and myself by Mr Dunlop[61] and Mr Collison obliges me to say a few words today prior to the beginning of the lectures tomorrow. I was immensely pleased to hear that Mr Dunlop and his helpers, both ladies and gentlemen, wanted to arrange this summer course of lectures on anthroposophy, and I hope that the content of the course will provide some degree of satisfaction for all of you gathered here, whom I also warmly greet.

Mr Dunlop's choice of subject gave me particular satisfaction. It will allow me to show you how the most ancient wisdom and the oldest spiritual life of humanity is connected with what anthroposophy has to say today about the present time and also the near future. From the point of view of our contemporary civilization and its spirit, I of course entirely appreciate the committee's plans. Nevertheless, there is one aspect that is not quite in keeping with anthroposophy itself, which is the main element of a conference such as this. In those most ancient gatherings—which we are so fond of remembering because they reveal the most venerable wisdom about human beings and the spiritual home of the human soul—an event like the present conference, in which that venerable wisdom was cultivated, meant that the participants had to take great pains to extricate themselves from their day-to-day activities dictated by the seasons of the year. Such gatherings took place at times determined by the cosmos, and there was no question of wondering what worldly affairs one might miss by gathering around the Mysteries for an event—a cosmic festival for

INTERNATIONAL
SUMMER SCHOOL

PROMOTED BY

THE ANTHROPOSOPHICAL SOCIETY

TO BE HELD AT

PENMAENMAWR, NORTH WALES

FROM AUGUST 18TH TO SEPTEMBER 1ST, 1923

PENMAENMAWR FROM THE WEST

PENMAENMAWR is on the Carnarvonshire coast. The combination of fine mountain scenery and sea is wonderfully beautiful. There is good bathing, and there are many lovely walks and excursions to be made. The summits of the mountains are crowned with the remains of ancient British fortresses and Druid circles. There are golf-links and a tennis club.

The School will be invited to study the Evolution of Humanity, past, present, and future, in the light of Anthroposophy cultivating the science of the spirit—whose timing was determined by the cosmos.

We should not be able to function in this manner, following the timing of the cosmos, since those of us who come together, for example, in summer schools do so because we have other things to occupy us in the winter. And so, since anthroposophy will only begin to influence civilization in the future, we have to gather during our summer holidays when we have nothing much else to do. We make trips and attend festivals in the summer and have to devote our holidays to the cultivation of anthroposophy.

Mr Dunlop has already mentioned all the things that can happen on a journey, such as losing one of our suitcases, but as we do not carry anthroposophy in a suitcase we should have managed to bring it here quite safely despite any such misfortune. Anthroposophy, after all, is what leads us above and beyond events that happen in space and time. As we discuss the subject chosen by the committee for this conference, anthroposophy will begin by leading us back to the most ancient times of human evolution, in which knowledge was the foundation for everything contained in civilization, in culture.

Dead ideas were not what human beings saw on the path of wisdom. They saw the living spirit itself, which was then able to flow into their artistic work and into their religious experiences. Through artistic creativity and religious experience the spirit led human beings up to realms where they could see those beings who otherwise speak perhaps enigmatically—though their message is clear—in the form of ethical, moral ideals.

During the course of human evolution, science, art, religion, and moral-social life, which had originally been wonderfully intermingled, became separated. The single tree of overall human evolution put forth four branches: science, art, religion, morality. This was necessary for human evolution because only in this way could each of these branches of civilization attain the strength it needed and indeed the strength that humanity needed.

Today we have reached an important point in human evolution in which human beings are no longer capable of bringing together all those one-sided elements that have evolved as a result of the original totality developing into several branches. Human beings can no longer unite these with what their whole being needs—out of soul, out of spirit, out of all unconscious and also subconscious inner powers— for the fulfilment of their overall humanity. So we have indeed reached an important moment in human evolution.

Science, art, religion, morality or social life are like brothers who have one mother. Having journeyed through the world alone for a while, they now yearn to return to the home where their mutual mother can be seen. But today we can no longer approach the spirit light of humanity along the paths used by human beings in ancient times. Humanity is in the midst of a living evolutionary process. Today's human beings differ from those who in the ancient Indian, Egyptian, Chaldean, Grecian Mysteries strove to find what had once been the Mother of all the knowledge and skills of humanity both in the spiritual and in the material world. We must find new paths today because we have become a new humanity.

These new paths to the spirit, ones that are fitting for the present time and can lead into the future, are something about which anthroposophy wishes to speak. Perhaps it will find the best way of discussing these things for the present and the near future if we succeed at least in outlining the subject chosen by your esteemed committee for this summer course of lectures.

It will be particularly satisfying to put on a number of performances of an art which is still, of course, only in its infancy; but perhaps for the very reason that it is still struggling for its own existence it will be the best way of showing how artistic work can be and is going to be created once again out of the spirit.

Naturally, in the short time at our disposal, we shall only be able to show you a small portion of all that we should have liked to bring to you. Nevertheless, when one's heart is full of a sense of urgency in letting anthroposophy stream into the world today, then this selfsame heart can also be filled with the warmest gratitude towards those who have made it possible for anything at all to be presented that anthroposophy wants to strive for in the service of furthering human civilization.

Knowing about all these feelings, you will believe how sincerely and warmly I want to thank Mr Dunlop, Mrs Merry[62] and all the members of the committee who have helped make this conference possible, especially as I understand only too well what great efforts must have gone into making the arrangements.

As little as you are likely to see the pains that will be taken in the coming days—I only want to mention these in passing—which will be going on behind the scenes to mount a eurythmy performance, so does one also frequently tend to forget all the worries far and near that a committee like yours has to cope with. Someone, though, who has participated in innumerable committees and sees, on arrival, the pale faces of the committee members, knows only too well what has gone before—what worries and cares pass through the souls of such committee members just before and also during an event like this one. Someone who can judge such things from his own experience and is thus able to make a professional assessment of the degree of pallor in the committee members' faces can express his gratitude with the utmost warmth. And this I now do, both on behalf of Frau Steiner, who has been accorded such a warm welcome, and also for myself.

I only hope that our contributions to the events of the coming days will make them as satisfactory for you as we are able and that we shall succeed in fulfilling at least a part of the expectations you have brought with you to this conference. For we also know that we do not lose our hopes if we lose our suitcases; however heavy they might be, we bring them with us, and it is then extraordinarily difficult to fulfil such hopes.

Anthroposophy itself, however, is to penetrate so deeply into the souls of present-day humanity, because of the needs in the soul of all those who bear a sense of their full humanity within themselves that even if lack of strength means that their contribution is relatively weak it can nevertheless fulfil a purpose. We need such a purpose. Wherever we look we see that the magnificent external material culture which humanity has founded over the past three to four centuries is no longer enough. This culture is like a physical body which has spread out over a great part of the earth in all its material perfection but which, like everything that is to live, is crying out for soul and spirit. In the end it will be anthroposophy which bestows soul and spirit on the physical body that has come into being in such a magnificent manner in the external, material civilization of recent times. Inspired as it is by spirit in everything it does, I hope that this spirit of anthroposophy will also reign during the days of our Summer School. Out of this spirit I would like to greet you all most cordially on Frau Steiner's and on my own behalf.

3. ADDRESS ON THE FUTURE OF THE ANTHROPOSOPHICAL SOCIETY IN GREAT BRITAIN

Penmaenmawr, 19 August 1923

The first lecture in the series took place on the morning of the next day. The meeting was chaired by Miss McMillan,[63] a highly esteemed educationist and social reformer about whose work Rudolf Steiner spoke in Dornach when he gave his report on this conference. In the afternoon there was a discussion about anthroposophical work in England during which Rudolf Steiner was also asked to speak. His words remain relevant today.

Once a number of views have been voiced in trying to reach a general clarification, it would be a good thing if I could have the opportunity to speak once more about today's discussion theme some time during the coming days or at the end of the discussion evenings. For today I should just like to make a few preliminary remarks.

There are most certainly a number of difficulties connected with the growth of the anthroposophical movement, indeed of anthroposophy altogether. However, these difficulties can be overcome if as large a number of individuals as possible can be found who can take to heart, in the sternest sense, the conditions that the anthroposophical movement needs. The anthroposophical movement cannot grow in the way other movements do by means of external organizational measures or through having an organized form. Modern individuals who are interested simply in spiritual, cultural life as such, and who hear some general things about the anthroposophical movement, might ask themselves whether they should participate in this anthroposophical movement. Such people might initially be rather put out when they gain the impression that the anthroposophical movement contained certain dogmas which would have to be acknowledged and when it seems as though the movement were expecting them to sign on the dotted line with regard to some thesis or other. One frequently hears statements like the following from the very midst of the Anthroposophical Society: 'Well now, he—or she—cannot be regarded as a proper anthroposophist because he—or she—has said something or other about this or that!' This makes it look as though the anthroposophical movement has something to do with a belief or even a confession. This is more damaging than anything else for a purely spiritual movement such as the anthroposophical movement is striving to be.

Of course such a movement needs to have some kind of organization; but in addition to having some kind of organization it must be as broadminded as it is possible to be. This broadmindedness, though, must live in the sensitivity, the tactfulness, of those who already feel themselves to be carriers of the anthroposophical movement, rather than in any fundamental principles. That is why I have always found it rather worrying that the anthroposophical movement has continued to uphold the three so-called principles that were carried on from the Theosophical Society (at the time of course with some justification, since the theosophical movement did exist). Now, though, they do rather support the prejudice that the anthroposophical movement has something sectarian about it. The fact that this opinion has been formed in the world at all, but worse—please forgive me for speaking openly about this—the fact that in many instances something actually emanates from the Anthroposophical Society itself that casts a sectarian light on the movement, this is what makes it so very difficult for outsiders to get close to the anthroposophical movement. To show that this is so, all we need do is compare it with the anthroposophical movement as it really is.

The day before yesterday I said over in Ilkley that if it were up to me I would like to have a different name for the movement every week. If this could be arranged easily from an organizational point of view this would be my favourite solution. The name is the very thing that initially puts people off: Anthroposophy . . . what is that? The name gets put down to those principles—one, two, three—and then all kinds of things are professed except the really important ones that involve what actually flows through the anthroposophical movement.

Perhaps this is not so obvious here in England, but over on the Continent you would soon discover how strong those prejudices still are in consequence of anthroposophy being seen as something sectarian, a sect even. On the Continent an immense number of articles and essays have been written about anthroposophy. You could say that every time you go into a bookshop and ask to be shown the latest writings there is sure to be another one on anthroposophy among them. When you read all these articles that speak out against anthroposophy—and even some that intend to show a positive attitude towards it—you really have to ask yourself what on earth has become of anthroposophy in all these various writings. Leaving aside the abominably hostile articles that have of course appeared in far greater numbers, I have to confess that even when I read those that have the appearance of wanting to present objective opinions about anthroposophy—and when I then ask myself what image of anthroposophy is presented, what image some theologian or philosopher, or all kinds of lay people of every hue have formed for themselves, and when I then consider this image in my mind's eye—I have to admit to myself that I would most certainly not wish to become an anthroposophist. People take these things at face value; they form opinions on the basis of what they have read and what the hostile camp has said, as well as all kinds of short reports of lectures. But the opinions they form are as inaccurate as it is possible to be.

What needs to happen is that the true content of anthroposophy must be enabled to find its way into the world to replace all those opinions which are the main obstacle hindering the spread of the anthroposophical movement. This is what really matters. The content of anthroposophy should really be brought before the world in a way which helps people realize that it is not something sectarian, not something which can be encompassed in a name. Those brief expositions that discuss the nature of anthroposophy over four or five pages must be countered with facts that show how anthroposophy is gradually spreading out into all kinds of areas.

Let us take the area we have been discussing in Ilkley over the past fortnight: education. The way we handle this is to elaborate our teaching and educational methods in the best way possible on the basis of the anthroposophical movement. The Waldorf School in Stuttgart where these teaching and educational methods are applied is not a sectarian school, not a school of dogmas, not what the world would have people believe to be a school for anthroposophists. We do not propagate anthroposophical dogmas in the school. What we do is seek to develop our educational methods in such a way that they are suitable for humanity in general, and in doing this we point quite specifically to anthroposophy.

There are many movements in the world today; in fact every individual, almost, represents his or her own movement, and we cannot claim that these movements are not perfectly reasonable. After all, one of the main characteristics of human beings today is that they are reasonable ... We have achieved a situation in which reasonableness is a general characteristic of human beings. So I can easily imagine 5, 10 or 15 clever people getting together to work out a programme of 12 or 30 points—all of which will be eminently reasonable—about the best possible kind of education ... I can well imagine that there would be nothing at all to say against such a programme. But in practice, in a real school, such a programme would be no help at all, for in practice what you need is an understanding of how a child develops year by year and how one can go out to meet each child's individuality. And even this would not suffice. Some of those exceedingly reasonable programmes for educational reform might also contain, for example, descriptions of what the teachers must be like. I can imagine wonderful, marvellous descriptions of what the teachers are expected to be like in those schools ... but if such teachers do not exist, if there is no prospect of finding teachers who would match up to the expectations of those reasonable programmes, then you have to accept whatever teachers there are and do your relative best with them. That is what you have to do in practice; you have to be practical in your choice of individuals and where you place them. So the moment anthroposophy wants to play a part in real life what it does is turn to what is generally human and avoid any kind of dogma; it wants to take hold of real life and bring it to awareness. You could say that the other reform movements want to do this too. But look at them and ask yourselves whether they really want this, or whether people who imagine themselves to be most eminently practical are not in fact the most theoretical of all because they make everything dependent on theory, on programmes. Paradoxical though this may sound, commerce and industry, all the so-called practical professions, are full of the greatest theoreticians. No one today who stands in the midst of practical life sees what is really practical but only what he imagines to be practical.

No wonder, then, that the carefully constructed systems of economic life, being wholly theoretical, are gradually collapsing. What we need now is a way of working directed towards real life and an ability to look at the real potential of the human being. It is this difference between the anthroposophical movement and other movements that one must strive to demonstrate to the world: its all-embracing nature, its lack of bias or prejudice, its freedom from dogma, and that it is purely and simply an experimental method endeavouring to work with all that belongs to human beings in general and with the overall phenomena of the world.

We can therefore ask: 'Where is there any dogmatism in the artistic field, in the Dornach building so tragically destroyed, in eurythmy performances?' In the Dornach building the forms that came into being were the best and clearest ones that could be derived from the wood itself. There you had an architectural style that was allowed to emerge from the actual life of human beings today. Eurythmy, in its turn, does not set out to teach people how to realize anthroposophical dogmas; what it shows is how to make the best movements arising directly out of the human organism so that these movements can become true speech, artistically formed. Thus in all kinds of areas anthroposophy strives for practical understanding and practical life that is deepened by the spirit. This is how anthroposophy differs from other movements in the world today.

That is why it would be so good if anthroposophy could have a new name every week, so that people would have no chance to get accustomed to all the things that arise when something is given a name. Consider the dreadful mischief that has arisen out of this name-giving in recent times. I do not know how this has been in England, but for example in the field of painting on the Continent we have been experiencing all kinds of 'schools' over the past decades. We have had the landscape painters, the Impressionists, the Expressionists, the Futurists, the Cubists and so on, and because such names have given things a context of some sort, people have grown accustomed to saying all kinds of things without mentioning anything at all about painting when painting was what was being done. When you are painting it is not a matter of being a Cubist or an Impressionist or any other kind of 'ist'. What matters, of course, is whether you can paint! The same applies in life. You have to approach life and deal with it in an appropriate way. That is why I would like to give anthroposophy a different name every week, because then instead of growing accustomed to a name people would get down properly to whatever matter was in hand. That would be the very best for anthroposophy.

Of course this is rather an extreme or radical way of putting it, but you know what I mean. It is really most important to be tactful about letting the world see what is all-embracing about anthroposophy, and not to involve people in something that might make them believe they have to accept some dogma or other when they sign their application for membership. We really must aim to let a broadness of outlook gain ground in the way we represent the anthroposophical movement. If we succeed in this, we shall find it easier to deal with the other questions than we think will be the case.

Recently the things that have taken place in the anthroposophical movement in all countries have made it obvious that the best thing is for anthroposophists in separate countries to form national societies—so here this would mean founding a British society. Then all the separate societies would unite in a general society which should have its seat in Dornach. One very difficult aspect of making an international society of this kind function satisfactorily is communication. I believe means of communication are coming into being as far as the subject matter goes. It is obvious that your journal *Anthroposophy*, founded by Baroness Rosenkrantz, has become a very good link between Dornach and here.[64] What we would need, though, would be an international means of communication. Whether this were a single journal or whether the journals of the national societies would serve the purpose—but the external form really would not matter much—the important thing would be to have the possibility of receiving from time to time something that would bring news of the anthroposophical movement all over the world.

The subject matter itself must of course flow through the anthroposophical society. But individual anthroposophists ought to be put in the picture about what is going on in the world in different places as regards anthroposophy. I have been asked about this more than about anything else in the different countries I have visited. Over and over again people have said that the Anthroposophical Society lacks any means of knowing what is going on in other regions, that there is no communication.

But such a thing cannot come about through organization, and indeed organization is something that wastes huge amounts of strength. When something gets established, committees are formed, and sub-committees; every committee then has to have a secretary, and of course it would be rather convenient to have an office as well, or even a whole palace from which communications are sent out in all directions, where addresses are stored and countless letters written which subsequently get thrown into waste-paper baskets or in some other way avoid being read, where infinite human effort is exerted daily and, above all, where a dreadful amount of money gets lost—this being something that also has to be considered in the Anthroposophical Society. Of course organization has to be appreciated (although if you are German you do not care too much for organization; but I say this in parenthesis). Respect should be paid where respect is due, but if something is to be established the most important requirement is that as many people as possible develop a lively interest in it; the rest will then follow on from that. It would be very good if there were a centre in Dornach where news from every country could be gathered. There would need to be individuals in every country who can write in various different languages. In Dornach arrangements would be made for things to be read and disseminated.

What must be developed in the world is interest in the anthroposophical movement. It is of course in the nature of the anthroposophical movement that this is more difficult than with other movements, for these others have indications as to what the aims are. The anthroposophical movement, on the other hand, although it is of general interest to all human beings, also has an aspect that goes beyond the individual. Of course it is only fair that individual hearts and souls should receive something; that goes without saying. But on the other hand the anthroposophical movement also has tasks to accomplish for civilization as such. That is why there must be interest in the movement as such; everything else will then follow on from that.

Time has gone on, so I would now like to bring these considerations to a conclusion, but whenever I have the opportunity over the next few days I shall go into more concrete detail on this matter.

4. QUESTIONS AND ANSWERS

Penmaenmawr, 20 August 1923[65]

The following two evenings were devoted to a discussion on the spiritual knowledge so far absorbed by the participants. Rudolf Steiner was asked to clarify some of the content that had not been entirely understood, for example the nature of Imagination, Inspiration and Intuition. He was only too willing to do so.

As regards difficulties involving the use of such a word as 'imagination', I should like to say the following.

When we choose a word to express an important content, we should really always go back to its original meaning, and not just ask what is its meaning in modern everyday speech—for, as a matter of fact, all modern languages have made words shallow. I already had to draw your attention to something this morning, and there was an inner justification for doing so. The word 'intuition' is also used in an everyday sense, but rightly so, because for the moral sphere the highest knowledge about the spiritual life must come down right into the simplest, most primitive human heart and soul. We cannot say exactly the same for the word 'imagination', and one should therefore first gain a clear idea as to all the aspects it contains. The moment you remove the prefix and suffix and look at what is left in the middle you arrive immediately at 'magic'. 'Magic' is contained in the word 'imagination'; it is a making inward of the magical. Going back to such an original meaning of the word, you find that its customary usage in the ordinary speech of today is quite adequate.[66]

I should like to know what one is actually to do in anthroposophy or indeed in any spiritual movement if one does not insist that all words are led back to their deeper meaning. Anthroposophy, you see, must be taken so seriously that one must really ask oneself whether it can be expressed at all in today's ordinary language. Can one say anything important about anthroposophy in any everyday language? Well, all familiar languages originally contained something deeper and so one can go back to those deepened meanings.

If one speaks of imagination when one means fancy, fantasy, one is simply using the word for what today amounts to people's sole understanding of inner experience. Most people think that inner experiences are fantasies, so they call fantasies 'imagination'. From their point of view they are quite right, but if one is not willing to go back to original meanings such as that contained in 'imagination', then it will be very difficult to express anthroposophy in language at all.

Many things, you see, are contained in the word 'magic'. First of all it contains something that I should like to describe as follows. Scientific curiosity today makes us look through the microscope, and when we do so we discover what is small in the world. Today's materialistic science is always curious about these small things, whether it is the longed-for atom, which is even being demonstrated experimentally now, or some germinating seed. But the moment we go to the actual causes of things, where the creative forces and powers are— there we arrive not at what is small but at what is great. To draw on what is great, to draw on what is powerful and imposing, on what embraces the creative powers that surpass the tiny human being, and to compress these into the human soul, that means to compress what is magical so that in its compressed state it can be received and experienced by the human soul.

With all the other words we use we should do what we have just done with 'imagination'. Today most people take 'inspiration' to mean a sudden bright idea—and why not? They have the right to use words at their own personal level. However, when it is given this meaning, the word 'inspiration' is not much use for interpreting higher knowledge. Let us then regard the words current in our present civilization as one used to regard human beings in general.

To go back to something quite recent, in the eighteenth century people here in England and everywhere on the Continent were very much occupied with what they called Martinism, the philosophy derived from Saint-Martin's *Des Erreurs et de la Vérité*, a book published in Edinburgh in 1773 and translated into every European language.[67] This book that dealt, in the manner of that time, with spiritual things, was a final straggler of the kind of spiritual reflection that was still possible in the eighteenth and early nineteenth century, but is no longer possible today.

The main idea of this book *Des Erreurs et de la Vérité* is that man in his totality as an earthly being has fallen from his original high estate. The Fall is still fully imputed to man. In the view of Saint-Martin man was once a mighty being girt with what he called the holy armour that served him magically, protecting him against all the powers and beings of the world, many of which were inimical to him. The human being lived at a place described by Saint-Martin as the Place of the Seven Holy Trees which in religious legends or earlier still, in the Bible, was described as 'Paradise'. He was endowed with the fiery lance through which he exercised his power, and so on, and so on. The book states that through his own pre-earthly guilt the human being lost all that was originally allotted to him. A frightful sin is ascribed to him in his pre-earthly state; even to name this sin in society today is somewhat shocking. So here we have the human being described as having fallen from his original high estate. Actually the whole of Saint-Martin's philosophy sets out to show what the human being could be if he had not fallen from his original high estate.

Well, such attitudes can no longer be brought to life today. They are the final stragglers of the way of looking at things that I described this morning as an ancient mode of perception. In modern initiation science we must start from the scientific mode of perception—not from science, but from the scientific mode of perception—for this alone will be able to satisfy people in the near future. As regards the special spheres, if we really wish to imbue the anthroposopical subject-matter—or the purport of any spiritual endeavour—with the necessary mood, the necessary exaltation of soul, with the solemn enthusiasm with which we should imbue it if we are to understand it, we must not take words from the customary familiar language, nor look on them as if all words had not undergone a fall on their way down to our civilization. Words today are not what they once were; they have become sinful beings. They have fallen into matter and no longer denote what they once denoted in the stage of humanity's evolution when they were used in the Mysteries. In a sense we must make an upward movement in our feeling for words. We must take pains not to remain at the level of ordinary everyday language, otherwise the colouring and timbre these words have in their familiar use will cling to them. Today it is easiest for the Hebrew language to rise up from words affected by the Fall to a kind of sacred meaning. For those languages that have been more employed in modern life with its completely unsacred interests it is naturally more difficult to look up to the sinlessness of words—if I may use this expression, which sounds more drastic than I mean it to—but in a certain respect we must do this. We must realize that the word 'inspiration' has fallen so far into sinfulness that any joke can be described as an inspiration. And why not? As a matter of fact writers and cartoonists in humorous journals need a good deal of inspiration in today's sense of the word—but it is profaned inspiration. If we go back, however, to the original meaning of the word, we are led into very profound regions of human endeavour.

Let me remind you of how a once marvellous and wonderful mode of knowledge has been preserved, now at a decadent stage, in India. It was formerly much more significant than it is today, and it did not, as is essential today, proceed from thinking but from a specific regulation, or 'disregulation' of the breathing process. The original yoga

method was concerned with raising the otherwise unconscious breathing process into consciousness. This can be
done by altering the rhythm of inhaling, holding the breath
and exhaling that comes about naturally when we pay no
attention to our breathing. If one gives the breathing rhythm a
different numerical ratio from the normal one, then inhalation
is in a different proportion to holding the breath and exha-
lation. What can be called the yoga method rested essentially
on a different manipulation of the breath which brought the
whole breathing process to consciousness. By altering the
breathing rhythm the person breathed consciously and the
currents of the breath entered consciously into the blood
circulation. The entire human being was interwoven and
pulsed through by an altered breathing rhythm. In seeing and
hearing we receive sense perceptions through the visual rays
and the auditory rays, in seeing we receive knowledge about
the colours of what surrounds us and in hearing we receive
knowledge about the sounds that emanate from what is all
around us. In the same way one who made the breathing
rhythm into an advanced perception of measure felt and
perceived in the breathing process how soul and spirit imbued
him. The moment the breathing process becomes completely
conscious in someone with a disposition of soul such as
existed in Southern Asia 8000 or 7000 years before Christ, at
that moment the altered rhythm, with its pulsing and undu-
lation, sends more than merely physical air into the body. Just
as we have soul and spirit in our physical body, so one sends
soul and spirit into oneself in this streaming breath and one
experiences these in so far as they are contained in the
streaming breath.

In the material sense one can of course say that inhalation is
'inspiration' (that is its literal meaning). If we spiritualize
inspiration we do what was done in ancient India. Then with
this super-spiritualized inspiration, with breathing filled with
soul and spirit, we shall experience through perception as a
thinking being. We are then working with what the word

'inspiration' has always meant, not only in India but in Europe too. So once again, in using the word 'inspiration' we must ascend to its sinless state.

For this reason, and in spite of proposals made from every side, I have always resisted writing so-called 'popular' books on anthroposophy. That would of course be a very easy thing to do, but even beginners should not be given altogether popular books on anthroposophy. Anthroposophical books should be something they have to break their teeth on (spiritually speaking), something they have to take an immense amount of trouble over because it is not at all easy. There is also another aspect in taking great pains, in struggling to overcome what has to be overcome if one wants to understand something that is difficult to grasp. If we were to receive anthroposophy in a popular way, in words of one syllable, we would have an entirely different taste, a different feeling in respect of the meaning of the words; we would drag the meanings down into their sinful state. But if we have to break our teeth over a difficult book for beginners, we acquire a taste for delving into the meaning of the words.

Think of a case in history. Read how wonderfully Jakob Boehme contemplates words deeply before he uses them. He first distils whole worlds, so to speak, out of the words before he uses them. So with Imagination, Inspiration or Intuition, or other words one uses, one forms one's attitude at a more profound level than is usually assumed. So I do not think we should try to substitute other words for ones that we use quite legitimately, such as Imagination or Inspiration. Instead, so long as we are dealing with anthroposophy, in communicating with one another about anthroposophy I think we should make efforts to raise these words to their sinless state—though there is no harm in descending to their sinful state again when we return to ordinary life. Such a mood as this in regard to a word could be extraordinarily beneficial for a deeper grasp of anthroposophy. What I mean is that someone who is conscious of what is encompassed in the word Imagination would even ultimately—if he were a fanatic—call for a law which would forbid the word 'imagination' to be used to denote 'a play of fancy', in order to retain it for the sphere where it is rightly employed.

When asked: 'Who is it who perceives? What is it in the human being that perceives?' Rudolf Steiner continued as follows:

Unfortunately these questions are more easily asked than answered. A great many things have to be mentioned in order to reply to such a far-reaching, all-embracing question. With such a question having been asked we shall have to gain a clearer idea of what this morning's lecture was about.

What we are talking about is how the human soul, which in its present incarnation exists in a human being, in a physical body between birth or conception and death, ascends gradually to perception—firstly of the etheric world of formative forces in Imagination, and secondly through the silence I described, through emptied consciousness in Inspiration. Then, in Intuition, which is achieved through a special development of the capacity for love, one arrives (I shall be describing this in my next lecture[68]) at the ability to see one's previous life, or several previous lives. As I described this morning, these lives are as objective to the human being as any external object or process in nature, or another human being whom one encounters. In ordinary social life I am related to another human being whom I meet through the fact of belonging to the human race as such, but this other human being is nevertheless quite objective to me. If I want to perceive my former incarnations truly, I must confront them as objectively as I confront another human being. Then, through a soul-spirit element that is not yet fully realized in my present earthly body, I get to know my true 'I', my ego, which passes through one earthly life after another.

The questioner seems to mean: Who is it, or what is it in the human being, that recognizes this true 'I' that passes through one life after another? Which member of the human being has this recognition? This question is not really a question; it has no properly concrete content. The question asks after the subject who does the recognizing. The subject who does the recognizing is the 'I', the ego, which is incorporated in the present incarnation. This 'I' or ego raises itself to a level where it perceives. The true ego can only be reached if one encompasses one's earthly life between birth and death with one's consciousness. In doing this one is living with one's ego on a specific level; one is living with this ego, but one does not recognize the true ego that passes through many births and deaths. However, by means of the methods I have described, this higher ego that one bears with one through life becomes capable, when it achieves independence, of recognizing the true ego.

You also have to take into account that as you follow this path of recognition or knowledge you are transforming the subject. First we have to do with the ego that lives between birth and death; this ego at first does not recognize the true ego. Then this ego ascends and becomes the one who recognizes the true ego, which passes through one earthly life after another. In this way it identifies itself with the true ego. Thus, by undergoing a metamorphosis this higher ego is raised up to the true ego. Only when it has been lifted up into the true ego can it recognize the true ego.

Thus we cannot ask: 'Who perceives, or what in the human being is it that perceives?' What in ordinary life perceives within the human being, this changes into something else, undergoes a metamorphosis through ascending from Imagination through Inspiration to Intuition. Only then does it become an actual ego that can be perceived. Yet the transformation is there in order that the true ego can be reached.

So in this way one can perhaps reach the true ego.

5. QUESTIONS AND ANSWERS

Penmaenmawr, 21 August 1923

Among the written questions on the next evening Rudolf Steiner
replied to one about the nature of sleep:

Perhaps it would be a good thing to begin by saying a few
words on this question. The questioner begins by stating his
surprise about how little concern is shown in the medical
profession for the processes of sleep. Actually this is not very
surprising since science today is for the most part not concerned with anything spiritual but only with things that are
not spiritual. The state of sleep and everything connected with
it, however, cannot be studied unless a path is found that
leads from the physical to the spiritual world. So it is quite
understandable that, at best, members of the medical profession discuss the borderline between waking and sleeping,
but not what goes over from the sleep state to the waking state
and vice versa. In my lecture tomorrow I shall be speaking
about these images, and it is better to deal with such matters
within a context.[69]

The next thing the questioner mentions is that there are
human beings who remember nothing during the state of
sleep. I would like to begin by asking: 'How does one know
whether what someone tells about his sleep when he wakes up
is all he could say? How does one know whether what he tells
is correct?' If such things are to be proved externally, then one
must investigate the degree of depth his sleep attained. It is
perfectly possible for elements of waking to play a part in
sleep. But such things are not easy to assess; they must be
accurately investigated so that one does not begin with the
general assumption that some people have all kinds of
experiences in their sleep. Everything must be carefully

investigated. I shall be saying a number of things during my lectures about what human beings experience in sleep. You will then see that what this questioner presumably means barely touches on what human beings really experience during the night between falling asleep and waking up. So as far as these questions go it will perhaps be quite good to wait for the coming lectures, as a number of things will then become clearer.

I should now like to spend a moment or two on a question from Mr K. Physical substances have certain spiritual forces in them. In ordinary sleep the ego and astral body separate from the etheric and physical body which remain lying in bed. I have pointed out that a human being sometimes thinks more cleverly when his soul life is not present than when it is.

Some physical substances[70] have the peculiarity of loosening the ego and astral body without putting the individual to sleep. In some instances ordinary alcohol has this effect. If there is a somewhat irregular connection between the etheric body and the organs of speech or thought (this is always so in the physical body as regards the organ of thought) then it is possible for a person to speak or write while his ego and astral body are loosened and set free. He then produces something that goes on outside the body and that can be far more significant than what he produces when he is in it. As we know, the astral body has cosmic connections. Of course one must not push these things to the point where they become practical measures. One must naturally not assert that anyone can be a good poet by becoming an opium addict, yet on the other hand these things are an absolute reality. This brings us to some really rather dangerous chapters of human life, and with regard to very many phenomena in the world it is quite essential to know how these things are connected. The achievements of some individuals cannot be understood at all if one is ignorant of the influences—purely external and material ones—that have affected them. It is possible, for instance in the case of Nietzsche and of Coleridge too—at least in one of his works—to interpret every turn of expression as the oscillation of the ether body going on independently. In fact we must admit that this ether body of ours is a very, very clever being, although it is prevented from expressing its cleverness all the time through the faculties in our astral body and ego when we are awake. One simply cannot imagine the total amount of cleverness present when a number of people have gathered together somewhere. Only the egos and the astral bodies prevent all this cleverness from coming to the surface. I have always said in my lectures that the ego is really the baby in the human being, the least developed of all.

The next question referred to the perception of smell.[71]

It has to be said in regard to the different sense perceptions we are accustomed to having in the physical world that these cannot be sought directly in the spiritual world in the way they exist here. It is for this reason that I have tried to speak very precisely when I have spoken about colours. I have said that you experience the same when perceiving a particular colour as when you have an experience in the spiritual world. I said that perceiving red in the physical world gives you a particular inner experience, a sensation of something approaching that is going to attack you, whereas with blue, for example, you feel that you must surrender with humility to what reveals itself in the blue. If we can be quite clear about these experiences—the attacking quality of red, the devoutness created by blue or blue-violet—then, if you have the same experience in the spiritual world as you have with red or blue in the physical world, you can speak of having the corresponding red or blue in the spiritual world. The moment you pass over to Imaginative Cognition you become one with the object and the whole experience is different from an experience in the physical world. With colour perceptions in the spiritual world, in particular, you really have the feeling of being within the colour and the whole experience has a different character.

Nevertheless, it is entirely justifiable to speak of colour perceptions in the spiritual world; you can really experience a red, a blue, a green, etc., when spiritual beings or entities appear. It is justifiable by reason of the fact that when colours appear in the physical world they are certainly not what physicists take them to be. Wherever they appear, colours are always projections, shadows out of the spiritual, astral world. When red is seen somewhere, this is the shadow, the physical shadow of a process in the spiritual, astral world which, in a direct experience, gives the impression of an attack on your own self.

So we can now say the following: If thinking becomes as inwardly alive as I described it a few days ago, then in a spiritual way it is like a sensation of touch. Perceiving in the etheric world begins with a kind of spiritual touching, and you go on from there. You distinguish between these touch perceptions and get to a stage where you can speak about colours and even musical notes and so on.

The questioner was asking about the perception of smells, and strange as it may seem, these perceptions of smells here in the physical world are those perceptions that are relatively the most influenced by the spirit. A perception of smell in the immediate physical world is actually always produced by a spiritual-astral element getting as close as possible to the physical. It is therefore true to say that fragrances are physical manifestations of the spirit. We can find correspondences in the spiritual world for all the other sense perceptions—spiritual perceptions of touch, of sight, of hearing and so on—but it is very difficult to speak of a spiritual perception of a smell because the perception of smell exists entirely in the physical world. The whole of it has arrived in the physical world. Speaking figuratively, when spirit comes down closest to the physical world, that is where the perception of smell arises.

For a perception of taste the spirit comes down somewhat less deeply, so that we can more readily talk of a spiritual correlation for a perception of taste than for a perception of smell. It would be possible to link this to what I began to say yesterday about language, but I shall only bring forward one aspect just now. There is a truly spiritual element in every language, and it is not merely a manner of speaking to talk about the genius of a language. This genius really exists. There is more in language than we as individuals can understand, for the most part. The way a language combines its sounds, the way it combines its letters, words and syllables, this has a spirituality all its own, a soul quality that belongs to it alone, and we grow up into this spirituality, this soul quality. Thus languages have expressions and terms that point towards deeper inner connections. So when we talk about aesthetic considerations it is not by chance that we speak of good or bad taste. This is an example of an ordinary perception of taste being transposed over into the soul realm. We cannot speak in the same way of a perception of smell being transposed into the soul world, however. A perception of smell is more or less complete in the physical world.

At best we might mention the distinguished German poet, Christian Morgenstern, who wrote both serious and humorous verses, and died in 1914 having been a member of the Anthroposophical Society for some time. He wrote about smell in a humorous and imaginative way that drew it up into the spiritual world. There is a humorous poem of his about an organ that expresses itself not in notes and harmonies but in smells, with all kinds of different fragrances proceeding from the various holes in the most varied ways. When you strike the keys, smells emerge from the holes, joining together to form harmonies and melodies. This is Christian Morgenstern's famous 'smell organ' about which the poem tells so amusingly.

This is simply a bit of fun, but actually we have to say that smell is something that is confined to the physical world. Smell is where the spirit has descended the lowest and surrenders to the physical world; it cannot be raised up in the way taste, but especially the other, higher, senses can. It is therefore quite right and entirely accords with reality to make evil spirits, who are so anxious to come into the physical world and do all sorts of things to people, give off a stink. You can find references everywhere in literature as to how obtrusive evil spirits are when it comes to the sense of smell. In this sense it is true to say that smell is confined to the physical world, although some slight mention can be made of it in the higher worlds too, though not very high. Smell only exists as a result of matter rising into the spirit through being pulverized into the tiniest possible particles. Another way of putting this would be to say that matter is at its most spiritual in fragrance. That is why in earlier times, when this was sensed more clearly, fragrance was felt to be a spiritual manifestation. This is all I can say on this in a few words just now.

Rudolf Steiner then spoke to a question asked by Miss O. about being wiser when asleep.[72]

I should prefer not to speak about the therapeutic method mentioned earlier, as that would lead to a subject which I do not care to discuss. It is not my habit to pronounce judgement on contemporaries in one field or another. So leaving aside this particular therapeutic method, I should like to indicate in a few words some other points of interest raised by the question.

The human etheric body is the bearer of thoughts. It is the bearer of our immediately present thoughts and also the agent that causes thoughts to be sent into memory and recalled from memory. It is essential for earthly human beings, however, that this etheric body should to some degree be enclosed in our physical body because as human beings on earth we need something that can provide resistance for what goes on in the etheric body. Just as we cannot walk on air, but need the ground to push against—the ground itself does nothing, but it is what we push against—so is it also for what takes place in our etheric body. The play of all our thoughts, the whole process of thinking, takes place in our etheric body. But it would not come alive while we are in a state of wakefulness if there were no resistance, if every movement of our living thinking did not come up against our physical body, which does nothing except provide the resistance. It is through this that our thoughts in external life come to our consciousness while we are awake.

When we fall asleep our physical and our etheric body remain in our bed while the play of thoughts continues. With our ego and astral body isolated from our physical and etheric body our etheric body still continues to think. It relies on rhythm and repetition with regard to the thinking and all the processes of revision going on within it, and is best able to retain content that is presented to it in a rhythmical way using repetition. That is why it is quite wrong to take oriental writings with many repetitions and give their content once only, as is our way here in the West. Oriental authors were not concerned exclusively with the content; it was not the main thing for them in the way it is for westerners. Having thought something once, westerners, Europeans, do not want to think the same thing over again. At most, perhaps, they do say the same Lord's Prayer day after day, but in the main, as far as content goes, Europeans do not experience their activity through rhythm. Every day they thus sin against what the etheric body really wants: repetitions. In the past, in the ancient Orient where people knew such habits, they were therefore fully aware about cultivating these repetitions because they knew what effect they would have. Perhaps this sin is not committed in England, but we have many strange translations in German which render the subject matter in an incredible way. When Buddha speaks in repetitions, the German translator only translates it once. Yet this entirely misses the point, for it is not the content of Buddha's talks alone that is important. The important thing is to take in these talks of Buddha and let every repetition run its course—again and again to let each repetition run its course. However many repetitions there are, the actual number is of significance. Such secrets were understood in former times, and those who make such prose translations show that they have not the slightest understanding of the essentials of oriental civilization and spiritual life.

The etheric body is also actually the healing principle in the human being, and if we apply an understanding of this to the manufacture of medicines, it will be something we shall take into account. Nowadays the medical profession is empirical in the statements it makes. Substances are tested, and if they work in such and such a percentage of cases then they are declared to be a remedy. If the percentage is low, then they are not a remedy. But no one investigates all the factors involved.

A wish has been expressed that I should give a lecture on 'anthroposophy and medicine' during this Summer School. This will enable me to touch on a number of things in this connection. The healing process itself is laid down in our medicines in such a way as to make them specially effective in the part of the body we intend to heal. Suppose someone has a liver complaint. We would help it to heal if we were to use a medicine that could make the etheric body of the liver active in a special way. The methods of applying pressure—so much employed nowadays, and rightly so—rest on this same principle of making the etheric body active. If there is a wound on a finger, for instance, and pressure is applied above the wounded place so that the limb 'goes to sleep', this is the simplest method of making the etheric body more effective there than usual; pressure applied in this simple way disconnects the etheric from the physical, and this enables it to assert itself.

Another method, especially for a westerner who is not used to employing repetition in life, is to make things aimed at bringing about healing repeat themselves in the right way; this will help the ether body find its way into a particular rhythm. The patient is disconnected from a habit, and this can arouse healing forces. This is certainly the case in many instances, but one must remember that such things can work well for a patient in the West because he is used to living without rhythm. An oriental patient, on the other hand, someone who specifically applies rhythm in his spiritual life, will be immune to such things and will have to look for other therapies.

If we want to use something as a remedy it must be something we are not accustomed to using in other ways in our life, something we rarely or never use. Hence—in chronic cases, not acute ones—if we have a remedy that is working effectively, it is even good to take the patient off it for a while so that he or she gets out of the habit of using it. Later on such a substance will then once more be all the more effective as a remedy. All these things are interrelated.

This is the best way of seeing how the material is connected with the spiritual. In this case we have a temporary repetition that has an effect on recovery by arousing the forces of healing in the patient's etheric body.

Of course we must realize that there is a great deal of amateur dabbling going on in this field at the present time. That is precisely why I do not care to speak about various therapies that are appearing on the scene. My concern is to show that without a thorough and penetrating knowledge of human beings with their physical, etheric and astral body as well as their ego, it is not really possible to discuss them from the therapeutic aspect.

6. ADDRESS FOLLOWING BARON ROSENKRANTZ'S LECTURE

Penmaenmawr, 24 August 1923

At Penmaenmawr Rudolf Steiner gave his lectures in the mornings. In the evenings there were discussions and some members gave talks. On the evening of 24 August 1923 Steiner gave a short talk[73] following Baron Rosenkrantz's lecture on 'Artistic Activity and the Sense of Colour'.[74]

Mr Dunlop has indicated that you would like me to follow Baron Rosenkrantz's interesting talk with a few words of my own about art and its future task, and also that I should give you an idea of what the Goetheanum will look like in the future.

Let me simply give you a few indications with regard to how artistic impulses might be developed in the future, although I do not mean that just anybody can bring forward an artistic impulse, whether arbitrarily or on purpose. From what is in preparation today you can work out where art, in particular, will have to find its orientation in the near future. I mean this in the following sense.

In our day, we see, on the one hand, how the old impulses in human activity and civilization continue their influence in all spheres of science and artistic activity, as well as in the sphere of religious feeling. But we also see, on the other hand, in the case of great numbers of human beings—and greater numbers than one would generally suppose—how undefined feelings and longings for an unknown something govern their soul life. If one works in the field of anthroposophy one would like to fathom these longings and find out what they are, and I do indeed have the impression that a great part of what is making itself felt in the present time in anthroposophy is in fact capable of satisfying those undefined and more or less unconscious longings of great numbers of human beings today.

It is because intellectualism has engulfed everything over the past three of four centuries—for intellectualism has taken a deeper root in human souls than one generally supposes—that it is so difficult for human beings of today to find the bridge leading from an undefined longing to something that in earthly activity can be revealed to this longing. This becomes obvious when we look at spiritual science itself.

In my lectures here I have often had to point out that although spiritual science has to be garnered from the spiritual world through Imagination, Inspiration and Intuition, nevertheless the results of this research are perfectly accessible to ordinary common sense. Only if we cling to old prejudices are we prevented from finding sufficient strength of soul to approach the results of spiritual research with an unbiased mind.

The objections so often raised against the results of spiritual research today are the product of an indefinable fear, deeply rooted in the soul. People today are afraid of the results of spiritual research.

Everything produced by human civilization over recent centuries so strongly contradicts this spiritual science that it appears to most people to be something entirely strange and unknown. People are always afraid of the unknown but they will not admit that they are afraid, so they clothe their fear in so-called logical refutations, logical criticism.

Once you see through this you realize that the logic of those who oppose spiritual science is in fact nothing but an excuse made by their soul for the fear they have of it.

The same applies in the sphere of art. How often do we hear people asserting that spiritual science strives to rise to higher worlds by way of ideas and scientific assertions and that science tends to crush unhampered artistic creation. Those who really want to create artistically should—so these people say—

be free of any ideas or acquired knowledge; they should create out of their own imagination.

There are very many poets, painters, musicians and artists in all fields who are terrified that their imagination will dry up if they have too much to do with spiritual science. They are afraid they would no longer be able to unfold their imagination freely but would only be able to reproduce in colours or notes those things that can be found in spiritual science.

A good many battles had to be fought in connection with the former Goetheanum building because individuals whose artistic impulse was not very profound made the mistake of thinking that spiritual science leads in some way to the use of symbolism or external allegory. I have to admit that there were very many anthroposophists and theosophists who looked for art in ideas that could be painted or, for that matter, composed in music, and so on. To enter an anthroposophical or theosophical meeting room decorated with symbols and allegorical pictures empty of any meaning was enough to make one despair. I also have to say that a good many no doubt very well-meaning friends wanted to decorate the old Goetheanum, now burnt down, with all kinds of symbols. I myself opposed this resolutely every time. I knew that in the case of the Goetheanum everything must be drawn from genuine artistic form. Every line, every shape had to arise as a result of seeing it with purely inner artistic feeling.

That is why the shapes and forms of the Goetheanum were there not to be interpreted but simply to be looked upon. When friends or other visitors from outside came to the Goetheanum they always wanted to be shown round by someone who would explain to them why the columns, the capitals and architraves had those particular shapes, and why things were painted in a particular way. They wanted to be given an inner meaning for everything.

When I myself conducted friends round the building, I used to say, as an introduction: 'I very much dislike saying to friends and visitors what I shall be saying to you.' In fact I was never so filled with distaste for my own words as when I was expected to explain the forms of the Goetheanum. These forms were not there to be explained, to be comprehended in concepts; they were there to be looked upon and grasped in an artistic and aesthetic way.

Why was this possible? This can best be explained by observing the human being. We can study the human being by basing our studies on what science has produced over the last three or four centuries, in its own field, as science. However, this brings us only to a certain point, it brings us at best as far as the physical organism. But when we want to ascend to the higher members of human nature we find it is not possible to do this unless we allow our contemplation of the world to become an artistic comprehension of the human being, for the world itself is a creative artist in all its spiritual activity. Thus no one can understand the human being unless in his own vision he is able to transform the scientific aspect into art.

Modern science then comes along and says: 'Those who let themselves be drawn away from science into art are departing from the paths and observations of logic that are essential for science. They are no longer scientists.'

However long people go on making this assertion, the fact remains that if nature reaches a point where it begins to be rather less naturalistically logical and works in an artistic way instead, then only those who also become artistic will, in the last resort, be able to keep pace with nature.

It is the same in the case of genuine anthroposophy. It is not in its nature to want or be able to be merely something that is alive; a moment comes when the living, scientific ideas it expresses become directly artistic and pictorial. So even if you only begin to describe the ether body—even if you do it in the scientific way that is appropriate for today—your description will immediately become an artistic creation, something that can be artistically shaped.

Once we have thoroughly grasped this we shall always find

that anthroposophy, in fact all genuine spiritual science, is not alien to art or even hostile to it but will in future lead over directly into something truly artistic.

This was shown in practice in the old Goetheanum. Its ground plan was symmetrical about an axis drawn through its centre, but other than this left-right symmetry there was no other.

The columns in the auditorium had capitals that were not all alike. They metamorphosed progressively, beginning with the comparatively simple shapes of the first capital on the left and on the right. The second capital was somewhat more complicated, and so on. The artists working on the capitals found that in their inner sense of the lines and curves they were able to let the forms in the second capital grow directly out of those in the first, and those in the third from the second. They surrendered themselves entirely to the life of the lines, surfaces and curves.

The upshot was that when it came to the seventh column the progression came to an end of its own accord with the lines and curves making a shape that did not go outwards but reached a standstill. But then people came along and saw the seven columns. They thought this must be a profoundly mystical number resting on some ancient form still alive in superstition, and so on. Yet this is not the case at all. If your work is entirely artistic you cannot help coming to an end at the seventh column. Just as the rainbow has seven colours and the musical scale seven notes from prime to octave (the octave being the repetition of the prime), so do you arrive at seven columns.

Something else also comes to light when your work is entirely artistic in this way. By experiencing the metamorphoses, the second capital arises out of the first, the third out of the second and so on until you have seven. Then you can stand back and look at the whole sequence. You look at your own work and discover all kinds of things you had not thought out beforehand. When I compared the seventh capital with the first, for example, I discovered that in an artistic way all the concave shapes in the first were convex in the last and all the convex ones in the first were concave in the last. By making a few adjustments here and there you could have fitted the last form inside the first, the seventh form in the first, the sixth in the second, the fifth in the third, while the fourth remained on its own in the middle. This arose entirely of itself.

This gave us the assurance that we had not integrated any arbitrary human ideas into the forms. We had worked together with the life that was in the forms themselves; we had united ourselves with the creative cosmic world itself. So we can also embrace this principle with regard to metamorphosis in plant shapes, comprehending what works and weaves in nature at a higher level. We had not created any allegorical expressions of human ideas; we had immersed ourselves in nature's creativity and begun to create as nature creates.

This is what genuine artistic creativity is. In future all arts will refer back to this to some extent. This is what artistic creation was in all the great epochs of art. This, too, is what shone out to us in all the different descriptions Baron Rosenkrantz gave us in his excellent lecture. This is what will always stand out wherever new artistic impulses make their appearance in earthly evolution. From these new impulses we can glean courage and hope that our experiences in spiritual science, too, can really lead us on to new forms of art.

I have been asked to give a separate lecture about how spiritual science has been the source of eurythmy.[75] Perhaps on that occasion I shall be able to add something to what I have said today.

7. FINAL ADDRESS AT THE SUMMER SCHOOL

Penmaenmawr, 31 August 1923

On 31 August Rudolf Steiner took leave of the Summer School and its participants with the following words.[76]

After the moving words we have just heard I would like to express my appreciation and gratitude at the end of this Summer School.

Looking back over the past days here in Penmaenmawr I can say that they have been a time of deepest satisfaction for me. This Summer School has been a wonderful opportunity to present anthroposophy here in Britain in a more extended way over a longer period of time. It is this above all else that fills me with such great satisfaction.

Basing our work on anthroposophy as we do, we must not underestimate ideas that lead to an enterprise of this kind. The idea out of which this Summer School arose was expounded to me by Mr Dunlop when I visited him while he was ill. He had already mentioned it briefly during my previous visit to London.[77] He was very keen to place amid all the multifarious and praiseworthy things that have been achieved on behalf of anthroposophy some event that would show the world what is central to the anthroposophical movement itself. He said to me at the time that he had the idea of putting on a Summer School that could show the world how anthroposophy can bring forward its content through the 'word' and also what has emerged from anthroposophy through eurythmy.

He also put forward a third idea which it was of course not possible to realize immediately since it was too comprehensive to be put into practice at the first attempt. Nevertheless it is very satisfying to have succeeded in bringing to the fore in its own right what is centrally anthroposophical, anthroposophy itself, and also eurythmy, which has emerged so intimately out of anthroposophy, especially in the way that became possible here in Penmaenmawr.

This does not mean that I want to underestimate all those other branches that have also arisen out of anthroposophy. But when you can look more deeply into all that is connected with the human soul and also into what can arise in the world out of a movement such as the anthroposophical movement, you realize that all the other branches can only become effective in the world to the extent that what is really central to anthroposophy can achieve recognition on its own account.

Believe me, dear friends, the education movement, in all its aspects is very dear to my heart indeed. But I should never be able to assure you that this education movement, which has grown out of anthroposophy, would be understood if it were brought out into the world as something in its own right, any more than I could assure you that by winning people's interest in the education that has grown up out of anthroposophy you would ever succeed in leading anyone to anthroposophy as such.

The opposite of this will be the truly correct way of going about things. A genuine understanding for something that has grown from anthroposophy—the education movement that is so important for the world—can only come about through anthroposophy itself, by means of cultivating anthroposophy as such in its most central position. That is why Mr Dunlop's words went so directly to my heart when he said that cultivating the source of everything must be given priority over cultivating the daughter movements.

An individual who is as deeply involved in this movement as I am can best give what he has to give if he is in no way constrained to force it on to the world, if he can give it because it has been asked of him, because it has been asked of him in the right way. This is a law that calls for far greater recognition: Mystery wisdom can only be given if it has been requested, if it has been asked for in the right way. And on that occasion it was indeed asked for in the right way.

I am therefore able to say that this Summer School in Penmaenmawr will prove immensely fruitful for the whole of the anthroposophical movement and its various branches in England, and that is why we can look back with such satisfaction over the time we have been permitted to spend here in Penmaenmawr. So from the bottom of our hearts Frau Steiner and I thank Mr Dunlop and those who worked with him in enabling us to present what is central in anthroposophy and, on its own account, eurythmy also, something that has grown from anthroposophy, to such a kind audience as the one we have had here. We both also want to thank you as an audience for your attentiveness that has been so sustaining for what we have wanted to bring to you. It is so very important on the one hand to be able to speak about what it has been possible to draw from the fountains of spiritual knowledge— for at the present time this is what should speak most deeply to human hearts and souls. On the other hand we are now living at a time when all sorts of signs can be seen testifying to the necessity for modern civilization to receive spiritual impulses; yet how little is what has come down to us from olden times still capable of carrying this civilization forward fruitfully. Without a new spiritual impetus civilization would recede.

I have to admit that when I am given the opportunity to speak from a background such as I have been able to express here and point out what is so necessary for our time, this fills me with the greatest satisfaction.

This morning[78] I was obliged to point out that civilization itself is threatened by a kind of 'occult imprisonment'.[79] In fact cultural and spiritual life as a whole is more threatened by this than we imagine; there are signs of it everywhere. This morning I referred to a talk given by Oliver Lodge in England a short while ago before a rather important gathering.[80] This talk was an example of how longings exist even in the most abstract science. If they are rightly understood and derive from the right inner attitude these longings lead directly to what spiritual science really is able to give—though I say this with all modesty. When we follow up such things as these we can see everywhere what it is that spiritual science must represent in such instances.

A most significant phenomenon has come about from the very midst of a mode of thought and frame of mind that is fully rooted in the most official scientific way of thinking. This phenomenon takes the form of a remarkable book, *Raymond*, by Oliver Lodge about the soul of his son after death. You are sure to know about this book, so I need not go into much detail.[81] The book relates how Lodge's son Raymond, who fell in the War, communicated with his father by means of a medium, saying things which Oliver Lodge reveals and which deeply affected the sorrowing father.

When this small book appeared, written by the celebrated Oliver Lodge about Raymond Lodge, the world was astounded, for in it he referred to the spiritual world in a profoundly scholarly way, springing from the most con- scientious and exact modern thinking. A great mass of documentary evidence was collected to prove the possibility of getting into the spiritual universe by means of mediumship, along lines analogous to any of the modern sciences.

The world was especially struck by the circumstance that Oliver Lodge was told by the soul of Raymond, through the medium, of the existence of a photograph taken of Raymond and his comrades in the war-zone in France. Two snaps had been taken of Raymond Lodge with his comrades, as photo- graphers often do, getting the subjects to change their pos- itions slightly to show their faces at a different angle. Nothing was known in England about these photographs as they had not yet arrived; Raymond had died before they came.

The book states that the soul of Raymond told Oliver Lodge and other members of the family, through the medium, about these photographs; no one here in England had seen them, but when they arrived three weeks later everything

proved to be true about the slightly differing positions in the
two snaps. What could be more striking than a description
through a medium given out to be coming from the soul of a
dead person, and giving details about something that has not
yet arrived. Nevertheless, a dreadful error did creep in.
Anyone who has explored these things is aware that under
certain circumstances there are possibilities of pre-vision.
What the circle around the medium saw, when they studied
the pictures after their subsequent arrival, could have been
seen by the medium in advance, without necessarily any
connection with the soul of the dead person—though this was
certainly a pre-vision of a very tender and intimate nature; but
it was a pre-vision.

You really do not even have to be a modern scientist in
order to be critical in the right way about revelations from the
spiritual world. Everything that is appearing in this field, even
this excellent, earnest and accurate work of Oliver Lodge,
tends rather to lead one away from a genuine comprehension
of the spiritual world than towards it. The habits of scientific
thought and research today are such that even when people
are trying to investigate the spirit they want to proceed as they
do in the laboratory, with every step based on material considerations. Such methods, however, do not lead to any
understanding. Only the purely spiritual path that has been
described here can lead to understanding. Those who
imagine that such methods will lead into the spiritual world
will find that although they do, in fact, discover something
spiritual it is only something spiritual that is taking place on
the physical plane. A pre-vision of two things that took place
in the physical world was described as purporting to have
been projected down from the spiritual world. The physical
world is of course everywhere filled with the spirit, but we
mistake the relation between the earthly and the super-earthly
world unless we have learnt to follow the true spiritual path of
research.

As I pointed out this morning, it is this current way of

wanting to draw solely on a kind of thinking that is purely scientific, and only allowing this kind of thinking any validity, that builds the walls of occult imprisonment. Inside these occult prisons people then make their experiments which actually go very wrong because instead of discovering truths they discover terrible errors that lead further and further away from the truth, especially when people are so strongly involved with their hearts as described in the book about Raymond Lodge. In the realm where the spirit begins to speak there is an immensely strong echo from human hearts, so because human hearts respond so strongly, and because all too human prejudgements very easily creep into human hearts, we must do everything in our power to prevent any possibility of the spiritual walls of occult imprisonment closing in upon us.

I would not speak about these things here if it were not that the very serious state of the times makes it necessary to do so. The truth is that humanity needs to make an energetic step in the direction of the spiritual world.

Many questions have been put to me during this Summer School. Some of these could not receive a full answer, not because the subject matter was too difficult but because the time has not yet come in the evolution of humanity when it is possible to speak of many things without arousing prejudice. This applies to the question asked about how the different nations relate to one another spiritually. In this connection I was asked what it meant to the spiritual world when one nation conquered another and reduced it to dependence.

Of course spiritual science is well able to give competent information on such subjects, but, believe me, the time has not yet come when these things can be discussed without any prejudice, or when the final consequences of such truths as the answer to this question would involve would be acceptable. We should ask ourselves whether the external view of one nation having made another dependent on it physically in matters of the world is the only angle from which to approach this situation. People do not always notice how a nation that has made another materially dependent upon it has in turn become spiritually dependent on the one it has subjugated. This, however, is only one of the first truths that must become common knowledge across the whole of the civilized world. Only when we really have the inner courage to admit the real spiritual truths can we acquire a universal understanding of such things, which will then attain their full significance for practical life.

The same situation also applies to the question as to whether there are individuals in the world today who are in possession of any higher truths and are bringing them to the world, individuals who are perhaps in contact with one another.

I have already indicated that the point is not solely whether truths can be given to the world by certain individuals, since this also depends on how far the world is ready to receive these truths. I have referred to various hindrances blocking the way today, which it has to some extent been possible to describe by saying: 'The Bodhisattva is indeed waiting, but a sufficient number of individuals must first make themselves ready to understand him.' You can ask the question: 'Do those who have spiritual knowledge communicate that knowledge to human beings?' If you ask this question, I can only reply: 'In itself the external printing of characters on paper signifies nothing.' I would simply like to say that today a great deal of the profoundest wisdom can be written on paper in printed characters, but the question always is: Are these words of wisdom understood? There are many means of communication and many are used. But reciprocal communication among individuals who do have something to communicate from the higher worlds was easier in the days when wisdom was given out from holy sanctuaries such as are hidden here in the Druid stone circles, and when the thought-waves from such circles moved through the world without encountering the waves of wireless telegraphy.

This is not meant in a reactionary way against wireless telegraphy which in itself is of course a great material blessing for humanity. The fact is, however, that if spiritual communications are really to find their way across the world, stronger powers are needed in an age when the spiritual waves meet up with the waves of wireless telegraphy than is the case in an age when this does not happen. We must realize that precisely in our own age, when our material culture has reached such a height for the blessing of humanity, it is all the more necessary for the spirit to inscribe itself more intensely, with more forceful intensity into human hearts, and travel forth again from those hearts.

A great and wonderful opportunity has been given for this to happen here in Penmaenmawr, for we have been living here as though in an atmosphere from which wonderful things radiated in the ancient sanctuaries. I was able to draw your attention to this as the lectures proceeded. The choice of this place was most fortunate, for here something that was once present in Central and Northern Europe, before the Mystery of Golgotha went on its way through the world, was able to come to life again spiritually. It had waited for the Mystery of Golgotha but then could not at first find any means of continuing when Christianity came up from the south, as I described this morning; in a sense it is still waiting.

We can truly say that in the wonderful solitude up there, where those stone circles stand, one is still met by the real echoes of what once worked with such strong power in these northern regions of Europe. In that stream of power there were many things that should now no longer exist, for human souls must go forward; in their progress today they would not be able to endure those things, they would be hampered in their freedom. In a sense the profound Mystery knowledge that was once sought in these holy sanctuaries has gradually passed into cosmic memories, which hover like luminous clouds in the hollows of the hilltops among which these holy relics are enshrined. That has been the source of the special atmosphere which has been spreading its mantle over all that can be willed here for a new spiritual life. All these things draw from Frau Steiner and myself the warmest gratitude for the efforts Mr Dunlop, Mrs Merry and the others have made so that this Summer School at Penmaenmawr can become an event which will make its mark in the anthroposophical movement.

We have already been told very nicely about all the things that have been necessary behind the scenes to make all this possible. Just as I warmly thank you, dear audience, for directing your wonderful attentiveness towards anthroposophy in this beautiful place, and towards eurythmy as well, so do I thank all those who have prepared this special event and continued to work behind the scenes while it has been going on. As I have already mentioned, I know from experience how much effort goes into bringing off such an event, so I know what I am talking about. And something else: In former times when those around me had to make preparations for events like this, they used to send their skin to the tanner's first—for actually it is usually not possible to give entire satisfaction. When you cannot satisfy everybody it is just as well for those working behind the scenes and bringing everything about to be in possession of a well-tanned hide.

Our anthroposophical movement really has grown up out of the smallest beginnings. A short while ago in Dornach I pointed to the time long ago—21 years or more—when the anthroposophical movement was introduced into the theosophical movement through the journal *Lucifer Gnosis*.[82] This journal did not perish; there was simply too much work to be done, so it was not possible to continue with it. It reached its not only extremely satisfying but indeed excellent number of subscribers at the very moment when I was no longer able to carry on with it. That journal, however, was the very small beginning of the anthroposophical movement. For the most part I wrote the articles. Then I had to go to the printers to correct the proofs. And once the magazines arrived Frau

Steiner and I put the wrappers round them and wrote the addresses—we did not even have a typewriter, let alone printed addresses. Then we loaded them all into a laundry basket and carried them to the post office. The anthroposophical movement did indeed have very small beginnings. The venues for the lectures, too, were not beautiful, elegant rooms like these. I once gave a lecture in a room with a floor full of holes; I had to watch every step so as not to get a foot caught in one of them. So as the town hall here also has holes, in the roof, I was not all that surprised, perhaps even felt a little nostalgic, when the rain came through the other day. Compared with the beginnings of the anthroposophical movement, events such as this Summer School are festive occasions indeed, quite unlike the days when things were not nearly so grand. I am not ashamed to remember an occasion in Berlin: because we could not find more suitable premises on the days set aside for some lectures, and also for various other reasons, I had to lecture in part of a room separated off by a screen behind which we could hear the clinking of glasses in a public bar. Once when even this was not available, because there were more important things going on in it, we were offered the only other available space, which was a cross between a cellar and a stable. Well, you can see that the anthroposophical movement has had to fight its way through a good deal, so the part of it that lives in human hearts knows how to be grateful. For our part we immensely appreciate all that has taken place here over the past few days.

I hope these words—with which I greet and thank you once more for these wonderful days in Penmaenmawr—will keep us close to one another for the future now that we have experienced such harmony together here, consecrated, I believe, by the historical memories this place holds.

8. ORAL DESCRIPTION OF THE 1923 VISIT TO BRITAIN

Dornach, 9 September 1923

In Dornach on 9 September 1923, Rudolf Steiner reported on his visit to Britain, a rich and varied experience.

This evening I should like to tell you a few things about our journey. Next week I shall have to be in Stuttgart, but in tomorrow's lecture I shall perhaps go a little more into the content of what I hope to describe to you today.[83]

First we went to Ilkley in the north of England, where there was to be a course on education showing how Waldorf methods are related to present-day civilization. Ilkley has about 8,000 inhabitants. It is customary in England to run what they call summer schools in towns like this, and this course was to take the form of a summer school.

On the artistic side we wanted to show how we have evolved eurythmy out of the anthroposophical movement. In addition, six teachers from the Waldorf school were going to show how they put into practice what was described in the lectures.

Ilkley itself is a kind of summer resort, but it is not at all far from towns that demonstrate only too profoundly the industrial and commercial culture of our time. Leeds is quite near, and so are places like Bradford and Manchester, cities which mirror the kind of life that has arisen today. They are places that give you a sense of the clear need for a more spiritual direction in our time, a spiritual direction, however, that should not be restricted to providing a few individuals with something for their own personal soul needs. Of course it is justifiable to regard the anthroposophical movement in this light, too, but I am referring to the sense that is reaching us very urgently from the world outside.

Culturally it would be paradoxical to recommend the inclusion of indigestible minerals, stones and so on, in the human diet, in other words to consider it perfectly possible that people should eat sand and similar things. Our conception of the human organism compels us to regard this as an impossibility. Similarly those of us who look more deeply into the way the world is constructed and arranged—this should be said once in a while out of genuinely anthroposophical feelings and sensations—will gain quite specific impressions from houses and factories being lumped together in ways that provide absolutely nothing for the aesthetic sensibilities of human beings, as is the case, for example, in Leeds where unbelievably blackened houses are strung together quite abstractly, where everything looks like a condensation of the blackest coal dust concentrated into the shape of houses in which people have to live. Linking this with human evolution and culture as a whole and regarding it in the same light as what I just said about having to eat sand, you cannot help feeling that it would be equally impossible for this human civilization to evolve inwardly and make any progress if such things came to be regarded as permanent features of it.

I am not saying that you have to be a reactionary if you are firmly rooted in anthroposophy. Such things must of course not be discussed in a negative way for they have, after all, come about as part of the earth's living evolution. But it is only possible for them to exist within human evolution if they can be filled and permeated by a genuinely spiritual life—if the spiritual life fills these things in particular and lifts them to some sort of aesthetic level, so that human beings are not totally separated from their inner humanness as a result of such things entering into the evolution of culture.

This kind of experience makes obvious how absolutely necessary it is that spiritual impulses should enter into our present civilization. Such things are not a matter of having some sort of general idea. They must be intimately linked with what is actually there in the world, but for this you have to have a heart that beats for what is actually there in the world.

Ilkley, then, is a place surrounded on the one hand by an atmosphere created entirely by these industrial towns. On the other hand, in the remains of dolmens and old Druidic altars lying around everywhere, it has traces of something that reminds one of ancient spirituality that has, however, no immediate successors. It is most moving to have on the one hand the impression I have just described and then, on the other, to climb a hill in this region so filled with the effects of those impressions and then find in those very characteristic places the remains of ancient sacrificial altars marked with appropriate signs. It is most moving. Quite near Ilkley there is a hill like this, with a stone at the top marked with what is essentially a swastika—although it is a little more complicated. Such signs were carved into stones sited in specific places. They indicate a spot where the Druid priest was filled with the ideas that were culturally creative about two or three thousand years ago in these parts. If you enter a place like this today and see the signs carved on a great stone, you can still sense from the whole situation that you are standing at a place where once a Druid priest stood and where he felt that in carving the stone he was giving expression to the consciousness he had as a result of his dignified office.[84]

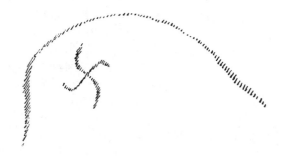

What can you read in these signs as you stand before a stone of this kind? You read the words that lived in the Druid priest's heart: 'Behold, the eye of the senses sees the hills and the places where human beings dwell. The eye of the spirit, the lotus flower, the spinning lotus flower (for the swastika is a sign of this), sees into human hearts and looks into the inmost parts of the soul. Through my seeing I desire to be united with those who have been entrusted to me as my congregation.' This is what you read when you stand before a stone of this kind, just as you otherwise read the text in an ordinary book.

This is more or less the environment in which the Ilkley conference took place. Each morning began with a lecture in which on this occasion I endeavoured to put before the audience the kind of education practised in the Waldorf school, basing this on the whole historical development of the art of education. My starting-point was to describe how in Greek culture education had arisen out of ordinary Greek life. This showed, I said, that no special methods or practices should be invented for use in schools, for schools ought to bring to the children what is there in the culture around them.

I do not want to be generally critical about, say, Fröbel's way of teaching little children, but I have to say that it is not right to invent special methods for doing things with children, methods that are unconnected with general cultural life and have not evolved from it. The right thing is for teachers to have a firm footing in general cultural life, to have a good feel and a good sense for it so that they can base their teaching on what is there in the culture into which the pupils will, after all, enter in due course.

So I wanted to show how education and educational methods must grow out of our own life, a life which is, however, filled with spirit. This led on to the opportunity to throw light on the Waldorf approach from another angle. What I have just mentioned was merely the starting-point. The actual content of the lectures was then the Waldorf approach as such, which you of course already know about.

Following the lectures there was a eurythmy performance by the children of the Kings Langley school, and performances in the Ilkley Theatre by professional eurythmists who had accompanied us there. It would probably have been better if the latter had taken place first. This would have been the appropriate order with which to demonstrate how eurythmy in school grows out of eurythmy as an art that exists in cultural life. Well, this kind of thing will gradually be better organized, so that even the external sequence will give a picture of what the goal really is.

The third element were the contributions from the teachers of the Waldorf school who had come with us. It has to be said that this part was met with the greatest of interest. For example Dr von Baravalle's demonstration was extremely moving for someone who cares deeply about the development of Waldorf education.[85] You probably know his book on teaching physics and mathematics. To watch him setting out his geometrical ideas in a simple way suitable for children; to follow a kind of inner drama in the way the Theorem of Pythagoras suddenly arose out of a sequence of metamorphosing planes that was both artistic and mathematical; to watch the audience, chiefly teachers, being led step by step without knowing where they were going, while various planes were shifted around until all of a sudden the Theorem of Pythagoras appeared on the blackboard—this was a most moving experience. The audience of teachers were quietly astonished, their thoughts and feelings evolved in an inner drama, and they were so genuinely enthusiastic about methods such as this coming into schools that it was truly moving to behold. Indeed, whatever our teachers brought forward aroused the most exceptional interest imaginable. We had taken along exhibits of the children's work such as modelling, toy making and painting. People were very interested indeed to hear how the children do this kind of work and how it is incorporated in the curriculum as a whole.

Fräulein Lämmert's description of how music is taught also met with great interest, as did Dr Schwebsch's explanations. Dr von Heydebrand's loving manner and Dr Karl Schubert's forceful way were also much appreciated. It all went to show that it is perfectly possible to place before teachers' souls in a vivid way what the essence of Waldorf education is. Fräulein Röhrle also gave a eurythmy lesson for various people, which rounded off the whole thing very well, so that the overall picture of the education emerged in the form of an excellent summary.[86]

There is no reason why I should not say this since I had nothing whatsoever to do with the arrangement of the programme. Our English friends put everything together in such a way that a truly excellent summary of the education as a whole as well as of some lesson subjects emerged.

As the conference progressed a committee was formed that sees its task in founding an independent school in England modelled on the Waldorf school. It is very likely that a day-school will come into being in addition to the school at Kings Langley; as you know, after the lectures I gave in Oxford last year[87] that school declared its intention to begin working along the same lines as the Waldorf school. As I mentioned earlier, it was children from the Kings Langley school who gave a demonstration in the Ilkley theatre of what they had learnt in eurythmy.

The interest these things aroused and the way they were accepted—even the understanding the eurythmy performances met with—is something about which we can be truly satisfied. The first half of August, up to the 18th, was spent in Ilkley. Then we moved over to Penmaenmawr.

Penmaenmawr is a place in North Wales, on the western coast of England where the offshore island of Anglesey is situated. It would have been impossible to find a better location this year for this anthroposophical project. Penmaenmawr is filled with an astral atmosphere that can be directly experienced. This is the atmosphere that gave form to the Druidic religion, traces of which can be found everywhere in the surroundings. It lies right by the coast where a bridge leads over to the offshore island of Anglesey. The bridge, by the way, is a technical achievement of genius. Hills rise up on one side of Penmaenmawr, and scattered amongst these are everywhere the remains of what people call sacrificial altars, cromlechs etc. Everywhere there are traces of the old Druid religion.

These scattered places of worship, if I may call them that, appear to be arranged in the simplest manner. Viewed from the side they are stones arranged in squares or rectangles with one lintel stone on top. Looked at from above, the stones are arranged like this [see drawing], and on top of them is one boulder making the whole into a small enclosed chamber.

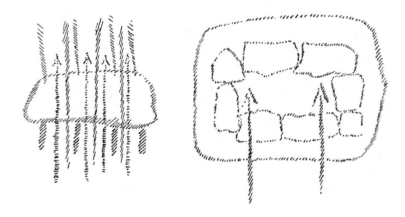

These things were of course also burial monuments, but in olden times burial places were everywhere functionally linked with religious practices that had a much wider scope. So I shall not hesitate here to speak about what we can learn from religious sites such as these.

These stones enclose a small chamber covered by another stone. It is dark inside; if the sun shines on it, the external physical light remains outside. But sunlight is filled with spiritual currents. These spiritual currents flow on, right into the darkened chamber. Because of the initiation he had received, the Druid priest was able to see right through the

Druid stones. He saw the currents flowing downwards, not the physical sunlight that had been blocked off, but the spiritual and soul qualities that live in the physical sunlight. This inspired him with all that flowed into his wisdom about the spiritual cosmos, the great universe. These were not only burial places, they were places where knowledge was revealed.

And there was more. What I have just described occurred at certain times of day. At other times of day the opposite happened; currents flowed up from the earth [upward arrows]. These could be observed when the sun was not shining on the place. In these upward currents lived the moral qualities of the congregation for which the priest was responsible, so that at certain times the priest was able to see the moral qualities of the congregation that surrounded him. Both the upward-streaming spiritual element and the downward-streaming spiritual element showed him things that enabled him to live within the circle in which he functioned in a truly spiritual way.

Such things are of course not written down in the explanations given by modern science about these places of worship today. But they can be directly perceived there because the power of the impulses emanating from the Druid priests—during the times that were still good times for them—was so strong that even today these things are still alive in the astral atmosphere of such places.

I was able to visit another kind of religious site with Dr Wachsmuth.[88] Leaving Penmaenmawr you walk up a hill for about an hour and a half until you get to a kind of hollow at the top. From this hollow there is a wonderful view of the hills all around, and also of the raised ground surrounding the hollow. In this hollow people have found what you really can call a place of sun worship of the ancient Druids. Everywhere there are traces of the standing stones with their lintel stones. These places have no enclosed inner chamber. Quite close together there are two Druid circles. As the sun goes on its way during the day the shadows cast by these stones fall in

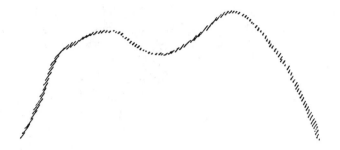

various ways, so that you can distinguish between, let us say, the Ram shadow as the sun passes through the constellation of the Ram, and then the Bull shadow, and then the Twins shadow and so on. Even today, those who can decipher these things can glean a clear impression of how in the qualitatively differing shadows cast by the sun in this Druid circle—which the Druid priest was able to read—the mystery wisdom resulted from what lived on in the shadow where the physical light of the sun was held back. Such a circle is like a cosmic clock speaking about the mysteries of the universe. The signs that arose and were brought about through the shadows spoke of cosmic, universal mysteries.

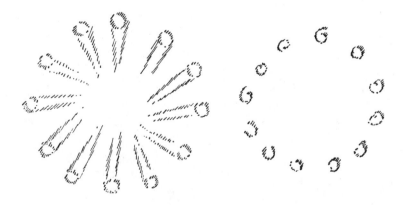

The second circle provided a kind of control for checking what arose in the first. If you were to look down on the two from an aeroplane high enough to eliminate the distance between them, these two Druid circles would have shown you the ground plan of our Goetheanum.

All this lies close to where the island of Anglesey is also located, which is where many of the things told in connection with King Arthur took place. The centre of King Arthur's activities lay further to the south, but a good many of the things that belonged to his work took place on the island. All this results in an astral atmosphere around Penmaenmawr that clearly makes it a special place, a place about which you could say that if you want to speak about spiritual things there, you will have to speak in Imaginations. What happens with Imaginations today is that as you form them in the course of explaining something they very quickly disappear again in the astral atmosphere of our present civilization. In attempting to portray something spiritual you are constantly battling against the disappearance of the Imaginations. You have to call up the Imaginations, but they evaporate very rapidly so that you are constantly having to recreate them in order to have them before your inner eye.

The kind of astral atmosphere that arises as a result of the things I have been describing is such that although it is more difficult in Penmaenmawr to form the Imaginations in the first place, spiritual life is made much easier through the fact that this difficulty is compensated for by the way the Imaginations, once formed, appear as though written into the astral atmosphere, so that they simply stay put. Once you have formed Imaginations there as expressions of the spiritual world, you have the feeling that they simply remain in the astral atmosphere of that place.

This circumstance reminds you in a very vivid way of how the Druid priests chose their special places where they could inscribe into the astral atmosphere the cosmic secrets they were obliged to shape into Imaginations. So travelling there from Ilkley was indeed like stepping across a kind of threshold. You went from a location very close to an industrial area where there were only traces of ancient Druid times and entered something that is purely and simply spiritual even in our present time. It is entirely spiritual. Wales is indeed a very special place on the face of the earth and is today the guardian of an immensely strong spiritual life. True, it is the memories of this spiritual life that still exist, but they are real memories that stand firm. So it is not inappropriate to say that the opportunity to speak in this place about anthroposophy as such, not in connection with any of its daughter movements but about anthroposophy in the truest sense, about the inner core of anthroposophy, can truly be counted one of the most important chapters in the development of our anthroposophical life.

That it was possible to make these arrangements and place such an important event into the midst of anthroposophical life we owe to Mr Dunlop's exceptional insight and energetic activity. He suggested the idea to me last year when I was in England and then stuck to the plan which he brought to fruition this August. Right from the start the plan had been to link purely anthroposophical subject matter with eurythmy.

Mr Dunlop also had a third impulse which, however, proved impossible to carry out. Nevertheless we can say that what did happen was only possible as a result of the spiritual insight that came into play in choosing the location. It is important, I think, to realize for once that such exceptional places exist on the earth where memories still so vividly show how a living sun religion once prepared for the later acceptance of Christianity in Northern and Western Europe.

Again the lectures were in the morning. Some of the afternoons were set aside for the participants to visit those religious sites, dolmens etc., the memories of which are linked with the astral atmosphere of the place. In the evenings there were talks on anthroposophical themes and also eurythmy performances, five altogether in Penmaenmawr. They were accepted on the one hand with great cordiality and on the other with the greatest of interest. Some of the audience were anthroposophists and some not.

The hilly terrain right by the sea made for tremendously variable weather which changed from semi-cloudbursts to bright sunshine and so on, sometimes almost hour by hour. The external conditions were rather like those here in Dornach in the carpenters' shop, and there was one evening when people had to make their way to the eurythmy performance through what was virtually a cloudburst. They sat there in the hall with their umbrellas, their enthusiasm being not in the least dampened. As I said in Penmaenmawr, we really can call the whole event a most significant chapter in the history of our anthroposophical movement.

One of the sessions in Penmaenmawr was again devoted to educational questions. In this connection I want to mention something you may have read about in the brief description I have already put into *Das Goetheanum*. When I arrived in Ilkley there was a book awaiting me, *Education through the Imagination*. Although initially I only had time to leaf through it, I was immediately captivated. One of our friends is already calling it one of the most important books in England. The author is Miss McMillan, and this lady chaired our meetings on the first and second evenings in Ilkley.[89] She gave the introductory address. This woman's enthusiasm and inner fire concerning the art of education was most elevating. And it was very satisfying indeed to find her fully in favour of one of the forms of education today that needs taking extremely seriously, namely, Waldorf education.

Over the subsequent days I read the book properly, and I have summarized my impressions in the article in *Das Goetheanum*. Last Monday, Frau Steiner and I were able to visit the place where this excellent lady works, in Deptford, near Greenwich, London. That is where Miss McMillan has what I would like to call her 'care and education institution'.[90] This institution takes in children from the lowest and poorest classes, including older children. Having begun with six many years ago, it now has 300. They come in at the age of two, dirty, neglected, ill, undernourished, suffering from rickets, typhoid-like symptoms and worse. The whole school is situated in a garden. Only a few steps in from one of the gates you come to some hutments rather like the ones we had for the Waldorf school before our opulent house was built. The hutments are temporary but they are beautifully and handsomely appointed. Only a few steps away on the streets where the population lives in the most dreadful poverty and squalor you can compare the children there with what is made of them in the institution.

The bathing arrangements are exemplary, and this is the main thing. The children come in at 8 a.m. and go home in the evening. The morning begins with a bath. Then there are a kind of lessons given with the utmost devotion and most moving attitude of benevolence with everything arranged in a most practical and suitable way. Miss McMillan considers that Waldorf education must one day enter into all this, so from this angle, also, we should be extremely satisfied, for there are things in the method of teaching that one would wish to change. But measured against the utter devotion [of the staff] this is quite irrelevant at the moment. Such things are always in the process of evolving.

It is quite remarkable how well-behaved the children become, especially at mealtimes. They help each other and the food is always served by one of the children. The fact that it costs 2/4d per child per week to feed these children, in the most delicious and homely way that tempts you to join them in their meal, is just one example of how practical all the arrangements are. Then it was also a wonderful experience when the older children who had been attending the institution for years were called together to perform a scene from Shakespeare's *A Midsummer Night's Dream* for us. They performed so seriously, and there was even some degree of acting ability. It was wonderful and moving to see these children performing so expressively and impressively with a good inner sense for the dramatic.

This performance of Shakespeare's *A Midsummer Night's Dream* took place almost at the very spot where Shakespeare and his troupe used to perform his plays before the royal court, for Queen Elizabeth had her court near Greenwich. Queen Elizabeth's courtiers even lived in premises where the schoolrooms now stand, as well as other rooms about which I shall speak in a moment. Shakespeare had to come out from London to perform his pieces for the courtiers. This was the very spot where those children gave us their performance of Shakespeare.

Linked with the 'care and education institution', on the same piece of land, is a children's hospital, also for the poorest of the poor. Six thousand children pass through it each year. And the chairman of this hospital is once again Miss McMillan. In this very poor and squalid district, a dreadful place, there is this personage working with the utmost energy and a wonderful understanding of what she is doing. I was therefore most gratified when Miss McMillan expressed her intention of coming to visit our Waldorf school in Stuttgart at Christmas with some of her staff if she could possibly manage to do so.[91] Her teachers are immensely devoted people, for you can imagine that caring for the type of children I have been describing is not easy.

So I found it most satisfying to have this lady chairing my lectures at Ilkley, and that she then also came to Penmaenmawr for the few days she could spare, where she introduced a discussion on education at which Dr von Baravalle and Dr von Heydebrand spoke. What took place at Penmaenmawr in this field was therefore also most satisfactory.

The third and final part of our trip were the days we spent in London. Dr Wegman had come over to London to help with my task there.[92] We were to describe the methods and nature of our efforts in anthroposophical medicine to a number of English medical doctors. Forty physicians had been invited, and most of them came, to the home of Dr Larkins.[93] I was able to give two lectures.[94] The first was about the special nature of our medicines in connection with the symptoms of illnesses and the inner nature of the human being. In the second I gave a basic view of the physiology and pathology of the functions of the human body; on this basis I also mentioned the way certain medicines work—for example antimony and mistletoe. I think it is true to say that what we said met with considerable understanding, also in a wider circle, judging by the considerable number of people who asked Dr Wegman for a consultation. Thus this side of our anthroposophical work was also given consideration.

The final event was a eurythmy performance at the Royal Academy of Arts, which I think I can say was exceptionally successful. The hall was not particularly large, but the seats were sold out and people even had to be turned away. The performance was received with tremendous enthusiasm. Really you can say that wherever it goes eurythmy gives a good account of itself. If only there were not such great obstacles everywhere nowadays!

When you see all these good things, for example the intention arising from the Ilkley event to start a kind of Waldorf school over in England, you cannot escape being deeply worried by the troubling, as yet uncertain answer to the question: 'Now that Germany is in such terrible danger, what is going to become of the Waldorf school which, after all, is the source of these educational efforts?' I am not referring to the pecuniary difficulties but to the extremely dangerous conditions within Germany itself. Some things have already come to such a pass that you cannot help asking whether any efforts, in particular those to do with the Waldorf school, can lead anywhere at all. If things continue as they have begun it will scarcely be possible to guide such things as the school through today's troubles unscathed.

It is so depressing to see how everything nowadays is based on short-sighted decisions without even an inkling of the way spiritual currents have to play a part in cultural evolution. By far the larger part of the population has got out of the habit of taking any direct interest or getting involved in things with any warmth of heart. Virtually everyone is asleep as regards the things that are gnawing so dreadfully at the roots of human and earthly evolution. Humanity is asleep, and people only complain if something directly affects them personally.

Yet nothing can be achieved without developing great ideas. The world is so apathetic towards any impulses that ought to be making a difference. Either people do not want to hear about anything, or they feel uneasy when you point to something like the very dangerous situation existing at present in Central Europe. They feel uneasy; they either do not want to talk about these things or they lead the conversation round to non-essential matters such as the question of guilt and so on. This is how people get things off their back. It is deeply upsetting to see humanity's general attitude to what is going on in the world. The cultural sleep that is spreading in every direction is truly pitiful. People are totally unaware of the earth being a single unit in its civilization even when such elemental events occur—but I do not want to go into this now—as the terrible tragedy in Japan brought about by the forces of nature.[95] When you compare the way humanity would have reacted to such things even comparatively recently with the way they look at them now, you cannot avoid telling yourself constantly how urgent it is for humanity to wake up.

This is especially poignant when you see what could happen if only people would take an interest, if people could get themselves to see things not in terms of different countries or states but in terms of humanity as a whole. When you consider what could be possible and then realize that virtually nothing is possible because of the general state of slumber, you find yourself looking most clearly at the signs of our times. This is how things stand at the moment; you cannot talk about one thing without at the same time relating it to the other side of the coin.

Today, dear friends, I wanted to give you an account of our journey. Tomorrow I shall speak about questions of spiritual life less immediately related to it but bringing you more the anthroposophical content.

9. PUBLISHED DESCRIPTION OF THE 1923 VISIT TO BRITAIN[96]

In *Das Goetheanum*

Margaret McMillan and her work

When I reached England on 4 August in order to give two courses of lectures, at Ilkley and Penmaenmawr, I found the book *Education through the Imagination* by Margaret McMillan awaiting me as a gift. Glancing through the first pages I felt at once how well this book was suited to the mood in which the first course of lectures was to be given, intended as they were to describe the art of educating and instructing children as practised at the Waldorf school in Stuttgart. It gave me genuine pleasure to read this book.

It is about discovering the forces that are fruitful for education and in doing so it looks beyond the various outer manifestations of life coming to the surface in children, towards that soul power of imagination which from within holds these together, illumining and strengthening them. It discusses how a child's thoughts are shadow pictures of the soul power from which they receive their life, and shows how the child's will in action depends upon the amount of formative imagination which flows into its life of feeling.

The 'imagination' here referred to is of course not that specific soul power so often written about in this journal, by which the first stage of supersensible knowledge is attained, but it is an instinctive reflection of it that works in every human heart and mind and is, especially in children, the bearer of the soul life. The 'man in the street does not hold the same opinion of this wonderful thing. For him the "imaginative" is nearly always a mere "visionary" or person who sees things that are not really there at all.'[97] 'To a man situated in practical life imagination is a kind of weakness.' Miss McMillan herself is not of that opinion. She seeks a path leading from revealed soul powers to those that are hidden, and in so doing she is led to say that the wonderful power of imagination is not to be found only in the creative minds of scientists and artists, but that it is also the driving force in all that we do in our daily life. '. . . It is as reasonable to say that there is light only on the summits of hills as to say that there is creative power only in the minds of artists and scientists. It streams and flows . . . The brain of every man and child is a kind of world in which degrees of creative power are represented.' As soon as the human being expands beyond mere routine the imaginative creative power comes into play that carries him through life as a thinking being.

In the child whose activity is not yet hampered by routine, imagination reveals itself as the real driving power of the soul—and this it is that the teacher should make use of.

With real genius for education, Miss McMillan seeks to penetrate the peculiarities of the child's mind. Her book is a treasure chamber of precious observations concerning the child's soul, and is full of guiding hints to those engaged in education. Such a chapter as that on 'The Child as Artisan' cannot be read without a feeling of deepest satisfaction.

After reading this book I felt sure that its author would thoroughly understand my saying that one capable of entering so deeply as she has done into education and training would be able to follow me in what I had to speak about in my lectures at Ilkley.

I therefore felt it to be most fortunate that Miss McMillan was to take the chair at our first meeting and to give the opening lecture herself. Her address was given with the fine enthusiasm which she expresses so intensively and this was interwoven with the other enthusiasm for the 'poorest of the poor' and their education. It is really a great experience to hear this lady speak upon the social question as it pertains to the education of children.

But still greater an experience is it to see her words transformed into acts. Today I was able to accept her invitation to visit the nursery and school established by her at Deptford, London. Three hundred children of the very poorest population, from the ages of two to twelve, are wonderfully cared for there by her. An exceptionally devoted, far-sighted and willing band of teachers surround her. The children are brought to this institution in the most neglected state, they literally are taken from the mire. Rickety, tuberculous and even worse, dumb of soul and asleep in spirit are these children when taken in, but, as the result of the care and attention they receive, one sees at work in the various classes youngsters who are spiritually active, happy in soul, well-behaved and growing healthy in body.

It is an equal pleasure to see these children at play, to see them learning, eating and resting after meals.

A number of older children were assembled in one of the classrooms. What is described in the book in the chapter 'The Child as Artist' was here developed in a practical way. In a delightful manner the children acted scenes from *A Midsummer Night's Dream*. The young actors were all soul, all dramatic expression. This artistic instruction is given by Miss McMillan herself.

The classrooms, quite simple hutments with thin wooden walls, stand in a kind of garden which is situated in a wretchedly poor part of the city. One emerges straight from the classrooms into streets where those other children can be seen who have not the good luck to be numbered among the three hundred cared for by Miss McMillan.

The institution lies near the spot where once upon a time the court of Queen Elizabeth stood, who herself lived at Greenwich nearby. Shakespeare apparently acted for the royal household almost in the identical place in which his works are now being so delightfully interpreted by these little ones.

Close to the school is another building, a sanatorium for

children, also headed by Miss McMillan. Six thousand children are yearly received and nursed here.

Over all this work there rests a lofty, hallowed atmosphere. In 1917 Margaret McMillan lost her dearly-loved sister Rachel. The institution is dedicated now to the memory of one whose favourite motto was: 'Educate every child as if it were your own.' Her spirit permeates every room, and Margaret McMillan, in her strong and loving work, lives entirely in that spirit.

The life of that institution is described in her book *The Nursery School*,[98] in which the preface contains the beautiful words: 'Every teacher is a discoverer. Everyone is an inventor, an improver of methods, or he is a mere journeyman, not a master!' Miss McMillan has a right to say these words.

That *she* should have taken part in such an appreciative way in the course of lectures on education and the methods of the Waldorf school fills me with profound satisfaction.

Another fragment from my visit to Britain

In response to the invitation from English friends of anthroposophy, the second series of lectures was given this summer at Penmaenmawr in North Wales.[99] To have chosen Penmaenmawr was a delightful idea on the part of Mr Dunlop who has for many years been a student of spiritual knowledge and is now a member of the Anthroposophical Society. It lies on the west coast of Britain, facing the island of Anglesey.

We were enveloped there in the supersensible atmosphere which emanates from what the ruins of prehistoric Druid sanctuaries can convey to us today. Among the Penmaenmawr hills and on the island of Anglesey lie tell-tale stones in spots chosen, as one can still observe today, with the greatest care. Here, in these places, nature reveals many of its secrets to human beings.

In the places of worship known as cromlechs, unhewn stones are placed in circles and covered with a larger stone, thus creating a small enclosed chamber, and in other places are the Druid circles themselves formed with similar stones.

There are two such circles to be found on ascending one of the hills at Penmaenmawr. As one follows the pathway leading to these circles, wonderful views over sea and hills are disclosed. On the summit of this hill there is a gentle decline, the top of the hill sinks down a little, so that one is enclosed as if by a rampart thrown up by nature itself, and from here the loveliest landscape stretches out in every direction. Here, side by side, are two of these Druid circles, a larger and a smaller one.

History regards these structures as memorials erected upon burial sites, and also admits that they were places of pilgrimage as well and places where assemblies were held for the purpose of discussing and ordering the affairs of the people and so on.

What I have to say about these places must appear fantastic to the point of view of present-day thought, but for me it is the outcome of that spiritual vision of which I have often spoken in this journal. It is of the same character as any other recognized knowledge. A visit to Penmaenmawr gives one rich encouragement to speak of such things.

Druid worship went through a period of degeneracy when it no doubt manifested very gross depravity. But at its zenith it consisted of regulations by means of which an ancient humanity was enabled to investigate in its own way the secrets of nature and to organize its life accordingly. The Druid sanctuaries certainly served the purposes attributed to them by external history, but they served other purposes as well. The sun cast shadows from these works of stone, and according to the direction and the forms of these shadows during the different seasons of the year and times of day, the path it followed could be deciphered. The relation of the earth to cosmic events could thus be interpreted. Solar force lives in all growth, in life and death and in everything living. A Druid priest could see the effects of the sun through the seasons according to the way in which this was perceptible in the santuaries. What was interpreted was the knowledge of sun activity as it streams back in what lives in the products of the earth. In such places the Druid priests received a kind of Inspiration; for reading the secrets of nature was a part of their worship.

To this sun Inspiration with which they were equipped was added what they could regard as moon activity. The origin of everything possessing life on earth was once sought for in sun and moon. The sun calls forth all budding and sprouting life. But what is thus brought forth would continue endlessly to grow were it not for the moon. The way in which the moon intercepts the activities of the sun, reflecting them, trans-muted, back to the earth, holds in check and gives form to what otherwise would grow beyond all proportion in plants and animals—in all nature, in fact.

These life-creating, form-building forces became to the spiritual vision of the Druid priest pictures which constituted their wisdom. They were indebted to the sun Inspiration and to what the moon brought about for their understanding of nature. They saw the result of the moon activities in the formative forces through which the plant sends out roots into the solid earth substance, penetrates the air with its leaves and, finally, aspires in freedom towards the sun in the unfolding of its flowers.

In the pictures revealed to the Druids, spiritual beings were seen actively working in all the forms of living nature. They did not think in an abstract way upon the working of nature's laws; they saw living, spiritual beings in hidden relation to sun and moon working actively in the roots, leaves and flowers of the plants. Living spirit was regarded as the origin of physical life.

These powers are manifested in the world in various ways. Nature spirits work beneficently on the roots of plants within the limits set out by sun and moon, but they can also escape beyond these boundaries. The force that draws the salts of the earth into the root, causing them to pass from thence into the form of the plant, is able to escape the boundary of what is plantlike and become independent. It then becomes rank growth, gigantic. Instead of remaining confined within the roots it expands to the wide sphere of nature happenings. Then it lives in the ravages of frost, in the savage effects emanating from the cold of the earth. Root spirits expand and become the giants of frost and hoar frost. Similarly, what the leaf of the plant passes on to the air becomes, when freed from its limits, giants of wind and storm. And what the plant liberates to the forces of the sun in the flower and fruit becomes, when independently rampant, the giants of fire.

Thus arose long ago in Northern Europe a conception of nature which saw giants of frost, storm and fire where today we see 'the forces of nature'.

During the visit to Penmaenmawr one was made aware of the activity that rose up from the earth as the workings of nature, what lived in the air, what streamed down in rays from the sun. Exquisite sunlight effects often alternated hourly with cloudbursts and rainstorms. Truly it is possible here to awaken the recollection of the nature giants who revealed themselves to those old Druid priests.

The Druid priests sought to derive beneficial effects from the beings of nature who so often grew into giants in such a terrible way. What worked in the plant *from within* through sun and moon moulded the plant into root, leaf and blossom. What expressed itself in the giant forces that had gained their independence: in the juices of hoar frost and dew, in the forms that arose on the earth through wind and weather, in the effects of the fire nature in charring and combustion—in all this, human craft finds means for treating the plants *from without*. In this way what often works harm and damage becomes a means of healing when turned to the proper use. The Druid priest became a healer, wresting from the giant-forces opposing the gods their powers when these became harmful and placing them again at the service of the gods.

The Druids brought order into life through entering into a relationship with the spirit of nature. The stones lying on the ground at Penmaenmawr speak of this search for the spirit. They tell in a most impressive way of this search for spirit so that it may be brought into the life of earth.

It was therefore a source of deep gratification to me to be allowed to speak in the atmosphere of memories such as these about the search for the spirit and how this search must be carried on in the present time.

PART FOUR

MEETINGS AND ADDRESSES

1. MINUTES OF THE GENERAL MEETING OF THE ANTHROPOSOPHICAL SOCIETY IN GREAT BRITAIN

London, 2 September 1923

ANTHROPOSOPHICAL SOCIETY

<u>Minutes of General Meeting</u> held at 46 Gloucester Place, London W.1., on Sunday Sept. 2nd, 1923 at 10.30 a.m.

<u>Chairman</u>. Mr Wheeler was asked to take the Chair. (Proposed by Mrs Drury Lavin, seconded by Dr Dubourg.)

<u>Opening Statement</u>. The Chairman expressed a hearty welcome to Dr and Frau Steiner, thanking Dr Steiner for coming to help us establish the Anthroposophical Society in Great Britain, and to give us advice <u>re</u> the international Society.

<u>Mr Collison</u> then made a statement to the Meeting, referring to the suggestion which had been put forward that he should be General Secretary of the newly constituted Anthroposophical Society in Great Britain.

Mr Collison drew attention to two matters within the Society which were prejudicing the movement in English-speaking countries, (1) an attack upon Freemasons; (2) the attitude taken by some members who in the desire to free themselves from their own group-soul went so far as to assume an unfriendly attitude to their own nation.

Mr Collison in conclusion expressed his regret but said that before accepting office in the Society he felt bound to make a plain statement of his views on these matters.

<u>Dr Steiner</u> then spoke and dealt among other things with the points raised by Mr Collison. If such movements as those indicated by Mr Collison existed, they were out[side] of the spirit of Anthroposophy and very much to be deplored.

Dr Steiner, referring to the great services Mr Collison had rendered to the anthroposophical movement in the English-speaking world, expressed his sense that the choice of Mr Collison as General Secretary would be most fitting.

<u>The Chairman</u> welcomed what Dr Steiner had said and then indicated what was the first item for settlement, namely the formal constitution and establishment of the 'Anthroposophical Society in Great Britain'.

<u>RESOLUTIONS.</u>
I. Mr Collison proposed and Mr Dunlop seconded:-
   'That we now at this meeting (representing all members of the Anthroposophical Society in this country) constitute ourselves "The Anthroposophical Society in Great Britain." '

                                   Carried Unanimously.

II. Mr Dunlop proposed and Mrs Drury Lavin seconded:-
   'That Mr Collison be the first General Secretary of the Anthroposophical Society in Great Britain.'

                                   Carried Unanimously.

Mr Collison thanked the meeting for their confidence and said that he would try to work, as far as in him lay, in the true impulse of Anthroposophy.

III. Mr Dunlop proposed and Mr Collison seconded:-
   'That Dr Steiner be asked to be President for life of the Anthroposophical Society in Great Britain.'

Dr Steiner expressed his readiness to accept this position, on the clear understanding that it should involve no special rights or powers but should be interpreted simply in the sense indicated by Mr Dunlop in proposing it, namely as expressing before the world the association of the Society in Great Britain with his work in Anthroposophy. He pointed out that his relation to the Society had always been and must continue to be determined simply and solely by the real needs that arose from his work and help.

The Chairman and a few other members felt that we were placing upon Dr Steiner an external position which was not called for by the real needs of the case.

After a short discussion the Resolution was carried, with a few dissentients. The Chairman thanked Dr Steiner and said that all, including those who had dissented, felt it a great honour that he should accept this position.

IV. Mr Dunlop proposed and Miss Pethick seconded:-
'That Mr Wheeler be elected Treasurer of the Anthroposophical Society in Great Britain'.
Carried Unanimously.

V. Council. The mode of electing or appointing the Council was discussed, but owing to the advanced hour the discussion could not be brought to a conclusion. It was therefore resolved:-
'That the present Council with the addition of Mrs Merry and Miss Beverley (and with power to coopt) continue in office until the end of January.' (Proposed by Mr Dunlop, seconded by Mr Collison.)

The Meeting was then adjourned (at 1.05 p.m.).

NOTE. Over 100 English members were present.

2. MINUTES OF THE FOUNDING OF THE ANTHROPOSOPHICAL SOCIETY IN GREAT BRITAIN

London, 2 September 1923

ANTHROPOSOPHICAL SOCIETY IN GREAT BRITAIN

President: Rudolf Steiner, PhD

FOUNDED at General Meeting of all Members of the A.S. resident in Great Britain, on Sunday September 2nd, 1923, in the presence of Dr and Frau Steiner.

PRESIDENT. At the Foundation Meeting Dr Steiner, with his consent, was elected President for life of the A.S. in G.B.

GENERAL SECRETARY. Mr Collison was unanimously elected the first General Secretary of the A.S. in G.B.

TREASURER: Mr Wheeler. SECRETARY: Mr Kaufmann (appointed by Council Meeting on Tuesday Sept. 4th, 1923.)

FUNCTIONS of General Secretary, etc. Extract from Minutes of Council Meeting, Sept. 4th, 1923. (Dr Steiner present.)

'... Dr Steiner gave the following points of advice and direction:- The Secretary General as the responsible Chairman of the Council, and acting in agreement with the Council, should look after the inner and outer affairs of the Society. Especially should he represent the Society to the outside world. The Secretary as his assistant should be

responsible more especially for internal management. ...
The Secretary General was the Convener of the Council.'

COUNCIL. At the Foundation Meeting the constitution and
mode of election of the Council was left undecided and it was
resolved that the present Council should continue in office,
with the addition of two members, till the end of January,
1924. As such, the Council consists of 'Group Leaders' ex
officio, Secretary and Treasurer ex officio, and seven elected
members.

The future mode of election was discussed by the Council
Meeting on Sept. 4th, immediately following the Foundation
Meeting. Extract from the Minutes:-
'Dr Steiner advised that the Council be elected by the
General Meeting of the Society, and that only the leaders of
Groups whose membership amounted to one seventh or
more of the total membership of the Society should be ex
officio members of Council.'

It remains, presumably, for a General Meeting in 1924 to
decide on the composition and mode of election of the
Council and to appoint the new Council. The Secretary
General (see Dr Steiner's advice above) is Chairman and
Convener of Council. The Secretary is Secretary to the
Council, thereby acting as Assistant to the Secretary
General.

SUBSCRIPTION. The subscription to the National Society
is 20s. per annum. This does not include any sub. payable to
the International Society. It goes to the maintenance of the
London Headquarters at 46 Gloucester Place, W.1., and to
the general work of the Society and the spread of Anthroposophy in English-speaking countries. The subscription
does not appear nearly to represent the full expenses of the
Society. Arrangements are now being made to supplement it

by a 'General Purposes Fund' to which members will be invited to subscribe on a voluntary basis. The regular subscription is now paid in annually through the Group Leaders, who are responsible for its collection. It includes the subscription to the Lending Library. (Cycles, Lectures and Books.)

MAGAZINE. The Magazine 'Anthroposophy' was founded in 1920 by Baroness Rosenkrantz, as a bi-monthly. In 1922 it was amalgamated with 'The Threefold Commonwealth' (started as a Fortnightly in 1920–21), and became a Monthly Journal, with Baroness Rosenkrantz and Mr Kaufmann as joint editors. In 1923 it has been made the official organ of the Anthroposophical Society in Great Britain. The subscription is 7s. annually (6d. per copy).

PUBLICATIONS. Mr Collison, on behalf of Dr Steiner, is Editor of the English translations of his works on Spiritual Science. Those that are not published by Putnams and other outside publishers, are now being published by the ANTHROPOSOPHICAL PUBLISHING COMPANY (registered in the name of Mr Collison), 46 Gloucester Place, London W.1. Mr Collison is assisted by a publications committee appointed after consultation with Dr Steiner in September 1923.

Sale and distribution of published anthroposophical literature is carried on by the BOOK DEPARTMENT at 46 Gloucester Place, W.1., of which Miss Beverley is Manager.

GOETHEANUM REBUILDING FUND. A number of English members, present at the Delegates Meeting at Dornach in July 1923, together guaranteed approximately £5000 on behalf of the English movement, to be paid in full by the end of 1924. This sum includes all amounts sent in since the

Fire. A large portion is already paid; a considerable amount however remains. The following is an extract from Minutes of Council Meeting, July 27th 1923:-

'... it was decided that the English guarantors (i.e. guarantors of the above sum, - the word does not here mean Group Leaders) should work by arrangement in the various Groups to raise the sums guaranteed by them, and it was proposed by Mrs Drury Lavin and seconded by Miss Groves that Baroness Rosenkrantz should be recognised as Secretary of the Goetheanum Rebuilding Fund in Great Britain. Carried.'

Subscriptions to the Fund are paid in through the Treasurer of the Society, Mr Wheeler.

CONTRIBUTIONS TO THE INTERNATIONAL SOCIETY. Extract from Minutes of General Meeting at the London Headquarters on Tuesday, October 23rd, 1923:-
'Dr Wachsmuth's letter in answer to the Council's inquiry as to the likely expenditure of the International Secretariat was read, and the suggestion of a 5s. annual subscription to Dornach considered. It was decided to express our willingness for a 5s. annual subscription. ... It was decided to endorse the Council's recommendation that the ENTRANCE FEE be abolished altogether.'

MEMBERSHIP OF THE SOCIETY. At the same General Meeting 'it was decided to endorse the Council's recommendation' on this point. The Council's recommendation (Minutes of Meeting on Oct. 11th, 1923) was as follows:-
'The Council decided to recommend the adoption of the Dutch proposal that membership cards be signed by the national General Secretary and finally countersigned by the International General Secretary. The Application Forms should express the fact that the new member joins the single

world-wide Anthroposophical Society, and thereby, ipso
facto in the normal case, his own National Society. The
possibility should not be excluded of joining the Anthroposophical Society without becoming a member of the
National Society of one's own country; but in every such
case the international Secretariat should first inform and
consult the National Society in question. Application forms
should still be signed, in the first place, by a Guarantor as
hitherto.'

REGISTER OF MEMBERS AT DORNACH. Extract from
Minutes of General Meeting on Oct. 23rd, 1923:-
'The Council's recommendation that a list of changes of
address and of new and retired members be sent to
Dornach regularly was read and confirmed. The question
whether this should be done annually or every six months
was left open.'

DELEGATES TO THE CHRISTMAS MEETING. Extract
from Minutes of the same General Meeting:-
'Mr Dunlop proposed and Mrs Merry seconded that the
Council's recommendation be accepted, namely:- That Mr
Collison as General Secretary be appointed the official
delegate, and that a certain semi-official status (enabling
them to take part in the special delegates' meetings) be
given to others at a later date, after he had had time to
consult with them.'

OTHER POINTS. Extract from Minutes of Council Meeting
on Thursday Oct. 11th, 1923, at 46 Gloucester Place,
London W.1.
'The Other Points raised in the preparatory remarks from
Dornach were postponed, or left for consideration at
Dornach. The Council were inclined to think that the
institution of AMBASSADORS (Point 5) at Dornach
would be superfluous and embarrassing.'

Note: The other points were the following:- (1) Reports on the foundation and constitution of the National Societies. Materials for this report are contained in these notes. (2) Statutes (if any) of the National Societies already founded. We are waiting till after the Xmas gathering for this. (4) International General Secretary—proposals. (5) 'Ambassadors'—see the above Minute. (9) 'Mitteilungen'—international journal of the Society. (10) Organisation of an effective defence against the world-wide attacks of the opponents of Anthroposophy and Dr Steiner. (11) Support of the undertakings—educational, medical, Art, research, etc.—which have arisen out of the Anthroposophical Movement. Reports on these various activities from the different countries.

3. ADDRESS AT THE FOUNDING OF THE ANTHROPOSOPHICAL SOCIETY IN GREAT BRITAIN

London, 2 September 1923

My dear friends!

The present need to constitute the Society in different countries arises out of the development the anthroposophical movement has undergone in recent years. Initially the anthroposophical movement began by working out of the spiritual life that it desires to communicate, and also for a long time it worked in collaboration with the theosophical movement. In recent years, however, it has to some extent become necessary for the anthroposophical movement to be more visible in the world at large. This has called forth a critical response and also, as a natural side-effect of that, a good deal of hostility. The whole appearance of the anthroposophical movement, not so much within but as it is seen from the outside, has changed.

The situation with regard to the inner laws of a spiritual movement such as the anthroposophical movement is that one only does whatever is necessitated by the spiritual life itself, in so far as one is able to recognize it. Therefore the movement cannot take account of things that come from outside, be they opposition and hostility or be they approval. The movement must be true to its own intrinsic meaning. It can only carry out what it recognizes from spiritual insight to be necessary for a particular age. To take account in any way of external influences, be they approval and recognition of success or be they opposition and hostility, would damage the spiritual life that ought to be fostered in a movement such as this. Inevitably this brings about a kind of inner division. On the one hand one must follow the inherent forces of the movement, and on the other one must do whatever is necessary for it to continue to exist in the world and not perish. The inner division this causes demands constant watchfulness on the part of the members. So the Constitution of the Society must allow for this watchfulness; it must create for the spiritual movement a kind of vacuum, an empty, vacant space in which it can unfold properly. This is only possible if the various groups and the links between them are organized and administered in the right way.

No spiritual movement in our time can flourish if its aims are specialized in any way. It is what you might call an occult law that every genuinely sound and fruitful spiritual movement must exist for humanity in a general way. It must be generally human or, as we say in ordinary life, international. In our time, if something is not generally human, if a number of individuals get together to form a kind of group ego to carry a spiritual movement, they damage the general progress of mankind; they do not serve mankind or help it to progress.

There is no point in discussing this, any more than it is meaningful to discuss a law of nature. It is purely and simply a spiritual law; if a spiritual movement is to help humanity to progress it must be generally human.

This, however, does not prevent such a movement from doing justice to all the many kinds of human groupings. You can be just as fair towards your own nation as to any other. It goes without saying that every nation has its own great impulse to bear in the context of overall humanity, some more, some less strongly. It is a mistake to imagine that being international entails despising one's own nation. The very fact of being international provides the opportunity for a proper evaluation and illumination of one's own national element.

So if Mr Collison is not mistaken in the observation he described to us, if it is indeed true that this is happening, then it would of course be an aberration if two groups were to form because one of them does not want to rely on its own sense of nationhood and wants to establish a kind of selflessness by standing against what is valuable in its own nation. If one is firmly grounded in anthroposophy, if one truly understands the nature of anthroposophy, then there can be no question of any differences of opinion in this matter, just as there can be no argument about whether mountain air is good or whether sea air is good, if you will excuse this rather trifling comparison. People have different constitutions, so some may benefit from mountain air to help them recover from their complaints while others find sea air more congenial.

If someone were sent to take the mountain air, it would be difficult to take him seriously if he began to rage against sea air. Similarly one would not expect a person's enthusiasm for a particular nation to diminish his understanding for all that is international, or that it would prevent him from being unbiased about all the things in the different nationalities that can work together rather than pulling in opposite directions.

Where there is a true understanding of the deepest anthroposophical impulse there can be no such division. So it has to be said: The most fundamental task of anthroposophical groups is to avoid such divisions and reach an understanding about these things. If one group turns against another saying that if it does this or that it is opposing what Dr Steiner has said and therefore its members cannot be proper anthroposophists, if these things rumble on beneath the surface and people keep on talking about the lack of homogeneous groups or general groups, then of course the outcome cannot be particularly fruitful. But why should it not be possible for such things to be candidly discussed and sorted out in the anthroposophical groups? This, you see, is what I would like to call the watchfulness that is needed inside anthroposophical groups, which has to be taken just as seriously as keeping an eye on whether the outside world is reacting to anthroposophy in a hostile or friendly manner.

In life you can either be awake or asleep. I am not referring

to the ordinary states of waking and sleeping, about which I
shall be speaking in the lecture,[100] but to our awareness of
what is going on in the world, for in this sense you can be
asleep even when you appear to be wide awake. To be asleep
amounts to the same thing as withdrawing your attention
from something, just as in our actual night-time sleep we turn
our attention away from all the things that concern us in the
waking world and pay attention instead to things we are as yet
incapable of perceiving consciously in the present stage of
evolution reached by humanity. This is the sense in which to
be asleep can mean the same as to turn one's attention away
from something. As anthroposophists, though, we ought to be
intensely interested in what is going on in the world. The
world is interested in anthroposophy; if we are not interested
in the world, the world turns hostile.

Watchfulness is what is required, and it is for the sake of this
watchfulness that the Anthroposophical Society as a whole
needs to be constituted in a certain way. I have been pointing
out for some time that the various national groups of the
Society need to form themselves into national Societies. This
has already happened in Switzerland, Germany, Czechoslovakia and Norway, and it is about to happen in Austria and
Holland this year as well. It is tremendously important that
this should also be done here, and that these separate national
Societies then join to form the international Anthroposophical Society, which in future can have its centre in
Dornach. The delegates' assembly at Dornach in July discussed plans for bringing the separate Societies together to
form an international Society at Christmas.

However, this will only be possible if the national Societies
have been formed first, for you cannot join things together if
they do not yet exist. So it would be good if our discussions at
this meeting could result in the constitution of the English
Anthroposophical Society as a national body with an intention of joining the international Society at Christmas, so that
there would be a national centre here in London and the

international one in Dornach, Switzerland. That would be a good thing.

For my part this is all I would like to recommend, for obviously whatever is done in detail must depend on what the friends here think would be the best way of dealing with the matter.

I do hope you will not mind my pointing out that in future much stronger cohesion and collaboration really must come about between anthroposophists from all the countries. Wherever I go I am made aware of a genuine longing to know what is going on in other places. It is no exaggeration to say that there are anthroposophists in almost every civilized country today, but they know virtually nothing about one another, even to the extent sometimes of a person living in one street being unaware that another lives just around the corner. They are unaware of each other's existence.

There is also a wish for an international organ of communication. But such an idea can only be put into practice if there are national groups that can join together to form an international group. Once this has happened we in Dornach will be able to find world-wide ways of communication. So far attempts to do this have remained in the abstract. When the journal *Das Goetheanum* was set up in Dornach the idea of course was that it should send news in every direction. But it cannot send news without first receiving some! Things need to be reported to Dornach first, so that Dornach can then spread news of them. Then we shall begin to have international perceptions and international opinions. This would be the way to go about things. But it cannot be done if it remains in the realm of ideas; it can only be brought about by genuine international collaboration.

In France, too, a national group has been founded with Mademoiselle Sauerwein as General Secretary.

As to the other questions mentioned, I really cannot see that any of the issues raised present the slightest problem as regards Mr Collison having the best possible qualifications for becoming General Secretary. I cannot see anything against this, and in particular the things he himself said about Freemasonry do not appear to be of any consequence. As with many other things in ordinary life that are inconsequential, and without wanting to trivialize the issue, I have always said that the direction from which people approach the anthroposophical movement—in this case Freemasonry—is entirely irrelevant. It is not where people come from that matters, but whether they are good anthroposophists once they have entered the anthroposophical movement. It does not matter in the least if a person also belongs to a guild of shoemakers or engineers. Belonging to a guild of shoemakers or engineers does not infringe a person's anthroposophical worth—this is not intended as a comparison but as a statement of principle. If he is a good anthroposophist, this is all that matters as far as the anthroposophical movement is concerned. Whether he is also a good or a bad or even an indifferent Freemason does not concern the Anthroposophical Society. Actually I find it rather strange that such weight is given to opinions someone or other appears to hold, if Mr Collison's supposition is correct. Ordinarily I say that such things do not occur amongst anthroposophists. But perhaps I shall have to modify this, for in ordinary life people do after all arrive at foolish judgements sometimes. One such foolish judgement would be to base an assessment of someone's value as an anthroposophist on whether he is a Freemason or not.

This was the viewpoint from which I answered Mr Collison in Holland a little while ago when he asked me about this. I told him that a number of our oldest and most valued members were Freemasons. I really cannot imagine any form of Freemasonry proving a hindrance to becoming a member of the Anthroposophical Society. In my opinion the anthroposophical movement wants to stand for something in its own right. Surely it would not be able to bear fruit if it did not work in a positive way out of its own seed. What matters is that it works positively. It is not a question of making comparisons.

When I buy myself a suit what matters is whether it is to my taste and provides what I intend. It is irrelevant if someone comes and tells me this suit does not look like the one someone else is wearing. The issue is that one should wear one's own suit and not someone else's. When you become an anthroposophist you do not dress up in Freemasonry. So really it is quite impossible to make that kind of judgement.

In actual fact there is something else behind all this. Forgive me for saying so, but in my opinion anthroposophy is not valued highly enough—often not even by the members themselves. There is a tendency today to attach greater value to things that are older, more spectacular, more secretive. When work is done with simplicity in an open, honest manner it fails to measure up to something that appears more showy in an undefinable way. The anthroposophical movement is degraded by the assumption that it could be damaged as a consequence of some member or other coming from a different movement. Imagine how terribly weak it would be if such a thing could really harm it!

These attitudes, I believe, are founded on the secret suspicions some people have of one individual or another not being a good anthroposophist. So then they cast about for reasons. People always tend to look for reasons why they like or dislike something. They do not look at a reason and then decide whether they like it or not; first of all they decide whether something is sympathetic or antipathetic and afterwards try to find reasons. So they come up with the reason that someone is a Freemason and can therefore not be a proper anthroposophist, and so on. What people ought to do is look to see whether the person is a proper anthroposophist, and on this they can then base their judgement as to whether he or she belongs or not. There is no point in looking to see whether someone is a Freemason, or anything else.

I am reminded of a judgement I once heard someone pass in Weimar, that enlightened city, and I do not mean to be ironical. I really did overhear two women chatting in the market-place. One of them remarked that the person they were talking about was a liberal. 'What makes you think he's a liberal?' asked the other women. 'I've known him for years, he's a shoemaker!'

This is just about the same kind of judgement as stating that Freemasons cannot join the anthroposophical movement.

For my part, if there is no opposition or hostility from other contemporary movements, I refrain from passing judgement on them. However, if a movement does express hostility, whether openly or covertly, then one must of course put forward one's own opinion, you could say in order to defend the honour of anthroposophy. But apart from this it is just not done to pass comments about other movements, whether officially or unofficially. In fact this is one of the inner developmental laws of movements such as the anthroposophical movement. If you are constantly hitting out in one direction or looking suspiciously in another you lose the inner space you need in which to develop the seed of your own movement in a positive way. You have to try and give yourself to your own movement's inner impulses without turning towards what is outside it. This is what your deliberations here should be based on, and if this can be the basis, I am sure that everything will turn out all right.

Given these views, which he surely shares, I believe that Mr Collison will agree to take on the post of General Secretary. He is the man who has done more than anyone else for the translation and promotion of anthroposophical literature here in England and in the colonies. In future he will continue to represent the impulses that live in the Society here and be in the best position to serve them. It goes without saying that someone like Mr Collison will not be able to write every letter himself; nor will he be able to attend every meeting or council meeting. So he will need a very capable secretary. How you arrive at the composition of your executive council here will best arise from the hearts of the members of your community if they will accept the basis of deliberations I have just described and forget for a while whatever other difficulties there might be. This I believe is the best I can do by way of contributing to solving this question.

With regard to Mr Dunlop's proposition that he should be asked to be President for life of the Anthroposophical Society in Great Britain, Dr Steiner said the following:

May I say a few words on this matter. It is precisely because of the form the anthroposophical movement has assumed as the years have gone by—about which I spoke just now—that it has always been difficult for me to get close to something that has an external designation. I mentioned that the anthroposophical movement has within it certain laws that are appropriate for a spiritual movement of this kind, and this fact is what makes me have to think very deeply about the suggestion that Mr Dunlop put to me the other day, or actually many months ago, in our discussions last year. So I should like to say a few words about this.

The anthroposophical movement requires alert representation towards the outside. Inwardly, as I have already said today, it must work entirely out of its own seed and must do nothing that does not conform with genuine occult laws. As regards the interrelationship between myself and the anthroposophical movement, this has been the reason why for a long time I have not wanted to play any role in the Society except the one for which I am absolutely necessary within it. In other words, I do not want to be anything within the Society except what comes about because there are certain things that have to be done by me.

To some extent this applies also to Frau Steiner. Over the years I have talked with her repeatedly about the fact that she, too, should not be anything else, should not be designated in connection with anything except those things which have to be done exclusively by her.

This is what defines the situation. It is a situation that ought not to be improved upon—or, more likely, made worse—by election or any other kind of method. What ought to happen is that relationships must arise directly out of the way in which individuals are needed.

Once this is fully understood within the Society then, amongst the things that are deemed necessary, one can appreciate grounds such as those put forward by Mr Dunlop. I will concur with this request and not resist it so long as the members understand that I do so only on the grounds put forward by Mr Dunlop regarding the representation of the Society towards the outside—grounds that involve identifying me to some extent with the Society—grounds that appear desirable at present for this part of the world. Taking on this designation is one side of the matter. The other is that the members of the Society really must understand that I draw no other conclusions from such an official designation than those which have anyway been a matter of course. I do not want to derive any kind of power or authority, or any rights whatsoever from such a designation; I wish to work in the Society solely in ways that arise out of the Society's intrinsic concerns. I want to be in the Society what it is my task to be as the one who is called upon to do certain things. So this whole matter is twofold. Adequate account must be taken of both sides.

This being the case—since the reasons which Mr Dunlop gave certainly showed that this was his intention—there is no reason why his proposal should not be accepted. I do not think that it will lead to anything other than what it is anyway my task to carry out without any deviation. The anthroposophical movement must remain an inner movement; its esoteric character must be such that nothing may be done by me except what arises directly out of its intrinsic cause. So it must be absolutely clear that I seek no power other than what arises out of the intrinsic cause itself. I must do this because such are the laws of a spiritual movement. The way in which the Anthroposophical Society and the anthroposophical movement exist in the world today calls for the strictest adherence to the path indicated by the inner laws of the movement itself, from which one must not deviate even by one step.

4. CONCLUDING WORDS OF THE LECTURE 'CHRIST AND THE METAMORPHOSES OF KARMA'

London, 19 November 1922[101]

Before saying good-bye, it is now my duty to make a few remarks which I would ask you to accept as concerning the groups.

Having been permitted to speak to you three times in a row I not only have the strong wish to thank all the dear friends who have made this possible—which I do herewith, most cordially—but I also feel that it is my duty to draw your attention to certain things in order to prevent any mis-understandings arising in the way our anthroposophical movement is regarded.

You will agree, I feel sure, that our anthroposophical movement is not intended to be a movement into which mystical, hazy, nebulous theoreticians can withdraw from the world, but rather one through which human beings introduce the spirit into virtually every sphere of life. It is thus deeply satisfying that something like the education movement started here has come into being. This is one of the streams through which anthroposophy can flow into the world; and there may be a number of other movements through which contact with the rest of the world will be sought. There is, however, one thing we must not forget: that we shall not achieve anything with all these movements which arise as a consequence of anthroposophy if we do not energetically further the impulse of anthroposophy itself. The anthroposophical impulse that truly seeks to bring anthroposophical knowledge and anthroposophical forces into the world in a way that enables anthroposophy itself to become better and better known—this is the impulse to which we must chiefly devote our attention.

My impression is that you have here a good soil on which anthroposophy itself can grow, where anthroposophical thought as such can be accepted.

Suppose by a miracle we were to succeed in founding many schools, what should we need for them? We should need teachers well grounded in anthroposophy. And if we were to found anything else, that too would have to be carried out of anthroposophy. So before we can consider schools that have a good effect we first need active anthroposophists. Then this would provide a good soil for a direct widening of the anthroposophical impulse itself. This is what we must regard as the main thing. Something that brings spiritual life into the hearts and souls of human beings is what we must regard as the main thing.

It might be thought, for example, that eurythmy can be promoted by putting it into the schools. Some people might be thinking: If eurythmy comes about inconspicuously through the schools, then this is how it can expand. It is much better, though, to place eurythmy before the world without hiding in corners with it, for eurythmy is something that arises directly out of anthroposophy. For this, too, you will find that there is good soil here if you yourselves get a good grip on anthroposophical initiatives—whether they are to do with art or more with the knowledge itself—if you really carry these into the world as anthroposophy.

For this to happen it will perhaps be necessary for our dear friends here to join together in an even more conscious way so that particularly here anthroposophy itself can be brought into the world in an even more lively way.

Please, dear friends, consider something I first said in Dornach. As part of the role that has come to be theirs after the terrible War, particularly the English-speaking peoples of the world have gained the great responsibility of spreading the life of the spirit in the world. This can indeed be done by taking a very strong hold of the anthroposophical impulse. The Society here may be small today—believe in ideal magic!—but it will be possible for it to grow large because precisely here there is much yearning for spiritual life. Behind all the terrible decadence, which you will not want to disavow, there is, perhaps quite unconsciously in many, a longing for spiritual life. If there were much enthusiasm and a great deal of liveliness in the anthroposophical impulse, then it would be possible, precisely here, to make good progress with anthroposophy as such.

I have the impression that you would rather leave anthroposophy in the background and promote the daughter movements instead. I do not want the misunderstanding to arise that this is *my* wish. The daughter movements will not flourish until there is a mighty impulse at work in anthroposophy itself. For this to come about it will be necessary for those friends—who have so kindly made these three lectures possible—to come together in an even more intensive way. I wanted to say this here to prevent any kind of misunderstanding.

5. FINAL WORDS AFTER THE LECTURE 'CHRIST AND THE METAMORPHOSES OF KARMA'

London, 19 November 1922[102]

Finally I must now turn to an awkward matter that it is my duty to mention to you, and I do so without in any way intending this as a hint. Through their great generosity, friends have made it possible for a centre for the anthroposophical movement to be created in Dornach, but this very fact is causing me ever greater worries. Now that [the Goetheanum] exists—and of course it is good that it exists, for the anthroposophical movement needed a centre—but through the very fact of its existence we shall quite soon be faced with the possibility of not being able to proceed any further, indeed of having to close things down in Dornach for lack of funds.

Please forgive me for mentioning these matters that are always under so much threat from Ahriman, but unfortunately they are there. I am sure you all agree that idealism is most estimable. However, there are two ways in which it can express itself. On the one hand one can say: 'My concern is with ideals. Money, on the other hand, is so shabby, so disgraceful, that when I think of ideals I cannot at the same time think of my purse.' That is one way of looking at things.

Another way of doing so is to think of the highest ideals while overcoming those feelings of distaste so that one can take out one's purse in order to create the basis on earth so much needed by those ideals.

In this sphere it is one's intentions that matter and, strange though this may sound, one can help Ahriman with money, but one can also hinder him. The intentions are what count. The only question that needs asking, therefore, is whether supporting Dornach is a good or a bad intention. In my opinion it is a good intention. It is because I am so terribly worried that I have to appeal to all our dear friends on occasions such as this one. To do so calls for the greatest inner battle with myself. I do not like doing it at all, but it is my duty to tell you that in the next few weeks we shall be faced with the possibility of having to close the Goetheanum in Dornach. Then, dear friends, we should be left without the centre we have had for the anthroposophical movement in Dornach. I am sure you can weigh up what it would mean for the anthroposophical movement if we had to close Dornach down.

It is my duty to draw your attention to this, and I do hope it will be possible to think in the right way about what I mean, so that perhaps this terrible worry may be lifted from my shoulders. It will be weighing on me very much over the next few weeks on behalf of the anthroposophical movement.

Forgive me for having to mention this now at the end of this conference. The heartfelt gratitude I want to express for everything that has been done to make these events possible is not diminished by it.

Another thing I want to say at this moment is that as we shall not be in touch with one another for a while, let us hold fast to the following thought: we know that we are together in soul and spirit even when we are physically apart.

With this feeling I close our conference made possible here at this branch by your efforts, and I hope that similar events will be possible in the future.

May I just say that if anyone were to feel moved in their heart in the near future, please get in touch with me direct. As this worry is a burden for my heart in particular, please do not contact anyone else, but if you are moved to do so, please turn to me direct so that I may retain a clear picture of the situation and also bear the responsibility for it.

6. CONCLUDING ADDRESS AFTER THE SECOND INTERNATIONAL SUMMER SCHOOL

Torquay, 22 August 1924[103]

We can look back with great satisfaction on the two Summer Schools that have been held here in England. In so looking back over the way they have been organized we get an inner feeling that because certain things have been revealed in them for the first time there must have been something present that can perhaps best be described by saying that we have felt 'at home' here in an occult way. From all we have felt during this last gathering, it seems to me that the intentions brought to bear by our friends Mr Dunlop and Mrs Merry stem from a background that our feelings tell us arises from a genuine will for spiritual science. Not only this year but also last year we have felt, so to say, 'at home' in an occult sense.

We have had the privilege of being in localities that tell of important ancient happenings, places that even today speak to us in ways that are most significant spiritually. In such an environment one's words come more freely and find the spiritual form that wants to approach those human beings who, through their membership of the anthroposophical movement or because of their sympathy for it, want to share in taking up responsibility for what has come from the spiritual worlds and been so frequently mentioned during these courses, namely, a comprehensive anthroposophical will that the signs of the times tell us must enter our present age and also the immediate future. We felt what flows through the anthroposophical movement joining together with all that our friends, Mr Dunlop at their head, have prepared and got ready for us here as a framework.

There is no doubt that some of the strength that lies in our friends' will to organize such gatherings as the one we have just had—for the purpose of an intimate occult representation of anthroposophy—has even been capable of paralysing the by no means occultly sympathetic or artistically inspiring atmosphere of this hall, for we have had no trouble in putting up with it. This is a kind of indirect proof—as they say in mathematics—of how very successful this event has been.

In expressing our warmest, most heartfelt thanks from the depths of our souls, I know that I am also speaking on behalf of Frau Steiner and the whole of the executive at the Goetheanum, intimately bound up as they are with the aims of the anthroposophical movement and with all that is done for anthroposophy out of genuine anthroposophical will. We shall foster the memory of our gratitude when we return to the Goetheanum; we shall store up all the love, all that was beautiful and heartfelt, and above everything also the strong will that has met us here.

The artistic side, too, has been so well and lovingly cared for in both these Summer Schools. Thus our eurythmy, which has arisen out of occult intentions and is, as I believe, of such importance both for the present and the near future, has also been enabled to make its mark here. Eurythmy is especially suited for generating appreciation for the spirit as well as for art.

It seems to me that the eurythmy had the strength to fight its way through the obstacles put in its path, for some of the performances appeared to be tests of one's occult understanding. I felt a desire during the performances to see among the other visitors also the physical bodies of our anthroposophical friends who have been participating in the course. However, on some of the evenings I had the distinct impression that the physical bodies of our anthroposophical friends were missing. Perhaps, I thought, this was a test to see whether one was capable of looking out for souls and spirits instead. So I looked around the hall for the spirits of our anthroposophical friends, and indeed found many—who were not there, despite the fact that they had been present at the lectures. Well, no doubt it was an occult exercise challenging us to prove that those who use occult sight can see those who are not there. As you see, I regard the matter entirely from an occult standpoint, and not from the obvious one!

Nevertheless, if we disregard these limitations, there is every reason to look back with the very deepest gratitude on all that has yet again been done here for anthroposophy. In giving this course of lectures I have been permitted to assert in a high degree what has been the foremost impulse of the anthroposophical movement since the Christmas Foundation Meeting. I was permitted to introduce an esoteric power into what it was my task to render here because I feel responsible— in whatever is said or done anywhere within the anthroposophical movement—towards those spiritual powers who want to give a certain measure of spirituality to humanity in the present and near future, and who alone decide the manner in which the anthroposophical movement shall be led.

It is precisely with this feeling, with the inner realization that what can and must take place did actually take place, that I express my most heartfelt thanks to all those who have played a part in these arrangements.

Most especially I thank our dear friend Kaufmann, who has been so visible beside me all the time in making sure in the most self-effacing and accurate way that what I have had to say could be adequately understood. So I thank Mr Kaufmann very specially this evening.

It is not possible to express to everyone personally the gratitude that I and all the members of the executive at the Goetheanum feel, and indeed this has already been done by others. I have often said on such occasions that those who work behind the scenes do just that, including seeing that it is not possible to thank everyone individually, which does not mean that one's gratitude is any the less. Those who work behind the scenes generally have the worst time of it. They have to miss much of what is going on, and often collapse under the strain into the bargain. But I know that I am met by nothing but grateful hearts when I express the warmest thanks to all those who have contributed to this Summer School in whatever way.

We have now reached the end of this Summer School. Many things that might still have been said will have to be saved up for some future time. But in conclusion I must assure you that the memory of the days we have experienced together here in Torquay will live on—just as the Penmaenmawr Summer School has lived on—in that we shall recognize what has come to meet us from loving hearts and from souls filled with anthroposophy as something to be very specially inscribed into the Golden Book of the anthroposophical movement. In the anthroposophical movement so much depends on the things we organize and bring about receiving a touch of anthroposophy, of spiritual science. This touch will continue to shine like a beautiful light in our memory—of that you may remain most heartily assured.

RUDOLF STEINER'S LECTURES AND ADDRESSES IN GREAT BRITAIN

Asterisks show items contained in the present volume.

1 May 1913, London
Lecture 1, 'Occult Science and Occult Development', in *Occult Science and Occult Development*, London: Rudolf Steiner Press 1966 (in GA 152).

2 May 1913, London
Lecture 2, 'Christ at the Time of the Mystery of Golgotha and Christ in the Twentieth Century', in ibid.

*14 April 1922, London
Previously 'Knowledge and Initiation', in *Knowledge and Initiation & Knowledge of the Christ through Anthroposophy*, London: Rudolf Steiner Publishing Company 1936 (in GA 211).

*15 April 1922, London
Previously 'Knowledge of the Christ through Anthroposophy', in ibid.

19 April 1922, Stratford-upon-Avon
Lecture 7, 'Education and Drama', in *Waldorf Education and Anthroposophy*, Hudson NY: Anthroposophic Press 1995 (in GA 304).

23 April 1922, Stratford-upon-Avon
Lecture 8, 'Shakespeare and the New Ideals', in ibid.

24 April 1922, London
'The Threefold Sun and the Risen Christ', in *Planetary Spheres and their Influence on Man's Life on Earth and in the Spiritual World*, London: Rudolf Steiner Press 1982 (GA 211).

16–25 August 1922, Oxford
The Spiritual Ground of Education, tr. D. Harwood, London:
Anthroposophical Publishing Company 1947 (GA 305).
16 August: 'The Necessity for a Spiritual Insight'.
17 August: 'Spiritual Disciplines of Yesterday: Yoga'.
18 August: 'The Spiritual Disciplines of Yesterday and
Today'.
19 August: 'The Body Viewed from the Spirit'.
21 August: 'How Knowledge can be Nurture'.
22 August: 'The Teacher as Artist in Education'.
23 August: 'Organization of the Waldorf School'.
24 August: 'Boys and Girls at the Waldorf School'.
25 August: 'Teachers of the Waldorf School'.

18 August 1922, Oxford
Lecture VII in *An Introduction to Eurythmy*, Spring Valley,
New York: Anthroposophic Press 1984 (in GA 277).

19 August 1922, Oxford
An introduction to a performance of eurythmy by children.
Not translated (in GA 305).

20–30 August 1922, Oxford
The Mystery of the Trinity & The Mission of the Spirit, tr. J. H.
Hindes, New York: Anthroposophic Press 1991 (in GA 305
and GA 214).
20 August: 'Meditation: The Path to Higher Knowledge'.
22 August: 'The Cosmic Origin of the Human Form'.
27 August: 'The Mystery of Golgotha'.
30 August: 'The Other Side of Human Existence'.

*26 August 1922, Oxford
Previously in *Threefold the Social Order*, Canterbury: New
Economy Publications 1996 (in GA 305).

*28 August 1922, Oxford
Previously in *Threefold the Social Order*, op. cit.

*28 August, address in Oxford.

*29 August 1922, Oxford
Previously in *Threefold the Social Order*, op. cit.

12 November 1922, London
'Life in the Spiritual Spheres and the Return to Earth', in *Planetary Spheres and their Influence*, op. cit.

16 November 1922, London
'Luciferic and Ahrimanic Powers Wrestling for Man', in ibid.

*17 November 1922, London
Previously in *First Steps in Supersensible Perception and the Relation of Anthroposophy to Christianity*, London: Anthroposophical Publishing Company 1949 (in GA 218).

*18 November 1922, London
Previously in ibid.

19 November 1922, London
'Christ and the Metamorphoses of Karma', in *Planetary Spheres and their Influence*, op. cit.
*The concluding words and the final words after the lecture are contained in the present volume.

19 November 1922 London
'Education and Teaching' in *Waldorf Education and Anthroposophy*, Vol. 2 (in GA 218), Hudson: Anthroposophic Press 1996.

20 November 1922, London
'The Art of Teaching from an Understanding of the Human Being', in *Waldorf Education and Anthroposophy*, ibid.

5–17 August 1923, Ilkley
A Modern Art of Education, tr. J. Darrell, G. Adams, London: Rudolf Steiner Press 1972 (in GA 307).
5 August: 'Science, Art, Religion and Morality'.
6 August: 'Principles of Greek Education'.
7 August: 'Greek Education and the Middle Ages'.
8 August: 'The Connection of the Spirit with Bodily Organs'.

9 August: 'The Emancipation of the Will in the Human Organism'.

10 August: 'Walking, Speaking, Thinking'.

11 August: 'The Rhythmic System, Sleeping and Waking, Imitation'.

12 August: 'Three Epochs in the Religious Education of Man'.

13 August: 'Reading, Writing and Nature Studies'.

14 August: 'Arithmetic, Geometry, History'.

15 August: 'Physics, Chemistry, Handwork, Language, Religion'.

16 August: 'Memory, Temperaments, Bodily Culture and Art'.

17 August: 'Education Towards Inner Freedom'.

17 August: Farewell Address in Ilkley. (Questions and Answers not translated.)

*10 August 1923, Ilkley
Also in *Waldorf Education and Anthroposophy*, Vol. 2, op. cit.

11 August 1923, Ilkley
Questions and Answers. No record.

14 August 1923, Ilkley
Questions and Answers. No record.

14 August 1923, Ilkley
Introduction to a eurythmy performance (in GA 307).

*18 August 1923, Penmaenmawr
Introductory address at the Summer School.

19–31 August 1923, Penmaenmawr
The Evolution of Consciousness as Revealed through Initiation Knowledge, tr. V. E. Watkin, C. Davy, London: Rudolf Steiner Press 1966 (in GA 227).

19 August: 'First Steps Towards Imaginative Knowledge'.

20 August: 'Inspiration and Intuition'.

21 August: 'Initiation Knowledge—New and Old'.

22 August: 'Dream Life'.
23 August: 'The Relation of Man to the Three Worlds'.
24 August: 'The Ruling of Spirit in Nature'.
25 August: 'The Interplay of Various Worlds'.
26 August: 'During Sleep and After Death'.
27 August: 'Experiences between Death and Rebirth'.
28 August: 'Man's Life after Death in the Spiritual Cosmos'.
29 August: 'Experience of the World's Past'.
30 August: 'The Evolution of the World and Man'.
31 August: 'The Entry of Man into the Era of Freedom'.
*31 August: Farewell address.

*19 August 1923, Penmaenmawr
Address on the future of the Anthroposophical Society in Britain (in GA 259).

*20 August 1923, Penmaenmawr
Questions and Answers.

*21 August 1923, Penmaenmawr
Questions and Answers.

*24 August 1923, Penmaenmawr
Closing words after a lecture by Baron Rosenkrantz 'Concerning Art and its Future' (in GA 284/285).

26 August 1923, Penmaenmawr
Discussion on education. No record.

26 August 1923, Penmaenmawr
A Lecture on Eurythmy, London: Rudolf Steiner Press 1977 (in GA 279).

28 August 1923, Penmaenmawr
Lecture *Polarities in Health, Illness and Therapy* (in GA 319), tr. G. Karnow, Mercury Press 1987.

*2 September 1923, London
Founding Address of Anthroposophical Society in Great Britain (in GA 259).

*2 September 1923, London
Previously *Man as a Picture of the Living Spirit* (including the closing words) (in GA 228).

2 September 1923, London
On Therapy and Method in the Manufacture of Medicines. Two lectures to doctors, Lecture I, Typescript R99 (in GA 319).

3 September 1923, London
Lecture II, in ibid.

*9 September 1923, Dornach
Rudolf Steiner's report on his trip to Britain.

11–22 August 1924, Torquay
True and False Paths in Spiritual Investigation, tr. A. Parker, London: Rudolf Steiner Press 1986 (in GA 243).
11 August: 'Nature is the Great Illusion. Know Thyself'.
12 August: 'The Three Worlds and Their Reflected Images'.
13 August: 'Form and Substantiality of the Mineral Kingdom'.
14 August: 'The Secret of Investigation into other Realms'.
15 August: 'The Inner Vitalization of the Soul'.
16 August: 'Initiation Knowledge. Waking and Dream Consciousness'
18 August: 'Knowledge of the World of Stars.'
19 August: 'Potential Aberrations in Spiritual Investigation'.
20 August: 'Abnormal Paths into the Spiritual World'.
21 August: 'Influences of the Extra-Terrestrial Cosmos'.
22 August: 'Spiritual Investigation.'

12–27 August 1924, Torquay and London
Karmic Relationships, Vol. VIII, tr. D. Osmond, London: Rudolf Steiner Press 1977 (in GA 240).
12 August: Address on the Christmas Foundation Meeting, Torquay.
12 August: Lecture I, Torquay.
14 August: Lecture II, Torquay.

21 August: Lecture III, Torquay.
24 August: Lecture IV, London.
24 August: Lecture V, London.
27 August: Lecture VI, London.

12–20 August 1924, Torquay
The Kingdom of Childhood (GA 311), tr. H. Fox, Hudson: Anthroposophic Press 1995.
12 August: Lecture 1.
13 August: Lecture 2.
14 August: Lecture 3.
15 August: Lecture 4.
16 August: Lecture 5.
18 August: Lecture 6.
19 August: Lecture 7.
20 August: Questions and Answers.

*22 August 1924, Torquay
Concluding Address after the Second International Summer School (in GA 260a).

28 August 1924, London
Lecture 1 in report form in *An Outline of Anthroposophical Medical Research* (in GA 319), London: Anthroposophical Publishing Company. No date.

29 August 1924, London
'Educational Issues' in *Waldorf Education and Anthroposophy*, Part 2, op. cit.

29 August 1924, London
Lecture 2 in *An Outline of Anthroposophical Medical Research*, op. cit (in GA 319).

30 August 1924, London
A lecture to the Education Union (in GA 304a).

NOTES

When lecturing in Britain, Rudolf Steiner usually paused twice for translation by George Kaufmann (see Note 55). Where known, the stopping places are marked with an asterisk.

GA = *Gesamtausgabe*, the collected works of Rudolf Steiner in the original German, published by Rudolf Steiner Verlag, Dornach, Switzerland.

Introduction
1. R. Steiner, *Karmic Relationships*, Vol. 8 (GA 240), tr. D. Osmond, London: Rudolf Steiner Press 1975, lecture of 27 August 1924.
2. R. Steiner, *The Evolution of Consciousness* (GA 227), tr. V. E. Watkins & C. Davy. London: Rudolf Steiner Press 1991, lecture of 31 August 1923.

Part One
3. Marie Steiner-von Sivers (1867–1948) was born in Russia and met Rudolf Steiner in Berlin in 1900 soon after which she became his most energetic supporter. They married in 1914. In addition to complete day to day involvement in his work, of which he regarded her as the co-founder, her central contribution lay in the development of eurythmy as a new art, drama and the renewal of speech as an art. In 1923 she became a member of the first Executive Council (Vorstand) of the newly founded General Anthroposophical Society. She founded the publishing house (Philosophisch-Anthroposophischer Verlag) that published Steiner's work, and after his death she was responsible for administering his literary estate. See Marie Savitch *Marie Steiner-von Sivers. Fellow Worker with Rudolf Steiner*. Tr. J. Compton-Burnett. London, Rudolf Steiner Press 1967. This book contains several descriptions of the visits to Britain.

4. Translated from R. Steiner *Das Sonnenmysterium und das Mysterium von Tod und Auferstehung* (GA 211), Dornach 1986. In the note to p. 141 the publishers stated: 'The shorthand reports of these [London] lectures are uneven in places and there may even be gaps in them.' In his 1922 English edition, H. Collison wrote: 'These lectures were given on Friday, April 14th, and on Saturday, April 15th, 1922. The ... translation is not from a verbatim report, but from very full notes made at the time.'

Harry Collison M.A. (Oxon) (1868–1945). One of the founding members of the first anthroposophical group in Britain, the Myrdhin Group, he was a lawyer, artist and freemason, and responsible for translating and publishing many of Steiner's lectures. He was chosen as Chairman of the newly formed Anthroposophical Society in Great Britain in 1923. When the Society split in the early 1930s he became leader of the English Section of the General Anthroposophical Society.

5. R. Steiner, *Knowledge of the Higher Worlds* (GA 10), tr. D. Osmond & C. Davy, London: Rudolf Steiner Press 1993. Or *How to Know the Higher Worlds. A Modern Path of Initiation*, tr. C. Bamford, Spring Valley, New York: Anthroposophic Press 1994.

6. R. Steiner, *Occult Science: an Outline* (GA 13), tr. G. & M. Adams, London: Rudolf Steiner Press 1979. Or *An Outline of Esoteric Science* (GA 13), tr. C. E. Creeger. New York: Anthroposophic Press 1997.

7. The great wooden building of the First Goetheanum was burnt down by arson on New Year's Eve 1922. Rudolf Steiner at once planned another in concrete, which now stands on the same site.

8. Galatians 2:20.

9. See lecture of 18 November 1922 in the present volume, and that of 19 November 1922 in *Planetary Spheres and their Influence on Man's Life on Earth and in Spiritual Worlds* (GA 218), tr. G. & M. Adams, London: Rudolf Steiner Press 1982.

10. Lectures of 14 and 15 April 1922 in the present volume.

11. See Note 9.

12. See lecture of 17 November 1922 in the present volume.
13. Ilkley, 4–17 August 1923: *A Modern Art of Education* (GA 307), tr. J. Darrell, G. Adams, London: Rudolf Steiner Press 1981. Penmaenmawr: 18–31 August 1923: *The Evolution of Consciousness*, op. cit.
14. Lectures of 17 and 18 November 1922 in the present volume, and the lecture of 19 November 1922 in *Planetary Spheres and their Influence on Man's Life on Earth and in Spiritual Worlds*, op. cit.
15. R. Steiner, *Occult Science: an Outline*, op. cit.
16. R. Steiner, *The Mystery of the Trinity & The Mission of the Spirit* (GA 214), tr. J. H. Hindes, New York: Anthroposophic Press 1991, lecture of 30 August 1922.
17. P. Ramanathan (Solicitor General of Ceylon), *The Culture of the Soul among Western Nations*, New York and London 1906.
18. Up to this point the lecture to members in London of 2 September 1923 is published in German in *Initiations-wissenschaft und Sternenerkenntnis*, GA 228, Dornach 1985. The concluding words that follow appear in German in *Das Schicksalsjahr 1923*, GA 259, Dornach 1991, p. 177.

Part Two
19. The other lectures Steiner gave during the congress are in R. Steiner, *The Spiritual Ground of Education* (in GA 305), tr. D. Harwood, London: Anthroposophical Publishing Co. 1947.
20. Mrs H. Millicent Mackenzie, MA, Professor of Education at University College, Cardiff, organizer of the lecture course at Oxford and chairwoman of the committee.
21. Robert Owen (1771–1858), a Welsh social reformer who founded the New Lanark mills in Scotland.
22. Franz Oppenheimer (1864–1943), a German economist and sociologist who founded co-operative settlements in an attempt to break the land monopoly of the great land-owners.
23. The reference is to H. Collison, MA (Oxon). See Note 4.
24. Leviticus 19:18.
25. Exodus 21 and 22.
26. Tribunes who attempted an agrarian reform in ancient Rome.
27. In 494 BC.

28. Diocletian (284–305), Roman emperor.
29. Adam Smith (1723–90), Scottish political economist and philosopher, creator of the subject of political economy. Main work *An Inquiry into the Nature and Causes of the Wealth of Nations*, 1776.
30. Karl Marx (1818–83), *The Communist Manifesto*, 1848; *A Critique of Political Economy*, 1859; *Das Kapital*, 1867.
31. Immanuel Kant (1724–1804). One of Kant's formulations of the categorical imperative is 'Act only on such a maxim as you can will that it should become a universal law'.
32. Peter the Great (1672–1725).
33. Vladimir Soloviev (1853–1900), Russian philosopher.
34. Herbert Spencer (1820–1903), English philosopher. *The Synthetic Philosophy*, 10 volumes, 1862–96.
35. Fyodor Mikhailovich Dostoevski (1821–81).
36. Vladimir Ilich Lenin (1870–1924). In 1917 he set up the dictatorship of the Bolshevik Party in Russia.
37. Rudolf Steiner first described the threefold physiological nature of the human being in *Von Seelenrätseln*, which has been partly translated in *The Case for Anthroposophy* (GA 21), tr. O. Barfield, London: Rudolf Steiner Press 1970. The first brief sketch of an analogous threefolding of the social order appeared in January/February 1919 in 'An Appeal to the German Nation and to the Civilized World', included in *The Renewal of the Social Organism* (in GA 24), tr. E. Bowen-Wedgewood & R. Marriott, New York: Anthroposophic Press 1985. Later the subject was tackled in greater depth in *Towards Social Renewal* (GA 23), tr. F. T. Smith, London: Rudolf Steiner Press 1977.
38. See Note 37.
39. See Note 37.
40. Roman Boos wrote in this connection: 'The "friends in Stuttgart" were industrialists and business people who were also members of the Anthroposophical Society in Stuttgart. They were deeply motivated by Rudolf Steiner's repeated and increasingly urgent warnings from 1917 onwards that the German people would only be able to achieve a healthy peace if they looked back to the roots of their spiritual being and made this spiritual being active. After the fall of Luden-

dorff and the abdication of the Kaiser, these friends had therefore tried to create conditions in Stuttgart which would bring about the will to speak and work in Germany and before the civilized world in a way that would enable the German people to be *politically* and *economically* accepted among the community of nations in the same way that German *cultural* life was already accepted because of its positive achievements.

'In Dornach on 25 January 1919 these three friends showed Rudolf Steiner the draft measures they were planning. During the meeting they urged Steiner to write a paper that would serve as a tool for what they were about to set in train, and give a detailed account of the plans.

'It was in answer to this request that Steiner wrote *An das deutsche Volk* ... and *Towards Social Renewal.*'

41. R. Steiner, *The Philosophy of Spiritual Activity: A Philosophy of Freedom* (GA 4), tr. rev. R. Stebbing, Forest Row, Sussex: Rudolf Steiner Press 1992. Or *Intuitive Thinking as a Spiritual Path* (GA 4), tr. M. Lipson, New York: Anthroposophic Press 1995.

42. *The Hibbert Journal*, July 1921, No. 4. The article is also included in *Aufsätze über die Dreigliederung des sozialen Organismus und zur Zeitlage* (GA 24), Dornach 1982.

43. Ernst Haeckel (1834-1919), zoologist and natural philosopher.

44. Michelangelo Buonarotti (1475–1564). The picture is *The Last Judgment* on the wall behind the altar in the Sistine Chapel, painted between 1536 and 1541.

45. See Note 29.

46. David Ricardo (1772–1823), pupil of Adam Smith.

47. John Stuart Mill (1806–73), English philosopher.

48. Among the lectures Rudolf Steiner gave to the workers at the Goetheanum were *Health and Illness* (GA 348), tr. M. St Goar, New York: Anthroposophic Press, Vol. 1 1981, Vol. 2 1983; *Learning to See into the Spiritual World* (in GA 350), tr. W. Stuber & M. Gardner, New York: Anthroposophic Press 1990; *The Evolution of Earth and Man and the Influence of the Stars* (GA 354), New York and London: Anthroposophic Press and Rudolf Steiner Press 1987; *From Elephants to*

Einstein. Answers to Questions (GA 352), tr. A. Meuss, London: Rudolf Steiner Press 1998. Translations of GA 353 and GA 354 are in production.

49. Rudolf Steiner's sculpture in wood of Christ as the Representative of Humanity had been intended as the focal point in the smaller dome of the First Goetheanum. It escaped destruction when the Goetheanum was destroyed by arson on New Year's Eve 1922/23 because it was unfinished and still in Steiner's studio at the time of the fire. It can now be seen in the Second Goetheanum building at Dornach in Switzerland.

50. See Note 19.

51. R. Steiner, *The Philosophy of Spiritual Activity: A Philosophy of Freedom*, op cit.

52. Ibid, Chapters 10 and 12.

53. R. Steiner, *Reincarnation and Immortality*, 'The Science of the Spirit and the Social Question' (in GA 34), New York: Multimedia Publishing Corp. 1974.

54. See Note 20.

55. George Adams (formerly Kaufmann) (1894–1963), mathematician and physicist. His immense gift for languages enabled him to give immediate renderings in English from notes he took of the lectures while Rudolf Steiner was speaking.

Part 3

Except for the two articles under number 9 (originally in *Das Goetheanum*, 9 and 16 September 1923), the items in Part Three are translated from *Rudolf Steiner und die Zivilisationsaufgaben der Anthroposophie*, Dornach: Philosophisch-Anthroposophischer Verlag 1943. The narratives are by Marie Steiner.

56. R. Steiner, *A Modern Art of Education*, op. cit. 1972.

57. R. Steiner, *The Evolution of Consciousness*, op. cit

58. Rudolf Steiner gave this lecture at the special request of English-speaking teachers during the 1923 education course for teachers at Ilkley, England. The other lectures are in R. Steiner, *A Modern Art of Education*, op. cit.

59. Emil Molt (1876–1936), proprietor of the Waldorf-Astoria cigarette factory in Stuttgart. Inspired by the movement for

the threefold ordering of society, he founded the independent Waldorf School in Stuttgart, initially for the children of his employees. At his request Rudolf Steiner agreed to establish and guide the school.

60. While the education course (5–17 August 1923) was under way in Ilkley two performances of eurythmy were given, one by schoolchildren from the Waldorf school in Stuttgart and one by a group of artists from the Goetheanum in Dornach.

61. Daniel Nicol Dunlop (1868–1935) was born in Ayrshire with a Quaker background. He trained as an electrical engineer and was director of the British Electrical and Allied Manufacturers' Association from 1911 until 1935. He founded the World Power Conferences (Now World Energy Council). From the Theosophical Society, where he met A.E. (George Russell), Thomas Lake Harris and W. B. Yeats, he moved to the Anthroposophical Society where he quickly became an organizer of conferences and editor of the journal *Anthroposophy* (1925–1933). He was General Secretary of the Anthroposophical Society in Great Britain from 1930 until his death. For a comprehensive biography of the man Steiner described as a 'brother', see T. H. Meyer, *D. N. Dunlop—A Man of Our Time*, London: Temple Lodge Publishing 1992.

62. Eleanor Charlotte Kynaston Merry (1873–1956), daughter of a classical scholar and Canon of Durham. She was well educated and studied music and art. From early interests in spiritualism and theosophy she soon became an anthroposophist and with her close friend D. N. Dunlop organized summer schools, gave many lectures, painted and wrote extensively on esotericism, Celtic and Arthurian themes, art and poetry. With Maria Schindler she developed painting techniques from Goethe's colour theory, for which they opened a painting school. See *Life Story: An Autobiographical Experience of Destiny*, London: Mercury Arts Publications 1987.

63. Margaret McMillan (1860–1931), founder and first president of the Nursery School Association. 'She died in the firm faith that the students of the [training] College will carry onwards the torch she has dropped and that the schools of her heart's desire will multiply and the children be comforted.' *The*

Times, 30 March 1931. Of her books she wrote that *Education through the Imagination* represented the theory and *The Nursery School* the practice of her work: 'Theory and practice alike owe much, if not all, of their original impulse to the work of Edouard Séguin, an exile from France finding refuge in America. [He] was . . . a follower of Pinel, Itard and Esquirol.'

64. The journal *Anthroposophy* ran from November 1920 to January 1926. It was succeeded by *Anthroposophy. A Quarterly Review of Spiritual Science*. Baroness Louisa (Tessa) Rosenkrantz (d.1944) was a Scot, the cousin of the Danish artist Arild Rosenkrantz whom she married in 1901. They lived in Dornach during Steiner's lifetime and later in London, where they were very involved with the building of Rudolf Steiner House. Tessa Rosenkrantz designed and made costumes for plays performed there. She edited the journal *Anthroposophy* from 1920 to 1925.

65. Formerly published in *Anthroposophical Movement*, Vol. XXIX, No. 5, May 1952.

66. The normal English usage of the word 'imagination' also contains the nuance of 'fantasy', which does not apply to the meaning *Imagination* has come to have in an anthroposophical context when the three soul faculties of *Imagination, Inspiration* and *Intuition* are under discussion.

67. L. C. de Saint-Martin (1743–1803), *Des Erreurs et de la Vérité*, Edinburgh 1773.

68. R. Steiner, *The Evolution of Consciousness*, op. cit., lecture of 21 August 1923.

69. Ibid., lecture of 22 August 1923.

70. From here this passage was formerly published in *Anthroposophical Movement*, Vol. XXIX, No. 5, May 1952.

71. This passage was previously published in *Anthroposophical Movement*, Vol. XXIX, No. 6, June 1952.

72. This passage was previously published in *Anthroposophical Movement*, Vol. XXIX, No. 6, June 1952.

73. Formerly published in *Anthroposophic News Sheet*, No. 4, 26 January 1936.

74. Baron Arild Rosenkrantz (1870–1964), Danish painter, worked with Rudolf Steiner on the paintings in the domes of the First Goetheanum.

75. R. Steiner, *A Lecture on Eurythmy* (in GA 279), London: Rudolf Steiner Press 1967.
76. Parts of this address were formerly published in *The Evolution of Consciousness*, op. cit.
77. In November 1922.
78. *The Evolution of Consciousness*, op. cit., lecture of 31 August 1923.
79. A very rarely performed operation of ceremonial magic by means of which an individual's higher activities can be paralysed in a kind of spiritual sleep.
80. Sir Oliver Joseph Lodge (1851–1940), English physicist who studied lightning and electricity. After 1910 he became increasingly prominent in psychic research.
81. O. Lodge, *Raymond, or Life and Death*, 1916.
82. The journal *Lucifer Gnosis* was published by Rudolf Steiner in Berlin from 1904 to 1908.
83. R. Steiner, *Man in the Past, the Present and the Future* (in GA 228), tr. E. Goddard, London: Rudolf Steiner Press 1982, lecture of 10 September 1923.
84. According to Helene Finckh's record of this talk, the swastika as Steiner sketched it on the blackboard is shown spinning in the opposite direction from that of the sign on the actual stone he was describing. It is not known whether he did this on purpose. However, the question of a swastika's 'direction' is very complicated. Some light is thrown on this in a lecture of 6 July 1906 in R. Steiner, *Kosmogonie* (GA 94), Dornach 1979. See also John M. Wood's important article 'A New Look at Old Stones' (*Anthroposophy Today*, Summer 1986), in which he states that Rudolf Steiner could not have seen the original carving as it would have been obscured by turf at the time.
85. Hermann von Baravalle (1898–1973), mathematician and physicist and a founder teacher of the Waldorf school in Stuttgart, wrote *The Teaching of Arithmetic and the Waldorf School Plan*, Rudolf Steiner College Publications 1991, and other books.
86. E. Schwebsch (1889–1953), music author and teacher; K. Schubert (1889–1949), remedial teacher at the Waldorf school in Stuttgart; C. von Heydebrand (1886–1938), teacher at the Waldorf school, wrote a number of books.

87. R. Steiner, *The Spiritual Ground of Education* (GA 305), tr. D. Harwood, Blauvelt: Garber Communications 1989.
88. Günther Wachsmuth (1893–1963). Studied at Oxford and Würzburg, scientist, author and biographer of Steiner. Wachsmuth was appointed as the first leader of the Science Section at the Goetheanum and was a member of the first Executive Council (Vorstand) of the General Anthroposophical Society at the age of 30. He sought to reconcile sciences and the arts and was a keen researcher into human destiny and the stars and also wrote historical dramas. His best-known book is translated as *Etheric Formative Forces in the Cosmos, Earth and Man*, London 1932.
89. See Note 63. M. McMillan *Education through the Imagination*, 1904, Second Ed. 1923.
90. Miss McMillan's school was a so-called Camp School, a type of school being established in cities by the English authorities at the time.
91. It is not known whether this visit took place.
92. Ita Wegman MD (1876–1943) was born into a Dutch family in Java. She began a medical training in Zurich at the age of 30, having met Rudolf Steiner in 1902 on joining the Theosophical Society when he was head of the German Section. She practised medicine from 1911 and opened her own clinic in Arlesheim, Switzerland, in 1921. She became one of Steiner's closest collaborators, not only in developing the anthroposophical medical work, but also as Recorder of the first Executive Council (Vorstand), and in carrying on the work of the School of Spiritual Science founded in 1924. She nursed Steiner during his last months. Later she became a focus of the tragic splits in the Anthroposophical Society. With her colleague Elisabeth Vreede she was expelled from the Executive Council in 1935 and also from the Anthroposophical Society. She continued her medical work in Arlesheim and Northern Italy, also founding the 'Sonnenhof', a home for children with special needs. See J.E. Zeylmans van Emmichoven *Who was Ita Wegman?*. Mercury Press 1995.
93. Dr Larkins practised in Harley Street, sometimes treating patients according to Rudolf Steiner's suggestions. Mrs C. A. M. Larkins supported the eurythmy work in London.

94. The lectures of 28 and 29 August 1924 survive in an abridged report, *An Outline of Anthroposophical Medical Research*, London: Anthroposophical Publishing Company 1926.
95. The earthquake struck Tokyo near noon on 1 September 1923. The estimated death toll was 74,000.
96. This report appeared in two consecutive numbers of *Das Goetheanum* (9 and 16 September 1923). Formerly in English in the journal *Anthroposophy*, Vol. II, Nos. 10 and 11.
97. This and the following quotations are from M. McMillan, *Education through the Imagination*, op. cit. See also Note 63.
98. Margaret McMillan, *The Nursery School*, London 1919.
99. See Note 2.

Part Four
100. 'Man as a Picture of the Living Spirit', London, 2 September 1923 (Lecture 5 in Part One of the present volume). Formerly *Man as a Picture of the Living Spirit*, London: Rudolf Steiner Press 1972.
101. These concluding words of the lecture on 'Christ and the Metamorphoses of Karma' are published in German in the Note to page 179 in the 1992 edition of *Geistige Zusammenhänge in der Gestaltung des menschlichen Organismus* (GA 218).
102. By the time the text of this lecture came to be reproduced in mimeographed form, the Goetheanum had been burnt to the ground. These final words after the lecture on 'Christ and the Metamorphoses of Karma' were therefore not included in the mimeographed record and were not published until they appeared in the *Nachrichtenblatt* of 14 October 1934, No. 41.
103. The Second International Summer School in Torquay (9–22 August 1924).

PUBLISHER'S NOTE REGARDING RUDOLF STEINER'S LECTURES

The lectures and addresses contained in this volume have been translated from the German which is based on stenographic and other recorded texts that were in most cases never seen or revised by the lecturer. Hence, due to human errors in hearing and transcription, they may contain mistakes and faulty passages. Every effort has been made to ensure that this is not the case. Some of the lectures were given to audiences more familiar with anthroposophy; these are the so-called 'private' or 'members' lectures. Other lectures, like the written works, were intended for the general public. The difference between these, as Rudolf Steiner indicates in his *Autobiography*, is twofold. On the one hand, the members' lectures take for granted a background in and commitment to anthroposophy; in the public lectures this was not the case. At the same time, the members' lectures address the concerns and dilemmas of the members, while the public work speaks directly out of Steiner's own understanding of universal needs. Nevertheless, as Rudolf Steiner stresses: 'Nothing was ever said that was not solely the result of my direct experience of the growing content of anthroposophy. There was never any question of concessions to the prejudices and preferences of the members. Whoever reads these privately printed lectures can take them to represent anthroposophy in the fullest sense. Thus it was possible without hesitation—when the complaints in this direction became too persistent—to depart from the custom of circulating this material "for members only". But it must be borne in mind that faulty passages do occur in these reports not revised by myself.' Earlier in the same chapter, he states: 'Had I been able to correct them [the private lectures], the restriction *for members only* would have been unnecessary from the beginning.'

Rudolf Steiner
FROM ELEPHANTS TO EINSTEIN
Answers to Questions

The remarkable discussions in this volume took place between Rudolf Steiner and workers at the Goetheanum, Switzerland. The varied subject-matter was chosen by his audience at Rudolf Steiner's instigation. Steiner took their questions and usually gave immediate answers. The astonishing nature of these responses—their insight, knowledge and spiritual depth—is testimony to his outstanding ability as a spiritual initiate and profound thinker. Accessible, entertaining and stimulating, the records of these sessions will be a delight to anybody with an open mind.

In this particular collection, Rudolf Steiner deals with topics ranging from elephants to Einstein. He discusses, among other things, ants and bees; shells and skeletons; animal and plant poisons—arsenic and lead; nutrition—protein and fats, potatoes; the human eye and its colour; fresh and salt water; fish and bird migration; human clothing; opium and alcohol; thinking, and bodily secretions.

RUDOLF STEINER PRESS
208 pages; ISBN 1 85584 081 2; £10.95

Rudolf Steiner
MYSTERY KNOWLEDGE AND MYSTERY CENTRES

Modern scholarship knows little of the mystery schools of antiquity. At most it is able to offer hypothetical explanations of their purpose, and to speak of externals. In these far-reaching lectures, Rudolf Steiner gives a penetrating description—from his spiritual research into the evolution and history of the human being, earth and cosmos—of the experiences people gained through the ancient mysteries. His survey takes us through the mysteries of Artemis in Ephesus, of Hibernia, Eleusis, Somothrace, and the Middle Ages. He also discusses the conditions which are required if initiation is to be achieved in our time.

After preliminary lectures on the nature and function of the human soul, a magnificent drama is presented of the development of the earth, including graphic descriptions of the metals, their connection with the planets and their curative properties. Steiner also outlines the origins of plants and animals and the connection of humanity with the earth, and gives a panoramic view of human evolution in the past, present and future.

RUDOLF STEINER PRESS
272 pages; ISBN 1 85584 061 8; £12.95

Rudolf Steiner
THE FIFTH GOSPEL
From the Akashic Record

From his clairvoyant reading of the supersensible Akashic Record—the cosmic memory of all events, actions and thoughts—Rudolf Steiner was able to speak of aspects of the life of Jesus Christ which are not contained in the four biblical Gospels. Such research, in that it is not based on historical records or extant documents, can be spoken of as a 'Fifth Gospel'.

After an intense inner struggle to verify the exact nature of these events, and after carefully checking the results of his research, Steiner describes many detailed episodes from the Akashic Record. He speaks, for example, of Jesus's life in the community of the Essenes, the temptation of Christ in the wilderness, and of a significant conversation between Jesus and Mary.

Steiner states that divulging such spiritual research is intensely difficult, but that, '... although people show little inclination to be told such facts as these, it was absolutely essential that knowledge of such facts should be brought to Earth evolution at the present time.'

This new edition has been retranslated, and features six lectures which have never before been published in English.

RUDOLF STEINER PRESS
264 pages; ISBN 1 85584 039 1; £11.95